**W9-AAC-086**

# Superior Perennials for the Great Lakes States
## David S. MacKenzie

### 3rd Edition

Published in U.S.A. by Hortech, Inc.
Spring Lake, Michigan 49456

Premium Plants is a registered trademark of Hortech, Inc.

Library of Congress Cataloging-in-Publication Data.

MacKenzie, David S.
Premium Plants / David S. MacKenzie

3rd Edition
Includes index.

ISBN 0-970 8800-0-6

Printed in China

# Foreward

Back in 1983, after I graduated from college, I got into the business of wholesale plant production in West Michigan and began growing and selling traditional ground covers (like English ivy and pachysandra). In time we at Hortech, Inc. added a few new ground covers and later embarked upon growing climbing vines, ferns, and ornamental grasses — at the time considered relatively unimportant plants, but traditionally grown by ground cover producers as filler items.

In the beginning it was innocent, just a few varieties. But things changed. We soon discovered dozens of "awesome" varieties, that we had to grow. And, like all plant lovers, well...you know the rest of the story...we tested thousands of plants, and ended up with a manageable palette of the "very best", only a few hundred exceptional varieties.

So, here they are, these are the plants that after lots of testing proved themselves to grow extremely well in the Great Lakes Region. "Premium Plants" are colorful, fun, interesting, disease and insect resistant, and easy to maintain. We know you will enjoy them as much as we do.

David MacKenzie
Hortech, Inc.

# Additional Resources

Perennial Ground Covers
David S. MacKenzie
400 pages
Timber Press
ISBN 0-88192-368-0

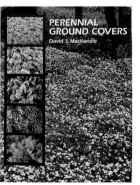

The Color Encyclopedia of Ornamental Grasses
Rick Darke
325 pages
Timber Press
ISBN 0-88192-454-4

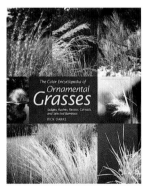

The Plantfinder's Guide To Garden Ferns
Martin Rickard
192 pages, 121 color photos, a must for anyone interested in these tough versatile, strikingly beautiful plants.
Timber Press
ISBN 0-88192-472-8

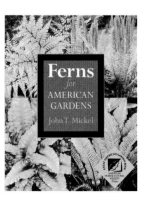

Climbing Plants
Jane Taylor
124 pages
Timber Press
ISBN 0-88192-221-8

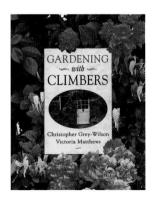

# An Introduction To

## Superior Perennials for the Great Lakes States

This book is about plants that are colorful, fun, and interesting. These plants grow especially well in the Great Lakes region, and since they are perennials, they become bigger, better, and more valuable with time — real estate appraisals support this.

But more importantly, perennial plants enhance the quality of our surroundings and thus the quality of our lives. These are plants that will surround you with their warm, classy richness and feed your eyes with an ever changing smorgasbord of color, texture, and beauty.

Section One, Climbing Vines, addresses a group of "upwardly mobile" plants that can add an important vertical dimension, of interesting foliage and showy flowers, to your landscape. Climbing Vines contains 61 color photos and 41 descriptions of the finest vines for the Great Lakes region. Hummingbirds and butterflies will thank you for using vines, as will your friends and neighbors who will benefit from their unique beauty.

Section Two, Ferns, talks about some fascinating, unusual, mostly shade loving plants. What first becomes apparent as you review the 38 color photos and 29 descriptions is that ferns come in an array of colors, shapes, and sizes that extends beyond what you might imagine. Read further and you will find that ferns are versatile and lend themselves to planting in every landscape. Indeed, some ferns even thrive in full sun, and many more are drought tolerant.

Section Three, Ground Covers, is a comprehensive treatment of superior plants for mulching and covering the soil. These are plants that oxygenate the air, control erosion, beautify the environment, and require little maintenance. No longer are ground covers just English ivy and Pachysandra — here you will find 423 photos and 348 descriptions of ground covers that range from clumping to vining, deciduous to evergreen, and pancake flat to 4 feet tall. Ground Covers will teach you about plants with colorful flowers and foliage in textures that range from needle fine to big fat and round — with colors ranging from green to red, blue, purple, silver, coppery, bronze, and gold. Variegated forms are also plentiful and some ground covers can even be walked on and used as substitutes for lawn grass.

Last but not least, Section Four, Ornamental Grasses, is all about the hottest plants, so far, in the 21st century. Ornamental grasses are superior plants with colorful wind responsive foliage, unique persistent flowers during summer, fall, and winter, and exceptional fall foliar colors. Most importantly, ornamental grasses bring constant change through the seasons. This makes them unusually exciting.

Ornamental Grasses, with 95 descriptions and 112 photos, will teach you the best ways to use ornamental grasses and about the finest varieties for use in the Great Lakes States. These are plants you can use as specimens, for accent, as ground covers, and for their unusual architectural features. You will also learn how to care for them (it's laughably easy) and about their effective pairing with such exceptional companions as cone flowers, ornamental oregano, sedums, black eyed Susan, asters, daylillies, yuccas, coreopsis, and other grasses.

I hope that you will enjoy viewing the picutres within this book and reading about these fine plants. More importantly, I hope that you will invite them into your landscape. If you do I am sure that you will be rewarded with everchanging color, texture, and beauty.

David MacKenzie

# Dedication

This book is dedicated to all who appreciate the aesthetic-, leisure-, economic- and environmental-significance of plants. Two such individuals who were important in my life were my father, Dr. Donald MacKenzie, and my dear horticulturist friend Ralph Shugert, both who left this world during the initial writing of this book (year 2000). This book is especially dedicated to them.

### Donald C. MacKenzie

I knew my dad for 39 years—though I don't remember much about the first five or six. He wasn't a horticulturist, but a medical doctor, or more correctly, an Osteopathic Doctor. My dad was a passionate person with many hobbies and interests. He threw himself into everything he pursued—including the interests of myself and my siblings.

My earliest memories of my dad are of us fishing in Lake St. Clair, back when we lived on the east side of Michigan. We didn't catch many fish but we worked hard on the boat (an old wooden Lyman that he was very proud of). I also remember lots of baseball, my dad the catcher, me the pitcher. In retrospect, I wonder if I was being groomed for a career in baseball. Maybe..., I never thought to ask.

We also spent a lot of time grooming the lawn, raking leaves, and weeding. And, more than anything, we gardened. I had a small garden plot in the field next to our house, but my dad had a 3 acre garden at his gentleman's farm in the country. At his, I got to sow, plant, fertilize, weed, hoe, harvest, run the rototiller, and generally get muddy, sunburned, and frozen. I never minded working on the farm (my Dad paid pretty well), and I loved the fresh air and renewal of spirit that came from being with the land, wind, and the plants.

These experiences, with my dad, had a lot to do with horticulture getting into my blood. Later, after having started Hortech, my dad came to work for me. Always a volunteer, and always part time, he did everything from propagation to planting, digging to delivery, and construction to consulting (he liked to give advice...sometimes I even asked for it).

It was a good experience to have Donald MacKenzie in my horticultural life, even better to have him for a dad.

*Gaura lindheimeri 'Siskiyou Pink'*

## Ralph Shugert

I met Ralph during the summer of 1983; just out of college and starting a new business, I was visiting Zelenka Nursery, where Ralph worked. He intercepted me, introduced himself, and for the next five minutes made me feel like the most important person in the world. He closed the conversation by saying "David, this is a special industry, one in which we help each other, if there is anything I can do for you, call or visit me".

Over the following 17 years, Ralph's phone rang and his office door opened countless times. And every time it was the same, "David my dear friend, how are you, what can I help you with?" Then, minutes of uninterrupted conversation, whereby I would become a better more knowledgeable person.

Ralph treated everyone this way, literally hundreds of fellow nursery people. He was the embodiment of enthusiasm, selflessness, and sharing. The expression, no matter how much you give, you never run out of love, certainly applied to Ralph. Ralph simply loved horticulture, and never stopped gushing about what a blessing it was to tend to God's beautiful creations.

As much as Ralph loved horticulture, his love for people was even more intense. Ralph viewed his colleagues with a sense of wonderment, awe, and appreciation. He spoke of the harvesters, shipping staff, and irrigators with a sense of reverence. He also impressed me with how respectful and appreciative he was of the owners of Zelenka Nursery. And, I doubt there is anyone who was more openly grateful to the educators, extension agents, researchers, and lecturers in our industry than Ralph. Ralph admired and was inspired by the horticulturists of yester-year. He was enamored with their history and respectful of their accomplishments. He seemed to find the best in everyone and every situation.

I am so proud and grateful to have known Ralph Shugert. He was such an unselfish person, and such a marvelous teacher. Ralph was a man of great enthusiasm, dignity, classiness and spirit. He was the greatest champion of horticulture I will ever know, and was at once cheerleader, coach, quarterback and referee. Mostly, however, Ralph was a once in a lifetime friend that I will always miss and never forget.

*'Ralph Shugert' Myrtle*

# Table of Contents

# Acknowledgements

Thanks to the following people for use of the following photos.

Sandy Green for the photo of Ralph Shugert

Janet Hendon for photo of Donald MacKenzie

Mary Walters for photos of Hemerocallis 'Rocket City', and Hosta 'Fire and Ice'

All other phototgrahy by David MacKenzie

# KEY TO SYMBOLS

## BLOOMING TIME

— **Blooming times** are approximate and typical and may vary depending upon weather and specific climate and microclimate.

## LIGHT CONDITIONS

— **Full sun**. Locations receiving full sun are exposed to direct, unshaded sunlight for at least six hours per day.

— **Light shade**. Light shade areas are exposed to partially filtered sun. Typically, the filter is an open-canopied tree, such as a honey locust, serviceberry, or birch. Usually such sites receive a few hours of direct sun during some part of the day.

— **Moderate shade**. Locations in moderate shade receive little direct sunlight. Reflected sunlight composes the bulk of the available light, such as underneath an oak or maple.

— **Dense shade**. Sites in heavy shade receive almost no direct sunlight. Nearly all the light available is reflected light, such as at the base of a north-facing wall or below dense evergreens.

NOTE: The light conditions reported in this book represent what is believed to be the best information available (obtained from experience, literature, and anecdotal information). Your particular experience may be affected by humidity, wind, surrounding hardscape features, microclimate, soil type, moisture content, and other environmental conditions. Use the information in this catalog as a general guideline, but realize that recommending light conditions is not an exact science.

 — Flowers attractive to hummingbirds.

 — Flowers attractive to butterflies.

 — Deer do not seem to relish this plant and seldom eat it. When extremely hungry, however, deer will eat about anything.

 — Foot Friendly® plants tolerate a fair amount of foot traffic.

— These plants tolerate occasional foot traffic.

— In addition to conventional uses, these plants are good for seasonal effect in decorative containers for patio and other hardscape decoration. NOTE: Most plants (although perennial when planted in the ground) will not survive winter in a container.

— Recommended for roof top planting (green roofs are common in Europe and are becoming more common in the United States).

— Great cutting plants providing flowers for live (sometimes dried) floral arrangements.

**NATIVE** — In this book, the term "Native Species" is applied to species that are known to have inhabited North America at the time of European settlement. Most of these plants inhabited the Great Lakes states (prior to European settlement) as well. The term native cultivar is applied to a cultivar derived from a native species.

# RECOMMENDED CONTAINER SIZES

100 RC rooted cutting flat
(with 2 half flats of 50 cuttings each)

50 cell pack (each 2 inches wide)

38 cell pack
(each 2-1/4 inches wide)

36 cell perforated (6 packs of 6 cells
each 2-1/8 inch x 2-3/8 inch)

*The perfect size for every need.*

6-Pack
(each cell 3 inches wide)

3-1/4 inch pot (18/flat)

#1 pot (8/flat) 5-1/4 inch square

1, 2, 5 gallon size containers

# Selecting, Using, and Maintaining Climbing Vines

*Lonicera sempervirens 'Blanche Sandman'*

Vines are unique for their flexible stems which make them useful for sprawling, trailing, and training in a multitude of directions. Without support, many vines make good ground covers. And, with support, they grow upright and thus take up little ground space. At the same time they introduce an interesting vertical dimension to the landscape. This is especially important in today's smaller landscapes where often the only direction to go is up. But vines do more than just cling and grow upward, and they have a great deal to offer in the way of ornamental appeal.

Vines offer a broad array of floral and foliar interest. Wisterias provide excellent color and a very classic look with their pendant trains of lavender flowers. But they also offer vibrant green fernlike deeply compound leaves. The trumpet vines (Campsis species) have large tubular flowers that appeal to hummingbirds—as do those of honeysuckles which range from white to pink to yellow and often are pleasantly fragrant. Honeysuckle leaves, by the way, range from yellow to green to purple. On the small end of the spectrum are the flowers of Boston ivies and Virginia creeper with their tiny green nearly invisible flowers. Such vines as these compensate for their tiny flowers with magnificent showy leaves that turn bright red or yellow during fall.

Some vines even produce interesting fruit. That of Boston ivy (Parthenocissus tricuspidata) is grapelike and persists through winter. The fruit of Akebias is colorful, large, and exotic, and that of trumpetvine resembles a miniature banana.

## Vines as Ground Covers:

Vines that work well as ground covers tend to grow rapidly and fill in to make a dense weed-impenetrable blanket. Hall's honeysuckle is a popular ground covering vine, and English ivy and purple wintercreeper are so popular as ground covers that they are often overlooked as climbers.

## Vines as Accents:

Used as accent plants, climbing vines help draw one's attention to other plants as well as such objects as trellises, pillars, light poles, chimneys, or other attractive ornamental features. For the purpose of accent, one or two plants are usually sufficient. The specific variety should be selected so as to contrast — through foliage color and texture or flowers, with the feature that is being accented.

## Vines as Screens:

Vines are wonderful for ornamental screening or concealment and there is a vine that will screen most anything. When using vines in this manner it is important to choose one with the proper growth characteristic so that it will effectively attach itself. It is also important to use a vine with the proper texture and leaf size to match the object being screened. Textures will vary according to the size and shape of the leaf, and there is a broad range of leaf sizes available.

## Vines For Decorating Walls, Fences, and Tree Trunks:

Vines are exceptional for adding color and textural interest to drab walls and harsh looking fences. They are also fantastic for dressing up the trunks of coarse barked trees, and for draping over the edges of retaining walls and planter boxes.

## Attracting Hummingbirds and Butterflies:

Vines with tubular flowers (like honeysuckles and trumpet vines) are hummingbird magnets. Others, such as climbing hydrangea, are good for butterfly gardening.

## Methods of Attachment:

*Twining Vines:* Twiners have stems that circle around other plants or objects to gain their support. These vines are good to use on chainlink fences, light poles, and trellises. They won't wrap around a large tree but they can overrun small trees and shrubs so be sure to use them in areas away from such plants.

*Clinging Vines:* Clinging vines attach themselves by aerial rootlets or adhesive disks and are great for attaching to flat surfaces. Those with aerial rootlets need a coarse surface to cling to, such as brick or coarse textured bark. They are good for use with large trees and brick walls and chimneys. Those with adhesive discs will attach to smooth (as well as coarse textured) surfaces and will climb just about anything.

## Maintaining Vines:
The maintenance of vines varies with each variety, its growth rate, and where it is planted. Ground covering vines usually need a simple trimming back once or twice a year to keep them in bounds. Those grown against a wall may need annual pruning to keep them away from windows and eave-troughs. Climbers growing on fences may go for several years without pruning.

## Planting, Spacing, and Watering.
Similar to ground covers. Please refer to the ground cover section of this brochure.

## Controlling Weeds in Vine Plantings:
Follow the directions in the ground cover section of this brochure.

## Fertilizing Vines:
Most vines are moderate feeders and should be fertilized in similar manner as ground covers (see ground cover section).

*Fruit of Wisteria sinensis*

# Lonicera japonica 'Aureo-reticulata' is an exceptional foliage plant.

A twiner, it is a fine selection for decorating a pole, trellis, or chainlink fence.

# Do Vines Damage Buildings?

*Parthenocissus quinquifolia*

Ever wonder if vines damage buildings? You are not alone as this is a subject of frequent debate.

The answer, according to experts who have studied century-old North American and European buildings, is no. What damage vines do cause is typically limited to fixtures such as downspouts, painted woodwork, and roof tiles — damage which would be avoided with timely pruning.

Rather than cause damage, these researchers found that a covering of vines reduces temperature fluctuations of brick walls (because of insulating and wind-breaking qualities), and thus reduces thermal contraction and expansion that can cause cracks in the underlying mansonry.

Vine covered walls tend to be cooler during the day and warmer at night and therefore help to save energy. A dense cover of Hedera helix (English Ivy) is said to bring about a 33 percent increase in R-value to poorly insulated walls and a 10 percent increase to those that are well insulated.

## VINE SELECTION CHART

Abbreviations: X = Applicable to this plant
P = Partially applicable to this plant

| NAME | METHOD OF ATTACHMENT | Full Sun | Light Shade | Moderate Shade | Dense Shade | Large Area | Moderate Area | Small Area | Controls Erosion | Tolerates Foot Traffic | Drought Tolerant | Moisture Tolerant | Tolerates Sandy Soil | Salt Tolerant | Spring Bloom | Summer Bloom | Fall Bloom | Evergreen |
|---|---|---|---|---|---|---|---|---|---|---|---|---|---|---|---|---|---|---|
| Akebia quinata 'Fruitful Combo' | twining | X | X | | | X | X | | X | P | X | | X | | X | | | P |
| Ampelopsis brevipedunculata 'Elegans' | tendrils | X | X | X | | | X | X | P | | | | | | | X | | |
| Aristolochia macrophylla | twining | X | X | X | | X | X | | | | X | | X | | X | | | |
| Campsis radicans and cultivars | aerial rootlets | X | X | | | X | X | | X | | X | | X | | | X | | |
| Celastrus rosethornianus | twining | X | X | | | X | X | | X | | X | | X | | X | | | |
| Clematis alpina 'Constance' | leaf stalks | X | X | | | X | X | | P | | P | P | | | X | | | |
| Clematis macrophylla cultivars | leaf stalks | X | X | | | X | X | | X | | P | X | | | X | | | |
| Clematis maximowicziana | leaf stalks | X | X | | | X | X | | X | | X | X | | | | | X | |
| Clematis montana 'Freda' | leaf stalks | X | X | | | X | X | X | | | P | | | | X | | | |
| Clematis tangutica | leaf stalks | X | X | | | X | X | | X | | P | X | | | | X | | |
| Clematis viticella cultivars | leaf stalks | X | X | | | X | X | X | | | X | | | | | X | | |
| Euonymus fortunei cultivars | aerial rootlets | X | X | X | X | X | X | | X | | X | X | | | | X | | X |
| Hedera colchica cultivars | aerial rootlets | X | X | X | X | X | X | | X | X | X | X | | | | X | | X |
| Hedera helix cultivars | aerial rootlets | X | X | X | X | X | X | | X | X | X | X | | | | X | | X |
| Hydrangea anomala varieties | aerial rootlets | X | X | X | | X | X | X | | | X | P | | | X | | | |
| Lonicera x 'Dropmore Scarlet' | twining | X | X | | | X | X | | X | | | | | | | X | | X |
| Lonicera x heckrottii | twining | X | X | | | X | X | | | | | | | | X | X | | P |
| Lonicera japonica cultivars | twining | X | X | | | X | X | X | X | P | X | X | | | | X | X | X |
| Lonicera 'Mandarin' | twining | X | X | | | X | X | | X | | P | P | | | X | | | P |
| Lonicera sempervirens cultivars | twining | X | X | | | | X | | P | | P | P | | | | X | X | |
| Parthenocissus quinquifolia | adhesive discs | X | X | X | X | X | X | | X | | X | X | | X | X | | | |
| Parthenocissus tricuspidata | adhesive discs | X | X | X | | X | X | | | | X | X | | | X | | | |
| Parthenocissus tricupidata 'Fenway Park' | adhesive discs | X | X | X | | X | X | | | | | | | | X | | | |
| Polygonum aubertii | twining | X | X | | | X | X | | X | | X | X | | | | X | X | |
| Polygonum aubertii 'Lemon Lace' | twining | X | X | | | X | X | | X | | X | X | | | | X | X | |
| Schizophragma hydrangeoides cultivars | aerial rootlets | X | X | X | | | | X | | | X | X | | | X | | | |
| Vitis vinifera 'Purpurea' | tendrils | X | X | | | X | X | | X | | P | P | | | X | | | |
| Wisteria brachybotrys cultivars | twining | X | | | | X | X | | | | P | P | | | X | | | |
| Wisteria floribunda | twining | X | | | | X | X | | | | P | P | | | X | | | |
| Wisteria macrostachya | twining | X | | | | X | X | | | | P | P | | | | | X | |
| Wisteria sinensis cultivars | twining | X | | | | X | X | | | | P | P | | | X | | | |

## Akebia quinata 'Fruitful Combo' (a-<u>kee</u>-bee-a kwi-<u>nay</u>-ta)
('Fruitful Combo' Fiveleaf Akebia)　　Zone 4

**Blooming Time**

20'-40' with support, 6" as a ground cover; full sun to moderate shade. In a single pot you may find A. quinata and A. quinata 'Alba'. A. quinata flowers deep purple and 'Alba' milky white. They bloom in spring and when grown together cross pollinate to give magnificently showy, colorful, bratwurst sized late season fruit. Durable and disease-free, fiveleaf akebia is an exceptionally attractive climber. A twiner, fiveleaf akebia grows well on a trellis or chain-link fence and unsupported, it is useful as an erosion controlling ground cover.
Rec. Size: 1 gal.　Space: (1 1/2'-2')

## Ampelopsis brevipedunculata 'Elegans' (am-pel-<u>op</u>-sis brev-i-ped-unk-you-<u>lay</u>-ta)
(Variegated Porcelain Vine)..................................................Zone 5

**Blooming Time**

Clinging 10'-15'; full sun to moderate shade. 'Elegans' has grapelike leaves ranging from 3 to 4 inches long, bears tiny flowers in early summer, and produces round berrylike fruit that is first yellow, later lilac, then bright blue. Quite famous for its lovely silvery white and green mottled foliage, the effect of the variegation is quite striking and attractive — especially in light to moderately shaded areas of the garden. With morning sun, it bears fruit more reliably, but afternoon sun should be avoided as it may cause the leaves to scorch.
Rec. Size: #1 Pot (8/flat)　Space: (1 1/2'-2')

This magnificent 100 year old specimen of **Campsis radicans, Trumpetvine,** exudes the characters of strength and endurance.

## Aristolochia macrophylla (a-ris-toe-<u>low</u>-kee-a mak-row-<u>fil</u>-a) a.k.a. A. durior.
(Dutchman's Pipe)..................................................Zone 4

**Blooming Time**

20'-30'; full sun to moderate shade. Simply extraordinary, Dutchman's pipe carries its massive heart shaped rich green foliage in overlapping fashion—making it the perfect screen. A twiner, Dutchman's pipe will cover chain link fences, climb poles, or decorate trellises. It is especially good against coarse bark, brick or block, and natural rough cut wood surfaces. Dutchman's Pipe is curious in bloom, with purple and yellowish-brown pipe-shaped springborne flowers underneath the foliage. Because the flowers are underneath the foliage, if they are to be appreciated, the plant must be carefully sited. An archway may be the best support from this standpoint as one can walk through and view the back side of the foliage, and therefore the flowers. Otherwise, one can simply lift up the foliage during spring to view them--they are really more of a curiosity than anything. The pendant fruit, when formed, is also interesting.
Rec. Size: #1 pot (8/flat)　Space: (2 1/2'-3')

## Campsis radicans (<u>kamp</u>-sis <u>rad</u>-i-kanz)
(Trumpetvine) NATIVE SPECIES..................................................Zone 5

**Blooming Time**

Climbing to 30'; full sun to light shade. A rapid grower, trumpetvine can be used to sprawl over the top of retaining walls or old stumps, or to cover a chain link fence. Its medium green, deciduous, compound foliage is arranged in opposite manner, and serves as a splendid backdrop to the flamboyant floral array of orange-tubed, scarlet petalled, hummingbird-attracting trumpets of July and August.
Rec. Size: #1 Pot (8/flat)　Space: (2 1/2'-3')

## Campsis radicans 'Flava' (<u>kamp</u>-sis <u>rad</u>-i-kanz <u>flay</u>-va)
(Yellow Trumpetvine) NATIVE CULTIVAR..................................................Zone 5

**Blooming Time**

Climbing to 30'; full sun to light shade. Similar to the species, this cultivar varies in that its summerborne flowers are a cheery yellow.
Rec. Size: #1 pot (8/flat)　Space: (2 1/2'-3')

### Campsis radicans 'Minnesota Red' (<u>kamp</u>-sis <u>rad</u>-i-kanz)
('Minnesota Red' Trumpetvine) NATIVE CULTIVAR.....................Zone 5

Climbing to 30'; full sun to light shade. An impressive cultivar, 'Minnesota Red' boasts rich velvety red hummingbird attracting trumpets throughout the summer months. These are enhanced even more by the outstanding foliage of this cultivar. Much deeper green than that of the species, the leaves of 'Minnesota Red' make a superb backdrop to its extraordinary flowers.
Rec. Size: #1 pot (8/flat)    Space: (2 1/2'-3')

### Campsis radicans 'MSU' (<u>kamp</u>-sis <u>rad</u>-i-kanz)
('MSU' Trumpetvine) NATIVE CULTIVAR......................................Zone 5

Climbing to 30'; full sun to light shade. A clone of the trumpet vine growing by the Vet. Clinic at Michigan State University, this is an awesome selection of C. radicans. Blooming during summer, 'MSU' boasts giant reddish orange flowers—way bigger than any other trumpet vine (over three inches wide), and to some degree similar to the larger flowered/less hardy species C. grandiflora. But, 'MSU' is extremely hardy, robust growing, stout stemmed, and highly desirable for its ability to flower during its first year from cuttings.
Rec. Size: #1 pot (8/flat)    Space: (2 1/2'-3')

# Aristolochia macrophylla, Dutchman's Pipe, is exceptionally course textured with massive heart shaped leaves. As a screen or accent, against coarse brick or covering chain link or a trellis, it is remarkably rich, and appears almost tropical.

### Celastrus rosethornianus (see-<u>las</u>-trus roze-<u>thorn</u>-ee-aye-nus)
(Loesener Bittersweet) ...............................................................Zone 5

40'; full sun to light shade. Compared to oriental bittersweet, this species displays glossier, darker green leaves (yellow in autumn) and narrower stems that arch over in pendant fashion. Most importantly, its late springborne non-ornamental flowers are bisexual and bear large quantities of bright-orange-seeded fruit without the need to pair male and female plants as is the case with C. orbiculatus and C. scandens.
Rec. Size: 1 gal.    Space: (3'-4')

# CLEMATIS

*Clematis maximowcziana seed heads*

*Compared to hybrid varieties, species clematis offer the important advantage of being drought and heat tolerant, and most importantly resistance to stem rot—the devastating disease that can kill many of the hybrid varieties. In addition to that, they are extraordinarily ornamental:*

*Species clematis offer unique features that make them highly prized. For starters, they are vigorous. Their strong stems grow quickly, attach effectively (to trellises, wire supports, poles, and chain link fence)—and act as strong supports to their attractive compound leaves. The foliage is different compared to many hybrid clematis. Instead of being sparse (and carried upon spindly stems) it is lush, robust, and sometimes quite colorful—a nice backdrop to the lovely flowers.*

*Some species, such as C. macropetala and C. montana, flower during early spring; C. macropetala with masses of bell shaped flowers, and C. montana with large, 4-petaled, sometimes fragrant flowers. Those of C. macropetala are followed by attractive feathery-appendaged seed heads. C. viticella blooms later and very heavily, beginning early to late summer and continuing until fall. It bears a tremendous quantity of large, highly colorful flowers. Then there's C. maximowicziana, sweet autumn clematis, which blooms like crazy during late summer and fall—many times with so many fragrant snow-white flowers as to obscure the foliage. These are followed by fuzzy wiry appendaged seed heads that persist through late fall into winter.*

## Clematis Selection Chart

| FLOWER COLOR/TONE | PRIMARY BLOOM TIME | | |
|---|---|---|---|
| | SPRING | SUMMER | FALL |
| White | | | C. maximowicziana |
| Pink | C. alpina 'Constance' C. macrophylla 'Markham's Pink' C. montana 'Freda' | | |
| Red | | C viticella 'Mme Julia Correvon' | |
| Yellow | | C. tangutica | |
| Blue | C. macropetala 'Bluebird' | | |
| Purple | | C. viticella 'Etoile Violette' | |

**Clematis alpina 'Constance' (<u>klem</u>-a-tis   al-<u>pie</u>-na)**
('Constance' Alpine Clematis) ...............................................Zone 5

Climbing 6'-8'; full sun to light shade. 'Constance' alpine clematis is a marvelously florific selection with fine textured medium green compound leaves. Like other alpine clematis, 'Constance' is disease resistant, quick to establish, and easy to grow. Unique for its masses of bright pink 1-2 inch long bell shaped flowers during April and May, the flowers of 'Constance' keep coming sporadically throughout summer and are followed by attractive seed heads. Flower buds are set in fall so prune early to mid summer.
Rec. Size: #1 pot (8/flat)    Space: (1 1/2'-2')

**Clematis macropetala 'Blue Bird' (<u>klem</u>-a-tis   mak-row-pe-<u>tay</u>-la)**
('Blue Bird' Clematis ).............................................................Zone 4

Climbing 8'-12'; full sun to light shade. If limited to growing just one clematis, this might be your pick. That's because 'Bluebird' blooms very early during spring (and a little bit again during late summer), with many large and showy 2-inch-wide bell shaped bright blue flowers. These contrast in such a beautiful manner with its superior fine textured three parted vibrant green foliage that they seem to jump right out of the plant. Later, the same flowers give rise to interesting feathery appendaged seed heads. Flower buds are set in fall, so prune early to mid summer.
Rec. Size: #1 pot (8/flat)    Space: (1 1/2'-2')

## Clematis macropetala 'Markham's Pink' (<u>klem</u>-a-tis mak-row-pe-<u>tay</u>-la)
('Markham's Pink' Clematis) ......................................................Zone 4

Climbing 8'-12'; full sun to light shade. This fabulous clematis selection is the pink flowered equivalent of Clematis 'Blue Bird'. Like 'Blue Bird', 'Markham's Pink' is early spring flowering with masses of showy 2-inch-wide frilly bell shaped pendant flowers. In this case they are a cheerful pink. 'Markham's Pink' is excellent covering a trellis or lattice, it displays pleasing vibrant green foliage and interesting seed heads, and it works well in combination with white- and blue-flowering clematis selections. Flower buds are set in fall, so prune early to mid summer.
Rec. Size: #1 pot (8/flat)   Space: (1 1/2'-2')

## Clematis maximowicziana (<u>klem</u>-a-tis maks-i-moe-witz-ee-<u>aye</u>-na)
(Sweet Autumn Clematis)........................................................Zone 5

1'-2' as a ground cover, climbing to 30' if given support; full sun to light shade. This is one of the fastest growing, most easily cultured and heaviest flowering of any vine hardy to the Midwest. As a climber, it is tenacious and will ascend quickly by tendril-like petioles, but its merits as a ground cover should not be overlooked. As such, it will easily spread 10 feet per year and forms a weed impenetrable mat. It does not root as it spreads, and therefore controls erosion only on gently sloping banks and level terrain. Flowering September and October, the blooms are very fragrant and plentiful.
Rec. Size: #1 pot (8/flat)   Space: (2 1/2'-3')

## Clematis montana 'Freda' (<u>klem</u>-a-tis mon-<u>tay</u>-na)
('Freda' Anemone Clematis ) ..................................................Zone 5

Climbing 25'-30'; full sun to light shade. Even without its masses of rich cheery pink, 2 inch wide, 4-petaled springborne flowers, this would be one of the most popular selections of clematis. That's because 'Freda' is prized for deep maroon-bronze foliage. And, regardless of how you use it, upon a trellis, topiary frame, or climbing up a pole, 'Freda' will add a unique element to the landscape. Flower buds are set in fall so prune early to mid summer.
Rec. Size: #1 pot (8/flat)   Space: (1 1/2'-2')

## Clematis tangutica (<u>klem</u>-a-tis tan-<u>gew</u>-ti-ka)
(Golden Clematis) ...................................................................Zone 5

Climbing 10'-15'; full sun to light shade. From China, this recognizable species is adorned with rich buttercup yellow, bell-shaped, 3-4 inch wide flowers. Blooming during June and July, golden clematis is considered one of the most handsome of the clematis species. A good bloomer and a fair foliage plant (leaves colored sea green), it is one of the very best for the showiness of its seed heads. Feathery appendaged, silky, and numerous, the seed heads of golden clematis rival the flowers that bore them, and indeed extend the unique qualities of this plant far into the fall season.
Rec. Size: #1 pot (8/flat)   Space: (1 1/2'-2')

## Clematis viticella 'Etoile Violette' (a.k.a.'Violet Star')
(<u>klem</u>-a-tis vee-ti-<u>kel</u>-la ee-<u>toil</u> vie-<u>oh</u>-let)
('Violet Star' Clematis).............................................................Zone 4

Climbing 10'-12'; full sun to light shade. From southern Europe, the species C. viticella is said to have contributed more to the popularity of clematis than any other species. It has been used to create many outstanding hybrids and is hardy and disease resistant. 'Etoile Violette' is among the finest selections of this species, unique in its vigorous growth habit and its multitude of bright purple 3"-4" wide, four-petaled summerborne flowers. Flower buds are set on new growth so prune during March or early April.
Rec. Size: #1 pot (8/flat)   Space: (1 1/2'-2')

## Clematis viticella 'Mme. Julia Correvon' (<u>klem</u>-a-tis vee-ti-<u>kel</u>-la)
('Mme. Julia Correvon' Clematis)...........................................Zone 4

Climbing 10'-12'; full sun to light shade. 'Mme. Julia Correvon' displays superb true-red flowers, in good quantity, throughout most of the summer season. In addition, it boasts a vigorous habit and attractive medium green foliage. Combined, these traits have made 'Mme. Julia Correvon' one of the most popular selections of clematis. Flower buds are set on new growth so prune during March or early April.
Rec. Size: #1 pot (8/flat)   Space: (1 1/2'-2')

## Hydrangea annomala `Mirranda' (hi-<u>dran</u>-je-a  a-<u>nom</u>-a-la)
(`Mirranda' Climbing Hydrangea) ........................................................Zone 5

20'-40'; light to moderate shade. The first variegated climbing hydrangea, `Mirranda' is a lovely selection with shiny deep green foliage decorated with a bright yellow irregular edge. Clinging by rootlike holdfasts to coarse textured bark and brick, `Mirranda' is a fabulous accent plant, and during summer produces white-bracted fragrant flowers. Expected to become a garden classic, `Mirranda' is still relatively new and rare. This is due somewhat to its initial slow growing nature. `Mirranda', like the parent species, takes a couple of seasons to get set. Thereafter it grows at a nice rate, not too slow and not too fast.
Rec. Size: #1 pot (8/flat)     Space: (2'-2 1/2')

## Hydrangea anomala ssp. petiolaris (hi-<u>dran</u>-je-a  a-<u>nom</u>-a-la pet-i-oh-<u>lay</u>-ris)
(Climbing Hydrangea) .............................................................Zone 4

Climbing 30'-50'; full sun to moderate shade. With root-like holdfasts and semi-twining habit, climbing hydrangea will cling to either trees, bricks, or fencing. Climbing hydrangea serves well for screening but can also be used as an accent or specimen plant, or when unsupported, as a small scale ground cover. Its deciduous rounded foliage is lush dark green, the perfect backdrop to its gigantic 6 to 10 inch wide white flower clusters — which burst into bloom during the months of June and July.
Rec. Size: #1 pot (8/flat)   Space: (2'-3')

## Lonicera x brownii 'Dropmore Scarlet' (lo-<u>nis</u>-er-a  brown-<u>ee</u>-eye)
(Dropmore Honeysuckle) ..................................................Zone 3

6'-8' when supported, or as ground cover 1-1/2'-2' tall; full sun to light shade. This extraordinarily hardy evergreen hybrid climbs by twining (or sprawls along the ground at a moderate pace). It is exceptionally attractive for its blue green foliage and numerous clusters of early summer — to fallborne, orange, scarlet throated, hummingbird attracting, trumpet shaped flowers.
Rec. Size: #1 pot (8/flat)   Space: (2'-2 1/2')

## Lonicera x heckrottii (lo-<u>nis</u>-er-a  hek-<u>rot</u>-ee-eye)
(Goldflame Honeysuckle) ..................................................Zone 5

Twining to 12'; as a ground cover 1'-2'; full sun to light shade. An outstanding sprawling vine that will climb with encouragement, goldflame honeysuckle is also exceptional as a ground cover when unsupported. Bright carmine flower buds open to yellow and are very pleasantly fragrant from mid-spring through late summer. Attractive to hummingbirds.
Rec. Size: #1 pot (8/flat)   Space: (2 1/2'-3')

## Lonicera japonica 'Aureo-reticulata' (lo-<u>nis</u>-er-a  ja-<u>pon</u>-i-ka)
(Yellow-net Honeysuckle) ..................................................Zone 5

Climbing 10'-15'; as a ground cover 12"-18'; full sun to light shade. Recipient of various awards for horticultural merit, yellow-net honeysuckle is a colorful novelty plant with leaves of bright green with brilliant golden veination. It is curious and colorful and makes an interesting plant for close-up viewing on a trellis, fence, stake, or container. Its white flowers are fragrant but borne sparsely during summer. Yellow-net honeysuckle greatly appreciates its soil being amended with liberal organic matter.
Rec. Size: #1 pot (8/flat)   Space: (2'-2 1/2')

## Lonicera japonica 'Hall's Prolific' (lo-<u>nis</u>-er-a  ja-<u>pon</u>-i-ka)
(Hall's Prolific' Honeysuckle) ..................................................Zone 5

Climbing 15'-30'; as a ground cover 1 1/2'-2 1/2'; full sun to light shade. A popular twining evergreen vine used for covering banks, large open areas, and trellises, 'Hall's Prolific' honeysuckle displays fragrant flowers which open pure white in early summer and gradually change to soft yellow. Not recommended in Southern Indiana and Illinois as there it may produce seed and end up in natural areas. Farther north in Zones 4-6 it does not seem to produce fruit or viable seed.
Rec. Size: #1 pot (8/flat)   Space: (1 1/2'-2')

## Lonicera japonica 'Purpurea' (lo-<u>nis</u>-er-a ja-<u>pon</u>-i-ka)
(Purple Leaved Japanese Honeysuckle)................................Zone 5

Climbing 10'-25', as a ground cover 1 1/2'-2 1/2'; full sun to light shade.

Similar to Hall's honeysuckle in habit and function, purple leaved honeysuckle is a bit slower growing and displays purple colored evergreen foliage. Floral appeal is also superb. Red in bud, the 1 inch long trumpets open to ivory white, then age to creamy yellow. Against the background of the purple leaves, the Juneborne flowers are magnificent, and their fragrance exquisite.
Rec. Size: #1 pot (8/flat)   Space: (1 1/2'-2')

## Lonicera 'Mandarin' (lo-<u>nis</u>-er-a)
('Mandarin' Honeysuckle) ................................Zone 3

Twining 15'-20'; full sun to light shade. From the breeding program at the University of British Columbia, 'Mandarin' boasts massive clusters of pleasantly fragrant, late-springborne, hummingbird attracting flowers of bright orange with yellow centers. Its foliage, also, is exquisite. First copperybrown then dark green, it is rounded, leathery, and provides a lovely foil as it twines on trellis or chain link.
Rec. Size: #1 pot (8/flat)   Space: (2'-2 1/2')

## Lonicera sempervirens 'Blanche Sandman' (lo-<u>nis</u>-er-a sem-per-<u>vie</u>-renz) NATIVE CULTIVAR
('Blanche Sandman' Red Honeysuckle)................................Zone 5

Twining 15'-20'; full sun to light shade. A robust grower, 'Blanche Sandman' ranges from evergreen to semievergreen. Its foliage is 2-3 inches long, oval to oblong, and depending upon the season is near burgundy to shiny bluish green. Of greatest interest, however, are the magnificent, late springborne, brilliant crimson flowers—providing not only color for our appreciation, but nectar for hummingbirds. Works well for screening or as a bank cover.
Rec. Size: #1 pot (8/flat)   Space: (2'-2 1/2')

## Lonicera sempervirens 'John Clayton' (lo-<u>nis</u>-er-a sem-<u>per</u>-vie-renz) NATIVE CULTIVAR
('John Clayton' Honeysuckle)................................Zone 5

Twining 10'-15'; full sun to light shade. A repeat bloomer that flowers early summer through fall, 'John Clayton' is a superb selection of yellow trumpet honeysuckle. Named for the colonial botanist, and discovered on the grounds of a 17th century church in Glouchester, VA, 'John Clayton' is clothed in bluish green deciduous foliage that looks nice as a backdrop to the bright yellow, hummingbird attracting, trumpet shaped flowers. A twiner, it is superb on a trellis, pole, or chain link fence.
Rec. Size: #1 pot (8/flat)   Space: (2'-2 1/2')

## Parthenocissus quinquifolia (par-then-oh-<u>sis</u>-us kwin-kwe-<u>foe</u>-lee-a)
(Virginia Creeper) NATIVE SPECIES ................................Zone 3

Climbing 40'-50'; as a ground cover 4"-8"; full sun to moderate shade. Clinging by tendrils, this lovely native will climb rough brick siding and coarse barked trees (doing them no harm) or cover large slopes as a ground cover. Chief among its attributes is its excellent red early fall color display. A summer bloomer, its tiny yellow flowers bear deep blue grapelike fruit in fall. It is attractive and a food source for various songbirgs.
Rec. Size: #1 pot (8/flat)   Space: (1 1/2'-2')

## Parthenocissus tricuspidata (par-then-oh-<u>sis</u>-us try-kus-pi-<u>day</u>-ta)
(Boston Ivy)................................Zone 5

Climbing to 60'; full sun to moderate shade. Boston ivy clings to nearly any surface by means of discettes borne from the ends of tendrilous holdfasts. Its rather coarse textured deciduous foliage is shiny green throughout the growing season. In fall it colors up nicely with striking hues of yellow, gold, and scarlet. Summerborne flowers are tiny and usually go unnoticed but the fruit which follows is dark blue, grapelike, and persists well into winter. By spring the fruit has usually disappeared, having eagerly been consumed by numerous species of songbirds.
Rec. Size: #1 pot (8/flat)   Space: (2'-3')

## Parthenocissus tricuspidata 'Fenway Park'
**(par-then-oh-<u>sis</u>-us   tri-kus-pi-<u>day</u>-ta)**
(Golden Boston Ivy)...................................................Zone 5

Clinging 20'-30'; light to moderate shade. Introduced by the Arnold Arboretum of Massachusetts, 'Fenway Park' is an exciting selection with bright golden yellow foliage (orange in fall) — exceptional for specimen planting and brightening up dark areas of the landscape, especially against brick walls, fences, and smooth and coarse barked trees. Blooming during summer, it sometimes produces grapelike fruit in fall.
Rec. Size: #1 pot (8/flat)   Space: (1 1/2'-2')

## Polygonum aubertii (poe-<u>lig</u>-oh-num   awe-ber-<u>tee</u>-eye)
(Silver-fleece Vine)...................................................Zone 5

Twining 15'-30'; full sun to light shade. This rapid growing twining vine has shiny, bright green, deciduous foliage. Its billowy masses of fragrant white flowers cover the plant from summer to late autumn and in fall its leaves pick up hues of purple. Excellent for planting along chain link fences and upon trellises.
Rec. Size: #1 pot (8/flat)   Space: (2 1/2'-3')

## Polygonum aubertii 'Lemon Lace' (poe-<u>lig</u>-oh-num   awe-ber-<u>tee</u>-eye)
('Lemon Lace' Silver-fleece Vine)...................................Zone 5

15'-25'; full sun to moderate shade. An exciting new introduction for brightening up the landscape, 'Lemon Lace' is clothed in vibrant lemon yellow foliage--in sharp contrast to its stems and petioles of purpled-red. Not only is 'Lemon Lace' a brilliant foliage plant, it puts on quite a floral show during late summer and fall when decorated with pendant chains of foamy white flowers. A twiner, 'Lemon Lace' is ideal for dressing up chain link fences, trellises, decorative poles, frames, arches, and entryways. It is also a great companion to colorfully flowered clematis.
Rec. Size: #1 pot (8/flat)   Space: (2 1/2'-3')

## Schizophragma hydrangeoides 'Moonlight' (ski-<u>zoe</u>-frag-ma or  skiz-oh-<u>frag</u>-ma   hi-dran-gee-<u>oy</u>-deez)
('Moonlight' Japanese Climbing Hydrangea)...................Zone 5

Clinging 15'-30'; full sun to moderate shade. Clinging by rootlike holdfasts, 'Moonlight' Japanese hydrangea is a splendid choice for growing against brick walls and upon the trunks of coarse barked trees. Its silvery-steel-blue overlaid, heart shaped leaves are deep green veined and attractive on their own. Yet, during mid summer, it also gives rise to large white-bracted florets for additional appeal.
Rec. Size: #1 pot (8/flat)   Space: (1 1/2'-2')

## Schizophragma hydrangeoides 'Rosea' (ski-<u>zoe</u>-frag-ma   or skiz-oh-<u>frag</u>-ma   hi-dran-gee-<u>oy</u>-deez)
(Pink Flowered Japanese Climbing Hydrangea)...............Zone 5

Clinging 15'-30'; full sun to moderate shade. Like 'Moonlight' (see above), this rugged climber bears its flowers during mid summer, but in this case the bracted florets are pink instead of white. Its foliage, also, is different. Colored a rich almost red-tinged deep green, it is quite handsome and can be used to great effect on coarse bark and brick. In any event, try to site it close to high traffic areas so that it may be appreciated by many.
Rec. Size: #1 pot (8/flat)   Space: (1 1/2'-2')

## Vitis vinifera 'Purpurea' (<u>vie</u>-tis   vie-<u>nif</u>-er-a)
(Purple-leaved Ornamental Grape)...................................Zone 5

30'; full sun to light shade. This rare vine bears attractive 6 inch wide, deeply lobed, rounded, richly colorful foliage—claret red in spring, deep red-purple by June, and translucent red-purple in autumn. A superb foliage plant, purple-leaved ornamental grape is useful for scrambling over retaining walls and terraces, covering fences and lattice (attaching by tendrils), and decorating pergolas, poles, and tree stumps. With tiny summerborne flowers, it seldom bears fruit.
Rec. Size: #1 pot (8/flat)   Space: (1 1/2'-2')

# Beautiful Mysterious Wisterias

*Wisteria floribunda 'Shiro Noda'*

Named for Caspar Wistar, a Philadelphia physician, wisterias are magnificently beautiful, hardy, long lived twining vines with head-turning, breathtaking floral effect—so as to win the affection of all who see them. They are plants of velvety, fragrant, pealike flowers arranged in sumptuous cascading racemes that remind one of colored icicles. After falling, and colorfully carpeting the ground, the thousands of flowers give rise to long pendant beanlike pods set against lovely, lacy, fernlike compound foliage—each leaf composed of 9 to 19 oval, vibrant green leaflets. Then, during fall, the pods turn coffee brown and jump out from the foliage which by then, often, has turned rich hues of yellow and gold.

Wisterias are mysterious, sometimes taking several years before blooming. Yet, there are tricks to reduce this time, and they are addressed below. Wisterias are confusing, though they shouldn't be. They are confusing because their names are all messed up, because garden writers have perpetuated mistakes in nomenclature, and because nurserymen have given long established varieties newer, fancier, unofficial cultivar names to enhance their market appeal.

Fortunately, however, Australian plant pathologist and horticulturist, Peter Valder, in his excellent book Wisterias (Timber Press 1995), has presented a definitive text on wisteria. Within its 160 pages, he discusses the different species, their history and lore, the mysteries of their blooming cycle, and the multitude of nomenclatural sins committed over the years by Japanese, Chinese, European, and North American nurserymen. It's amazing how many different names have been applied to identical plants (read on and you will get a feel for the magnitude of this).

## Popular Species of Wisteria

Kentucky wisteria, called W. macrostachya, takes its scientific name from Latin and literally means 'large spiked', the floral racemes being longer than the other native wisteria, W. frutescens. W. macrostachya also differs in having fewer leaflets per leaf than W. frutescens. W. macrostachya occurs naturally in swamps from Louisiana north to Illinois and was first used as a garden plant in France in the middle of the 19th century.

W. macrostachya is a slender, vigorous climber with stems turning counterclockwise (when viewed from above) and leaves composed of 7-11 leaflets. Its pale violet flowers are pleasantly scented and arranged in racemes of 70-80 flowers during late spring to mid summer. Cultivars range in color from snow white to lavender blue.

W. sinensis, Chinese Wisteria, in any manner; climbing a trellis, trained against a wall, trained as a shrub, or trained as bonsai, is one of the most famous and appealing of cultivated plants. It can become very tall, given support, and has been reported to reach 75+ feet in ideal conditions.

Chinese wisteria is popular throughout the world and performs well in climatic Zones ranging from 5 to 9. Chinese wisteria was originally brought to Europe in 1816 where it was well accepted, rapidly propagated, and soon distributed to other countries. Revered through the ages, Chinese wisteria has been depicted in a number of well known paintings, in Tiffany lamp shades, and in stained glass works throughout the world.

Chinese wisteria twines counterclockwise (when viewed from above). It is characterized by compound 16 inch long leaves of 9-13 ovate-elliptic to oblong leaflets, usually colored copper or bronze-green in youth, vibrant green in summer, and often pleasing yellow in fall. Its pleasantly fragrant 1 inch long flowers are colored blue-violet, violet, or reddish violet and are borne upon bare stems opening simultaneously in 25-95 flowered grapelike bunches as the leaves unfold during spring. Peter Valder, in his book, lists 29 cultivars ranging from 'Alba' to 'Yaezaki Shina Fuji'. Of these, 13 are described—meaning sixteen cultivars are the same, but misnamed versions, of the 13 with valid names.

Wisteria floribunda, Japanese Wisteria, reaches 35 feet tall with sufficient support, and is different from Chinese wisteria in that its stems, when viewed from above, twine in clockwise fashion. Its striking pendulous racemes are comparatively longer, sometimes more than 3 feet in length, and contain many 1/2" to 3/4" long sweet smelling flowers. Its leaves, composed of 11-17 ovate-elliptic to oblong leaflets are pale green or bronze-green in youth, medium green in maturity, and occasionally display good yellow fall color. Its flowers, usually violet, are arranged in many-flowered racemes. They begin opening, in succession from base (of the raceme) to tip, as the leaves begin to unfurl. Compared to W. sinensis, which opens its flowers all at once, the bloom period is drawn out, more artistic, and less bold—yet immensely exquisite.

Peter Valder lists 106 cultivars of Japanese wisteria, ranging from 'Akabana' to 'Yatsubusa'. Of these, 28 are described—meaning 78 are masquerading under errant names. In other words, for every legitimately named cultivar, there are nearly three that are misnamed.

There are other wisteria species such as W. frutescens and W. venusta. And, that which is of most interest for its ornamental features, is a W. brachybotrys. Peter Valder says that "if ever there was a plant deserving to be better known, it is this wisteria". He describes it as having broad racemes of heavily scented heavy textured flowers appearing early in the season. It comes in white, pink, and mauve cultivars and twines in a counterclockwise manner.

## The Secret to Having Wisteria Flowers

Flowering wisterias, with their vibrant colors and exquisite fragrance, are the envy of all who do not have them, the joy of those whose porch is bedecked with them, and the despair of him who has plants that have never bloomed. Written by Alfred Carl Hottes, in his book Climbers and Ground Covers, truer words have never been spoken. Wisterias may take as many as ten years to begin flowering, but this does not have to be the case. An understanding of the plant and its cultural needs, accompanied with appropriate pruning methods, can greatly reduce the time it takes wisteria to bloom.

**Fertilizing to Stimulate Flowering:** Wisterias belong in the pea family (Leguminosae) and like other members of the pea family they form nitrogen fixing nodules on their roots which allow them to supply their own nitrogen. This is important to understand when culturing them as they should be grown without the addition of nitrogen containing fertilizer—otherwise they will produce a lot of vegetative growth instead of flowers. Most authorities recommend planting wisteria in a well drained loam, amended with ample leaf compost, and fertilizing only with an annual application of superphosphate each fall. The superphosphate should be scratched into the surrounding soil at a rate of 1/2 pound for each inch of diameter of the main stem.

Wisterias should also be surrounded with a mulch, woodchips, bark, or stone, or ground cover that requires very little fertilizer. Do not allow wisterias to receive nitrogen containing fertilizer that's been applied to surrounding turf—in other words do not grow turf around them as turf requires regular nitrogen fertilization!

**Soil pH:** Wisterias prefer a soil pH in the range of 6.0 to 7.5. Regulating the soil pH in this range (via incorporation of lime or sulphur) will also help to keep wisterias healthy and predisposed to flowering.

**Proper Siting to Stimulate Flowering:** Wisterias will always flower sooner and better when grown in the sun, so avoid planting in even light shade. They should also be sited in locations sheltered from strong winds.

**The Maturation Process of Wisteria:** In youth wisterias expend most of their energy producing new growth and they store very little food. But, stored food is needed for flowering and fruiting. Therefore, young fast-growing plants do not flower. Only when wisteria makes sufficient growth to be able to store food does it begin to bloom. Left to its own devices, wisteria plants may take seven to ten years to reach this stage. Yet, there are pruning methods (both root and branch-pruning) that can facilitate the food storage process and thereby stimulate earlier flowering. Here is how it is done:

**Root Pruning to Stimulate Flowering:** Prune the roots in October in order to retard the top growth. Using a long sharp spade, sever the roots to a depth of 18 to 24-inches in a circle all the way around the main stem. The spade should be inserted one foot away from the trunk for each inch of the trunk's diameter.

**Branch Pruning to Stimulate Flowering:** Wisterias are like apple trees in that they flower near the main branches upon short lateral branches called spurs. Effective branch pruning of wisterias aims at building up a system of spurs. The more spurs, the more flowers. During the first couple of years one should concentrate on developing the main framework of the wisteria. Thereafter, pruning should be geared toward maximum spur development. Here is how you do it:

**Pruning Year One and Two:** Concentrate on developing a strong central structural support. Figure out where you want the main stem to grow—it may be straight up a pole, bent over an archway, trained as espalier against a wall, or left to climb up a tree. In any event, don't prune the branches that you want to become the main trunk and main structural branches until they have reached their desired height, shape, and length. The only pruning during year one and two should consist of a single summer pruning to cut back nonstructural branches to half their length. Then, in late winter, conduct a second pruning, this time cutting the same stems back another 1/2 their length. During either time (summer or winter), you should also cut out all useless cross branches, weak, or dead wood that may arise.

**Pruning Year Three and Beyond:** Now that most of the main framework of branches has been established, the lateral branches that arise from the main framework should be pruned each year to encourage the formation of flower buds. With the first pruning, after flowering (about midsummer), the long laterals should be cut back to about 6 inches of the main branches. During the second pruning, in midwinter, these again should be shortened, leaving only three or four buds to each lateral shoot (only the long young shoots required to extend the main framework of the climber are left unpruned). The shoots arising from the pruned stubs are treated the same way the following year, and so on. Gradually spurs are built up along the branches and the resultant buds will eventually be flower buds rather than vegetative buds.

By the time of its maturity a large wisteria will have a well developed system of short spurred branches with relatively few long extension branches being produced. Then maybe you will be able to boast of a wisteria such as this, described by Dr. John Lindley (1840) as recounted in Peter Valder's book Wisterias:

"[In China] there exists a magnificent [wisteria] specimen, 180 feet long, and covering about 1800 square feet of wall. The number of branches

was about 9000 and of flowers 675,000. Each flower consisting of 5 petals, the number of these parts was 3,375,000. Had all the petals been placed end to end they would have extended to the distance of more than thirty-four miles." Now that's a wisteria!

**Plant Selection for Flower Production:** In order to minimize the time until bloom, you should only use plants that have been vegetatively propagated (via cuttings, layering, or grafting) from adult (flowering) plants. If plants have been grown from seed they will take longer to mature and begin blooming. What's more, the flower color will be uncertain. Also, you should use only container grown plants as wisteria is set back severely when transplanted bareroot.

**Pruning Into Tree Form:** To train wisteria into tree form, simply stake the plants when young. Trim out all side shoots, leaving only the main one to be trained. When the main shoot has reached the desired height, usually 7 or 8 feet, tip it and let it branch out. Thereafter, prune as discussed above to encourage spur formation. In a few years the trunk will become so strong that the support may be removed. It will also be twisted and gnarled, increasing in rustic character, dignity, and strength as it ages—Robert Fortune, the noted plant explorer told of a W. floribunda which had a trunk measuring seven feet in circumference three feet from the ground. The vine covered a trellis 60 feet tall by 102 feet long.

## Landscape Use

Wisterias look splendid when planted on either side of a doorway and trained to grow over in archlike fashion. They are exceptional around and over patios and walkways. They train well against walls as espalier. They look nice in tree form and bonsai, and are wonderful growing up poles—but they can crush wooden poles, and are best grown on heavy (minimum of 4" x 4") pressure-treated wooden posts or metal supports. As specimens, accents, or screens, wisterias are superb in flower and foliage—their effect doubled when grown near, and their image reflected by water.

Wisterias may also be pruned into large self supporting topiary. At times they are allowed to grow up tall trees. This might be ok, but avoid letting them climb small trees, as they will eventually strangle, smother, and kill the small tree.

Wisterias are also great companions to spring blooming bulbs, Lamium, arabis, violets, Epimediums, Pulmonaria, early blooming honeysuckles, dogwoods of various flower color, redbud trees, Rhododendron, crab apples, and lilacs. Use your imagination and invent new creative ways to enjoy these beautiful mysterious plants.

**Peter Valder's Top Ten List of Wisteria:** In his book, Peter Valder took the brave step of announcing his favorite ten Wisteria. They are as follows:

1. **W. brachybotrys 'Murasaki Kapitan'.**
2. **W. brachybotrys 'Shiro Kapitan'** (a.k.a. 'Alba', 'Alba Plena', 'Plena', 'Shira Fuji', 'Shirobana Yama Fuji').
3. **W. sinensis 'Prolific'** (a.k.a. 'Consequa').
4. **W. floribunda 'Honbeni'** (a.k.a. 'Akabana', 'Alabama', 'Honko', 'Momoiro', 'Multijuga Rosea', 'Multijuga Rubra', 'Pink Ice', 'Rosea', 'Rubrum', 'Shinbeni').
5. **W. floribunda 'Kuchibeni'** (a.k.a. 'Alborosea', 'Carnea', 'Lipstick', 'Peaches and Cream').
6. **W. floribunda 'Lawrence'.**
7. **W. floribunda 'Macrobotrys'** (a.k.a. 'Kyushaku', 'Longissima', 'Multijuga', 'Murasaki Fuji', 'Muurasaki Naga Fuji', 'Naga Fuji', 'Naga-ho-no-fuji', 'Naga Noda', 'Penn Valley Long Cluster', 'Purple Patches', 'Rokushaku', 'Sanshaku', 'Ushijima').
8. **W. floribunda 'Royal Purple'** (a.k.a. 'Black Dragon', 'Eranthema', 'Hitoe Kokuryu', 'Kokuryu').
9. **W. floribunda 'Shiro Noda'** (a.k.a. 'Alba', 'Longissima Alba', 'Multijuga Alba', 'Sairo Nira', 'Shirobana', 'Shiro Naga', 'Showa Shiro', 'Silver Lace', 'Snow Showers', 'Wase Shiro Naga').
10. **W. floribunda 'Violacea Plena'** (a.k.a. 'Botan Fuji', 'Double Black Dragon', 'Flore-Pleno', 'Longissima Rosea Plena', 'Multijuga Flore-Pleno', 'Namban Fuji', 'Peony Wisteria' 'Pleniflora', 'Yae Fuji', 'Yae Kokuryu').

## Wisteria brachybotrys 'Shiro Kapitan' (wis-<u>tee</u>-re-a  bray-key-<u>bow</u>-tres)
('Shiro Kapitan' Silky Wisteria)..............................................Zone 5

15'-25'; full sun. Translated from Latin, brachybotrys means short racemed, in reference to the compact grape-like clusters of flowers on this species. 'Shiro Kapitan', from Japanese and Portuguese respectively, means white sea captain. This superb cultivar is exceptionally strongly fragrant with broad, pure white flowers of heavy substance arranged in 20-35 flowered racemes. Appearing during spring about the time the golden green juvenile leaves unfold, the flowers are known to rebloom, but with pink tinges, during the summer months.
Rec. Size: #1 pot (8/flat)    Spacing: (2 1/2'-3')

## Wisteria floribunda 'Honbeni' (wis-<u>tee</u>-re-a  flor-i-<u>bun</u>-da)
(Pink Flowered Japanese Wisteria) ..............................................Zone 5

20'-35'; full sun. Often errantly listed as 'Rosea' or 'Pink Ice', 'Honbeni', in Japanese, means True Red, which describes the rich lavender-pink highly fragrant flowers which it bears in 72-97 flowered 20+ inch long pendant, springborne racemes. An outstanding selection, 'Honbeni' is considered quite rare. It is exceptionally showy when planted alone yet combines exceptionally well with white flowered forms of wisteria.
Rec. Size #1 pot (8/flat)    Spacing: (2 1/2'-3')

This **Wisteria sinensis, Chinese wisteria** is a one of a kind specimen.

## Wisteria floribunda 'Shiro Noda' (wis-<u>tee</u>-re-a  flor-i-<u>bun</u>-da)
('White Flowered' Japanese Wisteria)..............................................Zone 5

20'-35'; full sun. 'Shiro Noda' is considered by Peter Valder to be "one of the most beautiful of all wisterias". This is because 'Shiro Noda' carries its multitude of ivory white late-springborne flowers in 20 to 26 inch long cascading racemes (129 to 153 flowers per raceme). Spectacular highlighted against a dark backdrop, the flowers of 'Shiro Noda' fairly jump out of the landscape. They are also superb with other flower colors suggesting comfortable companionship with other wisterias. Seed pods of this variety are exceptionally long and ornamental.
Rec. Size: #1 pot (8/flat)    Spacing: (2 1/2'-3')

## Wisteria floribunda 'Violacea Plena', commonly misnamed 'Double Black Dragon' (wis-<u>tee</u>-re-a  flor-i-<u>bun</u>-da)
(Double Purple Japanese Wisteria)..............................................Zone 5

20'-35'; full sun. This superb cultivar is highly sought after and, where available, exceedingly popular. Reported to be the only double flowered wisteria, this is also the darkest flowered—its pendant springborne racemes decorated with 75-86, double petaled, violet-tinged, rich purple flowers. Fall foliage color is a pleasing rich yellow.
Rec. Size: #1 pot (8/flat)    Spacing: (2 1/2'-3')

## Wisteria macrostachya 'Aunt Dee' (wis-<u>tee</u>-re-a  mak-ro-stay-kee-a)
('Aunt Dee' Kentucky Wisteria) NATIVE CULTIVAR....................Zone 5

15'-25'; full sun. Macrostachya means long spiked, in reference to its flower racemes being longer than those of the other native wisteria, W. frutescens. This highly fragrant selection of Kentucky wisteria flowers midseason, July-August, much later than the Chinese and Japanese species. Its highly fragrant flowers are colored light purple and carried on 7-12 inch long racemes.
Rec. Size: #1 pot (8/flat)    Spacing: (2 1/2'-3')

## Wisteria sinensis (wis-<u>tee</u>-re-a sye-<u>nen</u>-sis)
(Chinese Wisteria)............................................................Zone 5

**Blooming Time**
| J | F | M | A | M | J | J | A | S | O | N | D |
Winter | Spring | Summer | Fall

25'-50'; full sun. A sturdy Chinese twining species, this popular wisteria is noteworthy for its lovely, fragrant, 1 inch long, blue-violet pealike flowers. Carried in dense 6 to 12 inch long pendant racemes, they make a magnificent springtime floral show. The compound deciduous foliage of Chinese wisteria is composed of 9 to 13, 1 1/2 to 3 inch long, oval shaped, medium green leaflets.
Rec. Size: #1 pot (8/flat)   Spacing: (2 1/2'-3')

## Wisteria sinensis 'Prolific' (wis-<u>tee</u>-re-a flor-i-<u>bun</u>-da)
('Prolific' Chinese Wisteria)............................................Zone 5

**Blooming Time**
| J | F | M | A | M | J | J | A | S | O | N | D |
Winter | Spring | Summer | Fall

35'-50'+;   full   sun. Considered to be one of the very most spectacular flowering plants in cultivation, 'Prolific', a Dutch selection, is remarkable for its exceptional, iridescent blue-lavender, sweet scented springtime flowers which it carries upon pendulous 12 to 18-inch long racemes. In addition to this, its leaves are attractively colored bronze in youth, making it just that much more exquisite.
Rec. Size: #1 pot (8/flat)   Spacing: (2 1/2'-3')

Hanging like bunches of grapes from this arbor, the flowers of **Wisteria chinensis, Chinese Wisteria,** are not only a visual treat, but fill the air with a fragrance that is superior to any perfume.

# Selecting and Using Ferns

*Dryopteris atrata*

Among the first plants to inhabit the earth, ferns produce spores instead of seed and do not flower. Despite the lack of flowers, however, ferns are among the most versatile and attractive of plants. There are ferns that grow in sun as well as shade and water as well as dry sand. Not only do they range from small to large (a few inches to several feet), and deciduous to evergreen, they come in an array of colors. There are ferns with yellowish-, lime- and deep-green leaves, as well as copper — even those that are variegated silvery, green, gray, and burgundy.

Fern leaves or fronds are usually many segmented (compound) with a feathery appearance. But species and varieties exist that are nonsegmented (simple), crisped (frilled), succulent, and even beadlike.

In most cases ferns bear their spores in tiny dotlike structures (sori) attached to the bottom of the leaves. In other cases they are borne in beadlike segments carried either above the foliage or upon separate stalks—in which case they may be as ornamental as the nonspore-bearing leaves, as is the case with cinnamon fern (Osmunda cinnamomea) which is so named for the magnificent cinnamon-brown spore-bearing stalks.

**How Ferns Grow:**
Some ferns grow in clump forming fashion in which they form round hummocks or mounds, with leaves originating from the center or outside edge of the mound. On the other hand there are ferns that spread to form thick colonies. These types spread by underground stems called rhizomes which send up shoots as they spread.

## Ferns for Accent:

Like many perennials, ferns can be used for accent, to draw one's attention to other plants and landscape features. For the pupose of accenting, it is common to use one to five plants in conjunction with a boulder, bench, shrub, or tree trunk of contrasting color or texture. Ferns also look superb lining the edge of a wooded path or shady courtyard or patio.

## Ferns as Companion Plants:

Ferns make wonderful companion plants to other ferns, Ajuga, Astilbe, Bergenia, barren strawberry, black lily-turf, European ginger, geranium, Heuchera, hostas—especially blue leaved and variegated forms, Lamium, sedges, sweet woodruff, wintergreen, and wildflowers.

## Ferns as Ground Covers:

Ferns can be used to cover the ground just as vines, grasses, and other types of ground covers. Clump forming ferns may be planted close enough together that they cover the ground and exclude weeds. Those that spread to form colonies are best planted in moderate to large scale thickets and contribute a soft graceful texture to the landscape.

## Ferns as Container Plants:

Ferns make suburb, luxurious container plants. Some of the more hardy varieties may survive the winter in a container, and even if they don't, the cost of replacement is minimal. Ferns in containers, combine nicely with such ground covers as ajuga, creeping charley, dead nettle, black lily-turf, veronica, and selections of sedges.

## Planting, Spacing, and Watering:

Similar to ground covers. Please refer to the ground cover section of this brochure.

## Maintaining Ferns:

Ferns seldom need any maintenance. Occasionally the wintergreen types may look better if some of their older leaves are trimmed off as they become tattered. The deciduous types need no such care and their leaves need not be removed as they die back each fall. Better to let them rot, so that their nutrients may be returned to the soil.

## Controlling Weeds in Fern Plantings:

Ferns are sensitive to herbicides and thus weed control should be accomplished by any nonchemical means outlined in the ground cover section of this brochure.

## Fertilizing Ferns:

Most ferns are damaged when treated with low quality inorganic chemical fertilizers. On the other hand, they respond well to an early spring application of slow release fertilizer or a fall topdressing with leafmold.

## FERN SELECTION CHART

Abbreviations: X = Applicable to this plant  
P = Partially applicable to this plant

| NAME | GROWTH HABITS | Full Sun | Light Shade | Moderate Shade | Dense Shade | Large Area | Moderate Area | Small Area | Controls Erosion | Tolerates Foot Traffic | Drought Tolerant | Moisture Tolerant | Tolerates Sandy Soil | Salt Tolerant | Spring Bloom | Summer Bloom | Fall Bloom | Wintergreen |
|---|---|---|---|---|---|---|---|---|---|---|---|---|---|---|---|---|---|---|
| Adiantum pedatum | semi-spreader | | X | X | X | X | X | X | P | | | P | | | | | | |
| Athyrium angustum 'Lady in Red' | single crown | | X | X | X | X | X | X | P | | | P | | | | | | |
| Athyrium x 'Branford Beauty' | single crown | | X | X | X | X | X | X | P | | | P | | | | | | |
| Athyrium filix-femina cultivars | single crown | | X | X | X | X | X | X | P | | | P | | | | | | |
| Athyrium 'Ghost' | single crown | | X | X | X | X | X | X | P | | | P | | | | | | |
| Athyrium nipponicum cultivars | semi-spreader | | X | X | X | X | X | X | P | | | P | | | | | | P |
| Athyrium otophorum | single crown | | X | X | X | X | X | X | | | P | P | | | | | | P |
| Dryopteris affinis | single crown | | X | X | X | X | X | X | P | | P | P | | | | | | P |
| Dryopteris affinis 'The King' | single crown | | X | X | X | X | X | | P | | X | P | | | | | | X |
| Dryopteris atrata | single crown | | X | X | X | X | X | | P | | X | P | | | | | | P |
| Dryopteris crassirhizoma | single crown | | X | X | X | X | X | | P | | P | P | | | | | | X |
| Dryopteris erythrosora cultivars | single crown | | X | X | X | X | X | | P | | X | X | | | | | | X |
| Dryopteris f.-mas 'Linearis Polydactyla' | single crown | | X | X | X | X | X | X | P | | X | P | | | | | | P |
| Dryopteris f.-mas 'Parsley' | single crown | | X | X | X | X | X | X | P | | P | P | | | | | | P |
| Dryopteris f.-mas 'Undulata Robusta' | single crown | | X | X | X | X | X | | P | | P | P | | | | | | P |
| Dryopteris marginalis | single crown | | X | X | X | X | X | X | X | | X | X | | | | | | X |
| Matteuccia struthiopteris var. penn. | spreader | | X | X | X | X | X | | X | | | X | P | | | | | |
| Onoclea sensibilis | spreader | X | X | X | X | X | X | | X | | | X | P | | | | | |
| Osmunda cinnamomea | semi-spreader | X | X | X | X | X | X | | X | | | X | P | | | | | |
| Osmunda claytoniana | semi-spreader | X | X | X | X | X | X | | X | | | X | P | | | | | |
| Osmunda regalis | semi-spreader | X | X | X | X | X | X | | X | | | X | P | | | | | |
| Phyllitis scolopendrium 'Angustifolia' | single crown | X | X | | | | | X | | | P | P | | | | | | P |
| Polystichum acrostichoides | single crown | | X | X | X | X | X | X | P | | X | X | | | | | | X |
| Polystichum polyblepharum | single crown | | X | X | X | | X | X | P | | P | P | | | | | | X |

**Onoclea sensibilis, Sensitive Fern,** is a colonizing fern that brings lush bold texture to the shade garden and functions well as a ground cover. The photo at the right demonstrates its beautiful Fall colors.

## Adiantum pedatum (ad-ee-an-tum   pe-day-tum)
(Maidenhair Fern) NATIVE SPECIES.................................................Zone 3

1'-2'; light to dense shade. The deciduous leaves of maidenhair fern are soft textured, light bluish green, and uniquely arranged in the shape of horseshoes. Carried horizontally atop wiry ebony stems, the foliage contributes a delicate soft texture to the landscape. Maidenhiar fern is best in moist, acidic, organically rich soils performing well on shaded slopes as a ground cover and along woodland trails in combination with numerous wildflowers and perennials.
Rec. Size: #1 pot (8/flat)   Space: (10"-14")

## Athyrium angustum forma rubellum 'Lady in Red'  (a-thee-ree-um   an-gus-tum   rew-bel-um)
('Lady in Red' Lady Fern) NATIVE CULTIVAR..............................Zone 3

2'-2 1/2'; light to moderate shade. 'Lady in Red' is noteworthy for its shiny brilliant burgundy-red leaf stalks, which are visible from a long distance and offer exceptional contrast against the crisp green, lacy textured leaflets which they carry. 'Lady in Red' is a superior specimen fern and high contrast companion to other ferns, variegated hostas, sedges, pulmonarias, variegated Solomon's seal, epimediums, and countless ground covers, perennials, and wildflowers.
Rec. Size: #1 pot (8/flat)   Space: (14"-18")

## Athyrium x 'Branford Beauty' (a-thee-ree-um)
('Branford Beauty' Lady Fern).........................................................Zone 4

12"-24"; light to dense shade. Of hybrid origin, 'Branford Beauty' is the result of crossing Japanese painted fern and lady fern. The resulting plant is a beautiful selection combining some of the silvery leaf color of Japanese painted fern with the more upright habit of lady fern. Quick to mature but slow spreading, 'Branford Beauty' is an excellent choice for mass planting as a ground cover, for edging, and as an accent plant. It is carefree, disease resistant and easy to grow. Companions include such ferns as robust male fern and thick stemmed wood fern as well as hostas, wildflowers, sedges, and many other shade tolerant ground covers and perennials.
Rec. Size: #1 pot (8/flat)   Space: (1 1/2'-2')

## Athyrium filix-femina (a-thee-ree-um   fee-liks-fem-i-na)
(Lady Fern) NATIVE SPECIES.............................................................Zone 3

2'-4'; light to moderate shade. A very adaptable deciduous fern that will grow in open or dense canopied woodland sites. Tolerant to dry soils, this medium green deciduous fern is characterized by a lush, relatively fine textured appearance.
Rec. Size: #1 pot (8/flat)   Space: (14"-18")

## Athyrium filix-femina 'Encourage' (a-thee-ree-um fee-liks fem-i-na)
('Encourage' Lady Fern).......................................................................Zone 4

12" light to dense shade. The result of 8 years of hybridizing by Angelo and Carol Randaci, of the Fernery, is this superbly crested, uniformly tasseled, exceedingly lacy, apple-green, quite vigorous selection of lady fern. A standout, 'Encourage' is remarkable for imparting its soft textural quality and providing superior contrast to paving stones, coarse barked trees, and bold leaved shade lovers like hostas and ligularia.
Rec. Size: #1 pot (8/flat)   Space: (12"-18")

## Athyrium filix-femina 'Frizelliae' (a-thee-ree-um   fee-liks fem-i-na)
(Tatting Fern) NATIVE CULTIVAR......................................................Zone 4

10"-14" light to dense shade. 'Frizelliae' or tatting fern is really unusual with thin leafstalks surrounded at even intervals by frilly round leaflets (pinnae) that seem to whorl about the leafstalk. 'Frizelliae' is excellent as a specimen, edging, or small-container plant and makes a nice companion to other ferns, shade loving ground covers, perennials, and woodland wildflowers.
Rec. Size: #1 pot (8/flat)   Space: (12"-16")

FERNS

## Athyrium filix-femina 'Vernoniae Cristatum' (a-thee-ree-um fee-liks-fem-i-na)
(Miss Vernon's Crested Lady Fern) NATIVE CULTIVAR ......Zone 3 or 4

2'-3'; light to dense shade. Raised commercially since 1870, Victorian growers found an eager market for this prize among hardy ferns. Today, nothing has changed. Miss Vernon's crested lady fern is still prized and still resides in a class of its own. Indeed, after 100+ years of cultivation, its allure and charm have not diminished, for with its burgundy stems and overlapping, cool green, crested, tassel-ended leaflets, Miss Vernon's crested lady fern defers to none.
Rec. Size: #1 pot (8/flat)    Space: (12"-16")

## Athyrium filix-femina 'Victoriae' (a-thee-ree-um fee-liks fem-i-na)
('Victoriae' Lady Fern) NATIVE CULTIVAR.....................................Zone 4

1'-2'; light to dense shade. John Mickel, in his book Ferns For American Gardens, refers to 'Victoriae' as the "Queen of Green" and states that it is the most spectacular of all fern cultivars in its magnificent frond architecture—high praise from a man whose license plate reads FERNMAN. It surely is attractive—with unique 3-inch-wide, vibrant green, arching fronds composed of dramatically forked leaflets—often leading to a delicate crisscross network. 'Victoriae' is great in combination with other ferns, wildflowers, variegated Solomon's seal, hardy geraniums, and countless other ground covers and perennials.
Rec. Size: #1 pot (8/flat)    Space: (14"-18")

## Athyrium 'Ghost' (a-thee-ree-um)
('Ghost' Lady Fern) ...................................................................Zone 4

1 1/2'-2 1/2'; light to dense shade. The qualities that make for a popular fern are strong performance and attractive appearance. 'Ghost' rates high in both these categories; it grows and displays well, and is durable and long lived in the landscape. What's more, it is unique in appearance—leaves ghostly silver-gray (like Japanese painted fern without the burgundy) forming a neat semiupright habit. Effective enmasse as a ground cover, alone, or in small groups for specimen or accent, 'Ghost' combines nicely with other ferns, wildflowers, hostas, astilbes, black lily turf, barren strawberry, and countless other ground covers and perennials.
Rec. Size: #1 pot (8/flat)    Space: (14"-18")

## Athyrium nipponicum 'Pictum' (a-thee-ree-um ni-pon-i-kum)
(Japanese Painted Fern)...............................................................Zone 5

1'- 1 1/2'; light to dense shade. Even the most demanding gardener will appreciate the uniqueness of this colorful Asian exotic. Once you see how lovely the bluish gray and maroon flushed fronds appear when elevated upon deep wine colored petioles, you will find multiple homes for this fern in your landscape. Japanese Painted fern combines particularly well with hostas and Japanese maples (especially green leaved selections).
Rec. Size: #1 pot (8/flat)    Space: (1'-1 1/2')

## Athyrium nipponicum 'Silver Falls' (a-thee-ree-um ni-pon-i-kum)
('Silver Falls' Japanese Painted Fern) ......................................Zone 4

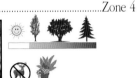

12"-15'; light to dense shade. Compared to other selectons of the classic cultivar 'Pictum' (the original Japanese painted fern), this may be the most distinct. Its foliage, overlaid in silver and accented with burgundy and purple, appears luminous and makes it jump right out of shady settings. It is this quality that makes it a superior ground cover for brightening up shady borders and superb as an edging for marking shady pathways. Excellent compaions include hostas with big bold foliage, especially with blue and rich yellow tones.
Rec. Size: #1 pot (8/flat)     Space: (12"-18")

## Athyrium otophorum (a-thee-ree-um oh-toe-fore-um)
(English Painted Fern)................................................................Zone 5

12"-18"; light to dense shade. Popularized in English gardening, this native to Japan and China is drought tolerant and durable. And with frosty gray green fronds striped burgundy in youth, English painted fern is among the most colorful of ferns. Each frond, shaped like a triangle, is flattened and thick in substance (almost plasticlike to the touch).
Rec. Size: #1 pot (8/flat)    Space: (12"-16")

*FERNS*

**FERNS**

## Dryopteris affinis (dry-<u>op</u>-ter-is  a-<u>fey</u>-nis  or  <u>af</u>-i-nis)
(Golden-scaled Male Fern) ........................................................Zone 4

2'-3'; light to dense shade. Impressive and stately, each spring golden-scaled male fern sends up tender light green fiddleheads from the center of its broad crown. A month later they develop into distinctly lance shaped, leathery, deep green, stately fronds. Golden scaled male fern takes its common name for the shaggy covering of golden-brown furry scales that cover its leaf stalks. Easily cultivated, it is clump-forming, semiwintergreen, hails from Europe and Asia, and is an excellent companion to other clump forming ferns, variegated hostas, epimediums, and ligularia.
Rec. Size: #1 pot (8/flat)   Space: (1 1/2'-2 1/2')

## Dryopteris affinis 'The King' (dry-<u>op</u>-ter-is  a-<u>fey</u>-nis  or  <u>af</u>-i-nis)
('The King' Golden Scaled Male Fern) ............................................Zone 4

1 1/2'-2 1/2'; light to dense shade. A stunningly handsome selection, 'The King' is the most popular of the D. affinis selections, and with good reason—its graceful, arching, durable, wintergreen, deep green fronds may reach over 3 feet long by 6 inches wide, and remarkably each of their segments is decorated with a frilly crest. This is a plant that is unique and attractive but also drought tolerant and durable. It combines nicely with other ferns, hostas, wildflowers, ajugas, and countless other shade loving ground covers and perennials.
Rec. Size: #1 pot (8/flat)   Space: (12"-16")

## Dryopteris atrata (dry-<u>op</u>-ter-is  a-<u>tray</u>-ta)
(Black Wood Fern) ........................................................................Zone 5

1 1/2'-2'; light to dense shade. A relatively uncommon fern, black wood fern displays stiff, leathery, semi-wintergreen, medium goldish-green fronds. Each is feather shaped in outline and divided into shallowly toothed leaflets that are backed by prominent dark black sori. The leafstalk is also interesting for its coarse black hairs. Black wood fern spreads slowly by expanding crowns, prefers moist, rich, well drained soils, and combines nicely with other clump forming ferns and shade loving perennials.
Rec. Size: #1 pot (8/flat)   Space: (1 1/2'-2')

## Dryopteris crassirhizoma (dry-<u>op</u>-ter-is  kras-i-rhi-<u>zome</u>-a)
(Thick-stemmed Wood Fern) ........................................................Zone 4

2'-3 1/2'; light to dense shade. With tall stature, erect vase-shaped habit, and coarse textured semievergreen fronds, thick-stemmed wood fern is an imposing species useful for making a strong statement in the shade garden. Give it a try for edging stone and brick pathways, stairways, and woodland paths. It will add a rich natural look. Companions include other ferns, Pachysandra procumbens, wildflowers, bleeding heart, epimediums, blue- and variegated-leaved hostas, pulmonarias, astilbes, ivies, and plumbago.
Rec. Size: #1 pot (8/flat)   Space: (14"-18")

## Dryopteris erythrosora (dry-<u>op</u>-ter-is  e-rith-<u>roe</u>-soe-ra)
(Japanese Sword Fern) ..................................................................Zone 5

1 1/2'-2'; light to dense shade. An outstanding wintergreen species, Japanese sword fern is superbly colorful and remarkably tough. Its color display begins in spring with coppery pink fiddleheads. In time these unfurl to pinkish golden green fronds — later becoming coppery green, and backed with bright red sori. With fall comes a deepening of the copper hues — to the point of appearing russet. Use Japanese sword fern in large masses in deciduous woodland settings. Drought tolerance is fair and it appears adaptable to most acidic well drained soils.
Rec. Size: #1 pot (8/flat)   Space: (1 1/4'-1 1/2')

This closeup of **Dryopteris erythrosora, Japanese Sword Fern,** details its exquisite leaf color.

## Dryopteris filix-mas 'Linearis Polydactyla' (dry-<u>op</u>-ter-is <u>fee</u>-liks-mas)
(Lace-leaved Wood Fern) NATIVE CULTIVAR ...............................Zone 4

1 1/2'-2 1/2'; light to dense shade. With amazingly slender leaflets, this cultivar has real character. Its medium to deep green fronds are open and airy, making it wonderful for specimen or accent use. Along these lines, it is unique (among ferns) in its landscape usefulness, in that it can be used as a veil in the foreground of other shade lovers such as wildflowers, ajuga, other ferns, and colorful sedges. As such, one can look right through lace-leaved fern and appreciate the background plants at the same time. Because it is so unique, you will want to locate it in areas that are up close and personal to those who will be walking by.
Rec. Size: #1 pot (8/flat)    Space: (1 1/2'-2')

## Dryopteris filix-mas 'Parsley' (dry-op-ter-is   <u>fee</u>-liks-mas)
(Parsley Leaved Male Fern) NATIVE CULTIVAR ...........................Zone 4

1 1/2'; light to dense shade. Little is known about this eye-catching fern. It was given to us (at Hortech) years ago under an errant name, and for years it has been the most intriguing fern in our trial, gardens—and in much demand. But, we had no source for it. Now, thanks to tissue culture, it is available in limited quantities. Parsley leaved fern displays superb, richly ruffled, deep green fronds that resist wind, insect, and disease damage and look superb throughout the growing season.
Rec. Size: #1 pot (8/flat)    Space: (14"-18")

## Dryopteris filix-mas 'Undulata Robusta' (dry-<u>op</u>-ter-is   <u>fee</u>-liks-mas)
(Robust Male Fern) NATIVE CULTIVAR ........................................Zone 4

1 1/2'-3'; light to dense shade. An exceptional cultivar of the stately male fern, this strong grower displays wavy edged, sturdy, semi-wintergreen fronds that reach 3 feet long. A clump former, it makes a nice backdrop for Japanese painted fern as well as blue leaved and green-white variegated hostas and other shade loving ground covers and perennials.
Rec. Size: #1 pot (8/flat)    Space: (1 1/2'-2 1/2')

## Dryopteris marginalis (dry-<u>op</u>-ter-is    mar-ji-<u>nay</u>-lis)
(Leatherleaf Wood Fern) NATIVE SPECIES.................................Zone 3

1'-1 1/2'; light to dense shade. Useful for accent or ground cover in wooded settings, the foliage of leatherleaf wood fern is wintergreen, twice divided, and borne in crowns. Remarkable for its adaptability, leatherleaf wood fern performs well in moist humus-rich soils as well as sandy dry conditions.
Rec. Size: #1 pot (8/flat)    Space: (1 1/4"-1 1/2")

## Matteuccia struthiopteris var. pennsylvanica (ma-<u>too</u>-see-a strew-thee-<u>op</u>-ter-is)
(Ostrich Fern) NATIVE SPECIES .....................................................Zone 2

3'-5'; light to dense shade. Ostrich fern is so named because its fronds are reminiscent of giant ostrich feathers. Tall, tough, hardy, and as graceful as any, ostrich fern excels not only as a specimen or accent plant, but also as a colonizing ground cover underneath large deciduous trees, along property borders in broad sweeping beds, or close to buildings as a foundation facer.
Rec. Size: #1 pot (8/flat)    Space: (2'-2 1/2')

## Onoclea sensibilis (on-oh-<u>klee</u>-a   or   a-<u>nok</u>-lee-a sen-<u>si</u>-bil-is)
(Sensitive Fern) NATIVE SPECIES.................................................Zone 3

1'-2'; full sun to dense shade. Interesting for its deeply lobed, deciduous, yellow-green foliage, sensitive fern excels in moist woodland borders. Its fertile fronds are brown, beadlike, and excellent in dried flower arrangements. Sensitive fern is a creeper that in time will colonize. Because of this it makes a terrific ground cover.
Rec. Size: #1 pot (8/flat)    Space: (1'-1 1/2')

*FERNS*

## Osmunda cinnamomea (oz-<u>mun</u>-da sin-a-<u>moe</u>-mee-a)
(Cinnamon Fern) NATIVE SPECIES.................................................Zone 3

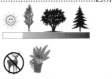

2'-5'; full sun to dense shade. Commonly called cinnamon fern because of its cinnamon brown upright fertile fronds that arise in spring, this robust deciduous fern is stately in appearance and may reach five feet tall. Best in rich, moist soil.

Rec. Size: #1 pot (8/flat)    Space: (1 1/2'-2')

## Osmunda claytoniana (oz-<u>mun</u>-da klay-<u>toe</u>-nee-aye-na)
(Interrupted Fern) NATIVE SPECIES.................................................Zone 3

2'-4'; full sun to dense shade. Medium green, the tall deciduous fronds of this upright growing fern are "interrupted" in the center by spore-containing fertile leaflets which mature to brown, liberate their spores, then fall off, thus leaving a gap or interruption in the featherlike nature of the fronds. Exceptionally striking, interrupted fern is a superior edging or background plant outstanding for use along the edge of a stream or pond. Of course 3 to 5 specimens planted together are impressive and commanding for accent or specimen uses.

Rec. Size: #1 pot (8/flat)    Space: (1 1/2'-2')

## Osmunda regalis (oz-<u>mun</u>-da ree-<u>gay</u>-lis)
(Royal Fern) NATIVE SPECIES.................................................Zone 3

2'-5'; full sun to dense shade. A large graceful fern for use in any shade garden, royal fern is exceptionally good along waterside or in bog-like growing conditions. Its locust-like leaves emerge wine-red and later become green. Its most lush and impressive appearance is attained when grown in constantly moist, acidic, humus rich soil.

Rec. Size: #1 pot (8/flat)    Space: (2'-2 1/2')

## Phyllitis scolopendrium 'Angustifolia' (fi-<u>lye</u>-tis sko-lo-<u>pen</u>-dree-um)
(Narrow Leaved Hart's-tongue Fern).................................................Zone 5

8"-14"; light to moderate shade. Unusual for its wavy edged, tongue-shaped leaves and the herringbone pattern of its spore laden sori (underneath the leaves), 'Angustifolia' is an exceptional cultivar that looks more like a conservatory specimen than a hardy wintergreen selection. Yet, it is hardy and rugged — relatively drought tolerant, and accepting of sandy and rocky acidic and alkaline soils. 'Angustifolia' grows well in the cracks of rock walls and planters or in mixed plantings with shade loving perennials and bright leaved, low growing ground covers and sedges. Black mondo grass and a variety of sedges are great in this respect. By the way, scolopendra is Greek for "centipede," in reference to the two rows of sori on the lower surface of the fronds which look like the legs of a centipede.

Rec. Size: #1 pot (8/flat)    Space: (10"-14")

## Polystichum acrostichoides (po-<u>lis</u>-ti-kum a-kros-ti-<u>koy</u>-deez)
(Christmas Fern) NATIVE SPECIES.................................................Zone 3

2'-3'; light to dense shade. A popular native fern with dark, leathery green, wintergreen fronds, in spring the fiddle-heads of Christmas fern are an attractive silvery-gray. It is easily cultured, slow to spread, and very low maintenance.

Rec. Size: #1 pot (8/flat)    Space: (1 1/4'- 2')

## Polystichum polyblepharum (po-lis-ti-kum pol-li-blef-a-rum)
(Japanese Tassel Fern).................................................Zone 5

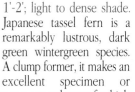

1'-2'; light to dense shade. Japanese tassel fern is a remarkably lustrous, dark green wintergreen species. A clump former, it makes an excellent specimen or accent plant which can be massed for planting as a ground cover for high contrast — especially when used with light colored variegated selections such as blue, golden, or variegated hostas, variegated pachysandra, or variegated aegopodium. Although Japanese tassel fern is fairly resistant to drought, it is at its best in a rich loam with constant moisture.

Rec. Size: #1 pot (8/flat)    Space: (1 1/4'- 2')

*FERNS* (left margin)

# SELECTING, USING, AND MAINTAINING GROUND COVERS

Ground covers are employed in a number of different ways — limited only by the imagination. Popular uses include the following:

### As a Turf Substitute / Living Mulch.

The most important application of ground covers is to use them to eliminate or reduce the amount of turf grass in the landscape. Not only is this better for the environment (less mowing = less noise and air pollution, not to mention less irrigation and fertilizer), in the long run it saves time and money. It also helps give the landscape a unique character that can not be created with turf grass.

### For Easing Transition and Creating Unity.

Using ground covers of intermediate height, color, or texture between and surrounding two contrasting elements (such as a beech tree with smooth gray bark and an oak with coarse dark brown bark) eases the perception of change and unites the features. Ground covers can be used in this manner to join the house with a surrounding woodlot, shrubs with trees, ornaments or benches with walkways, etc.

### For Controlling Erosion.

Densely rooted ground covers are excellent for holding soil in place on slopes and areas of water runoff.

### As Edging/Hedging.

Nonspreading types of ground cover can be used as edging or dwarf hedges to create geometric designs, direct traffic, and define borders and property lines.

### As A Filler Between Steps and Paving and Patio Stones.

Low growing "Foot Friendly" ground covers tolerate foot traffic and look fantastic in the cracks between steps and stones in the landscape. Here they add an element of color and softness. They also exclude weeds, prevent erosion, and in some cases release pleasant fragrances when stepped upon.

## For Accent.
Used as accent plants, ground covers can be used to draw the eye to such features as statuary, benches, brickwork, entryways, steps, and other plants.

## As Specimens.
The more unusual/showy ground covers can stand alone as specimens and should be sited in locations where the eye naturally falls such as atop a terrace, by a building entrance, outside of windows, and along the edge of steps.

## As a Facing.
When sited in front of other plants, benches, statues, ornaments, and building foundations some of the taller ground covers do an excellent job of concealing the bases of these elements — a practice known as facing. Employed this way, they also help ease the transition between such elements and the space that surrounds them.

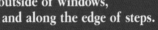

## To Reduce Glare.
Ground covers absorb light and reduce glare, therefore when used along boulevards, roadways, parks, and parking lots they increase visibility and safety.

## For Cooling Air and Controlling Snow Drifting.
Through transpiration (evaporative cooling) ground covers are natural air conditioners. During the winter (especially grassy types and those with woody stems) they trap snow and reduce blowing and drifting.

## What Are Ground Covers?

Ground covers are plants, which when properly cultured and established, require little maintenance and densely cover the soil in a manner that discourages or prevents the growth of weeds. For the most part, without pruning, ground covers range in height from less than an inch to about 4 feet tall. Ground covers may be succulent, herbaceous, or shrubby. They can be clumping, vining, or sprawling, and may be deciduous, evergreen, or semievergreen. Even some ferns and grasses can function as ground covers.

Ground covers are available in a broad array of colors and textures. In addition to green-leaved forms, there are red, blue, purple, silver, coppery, bronze, and gold leaved selections. Multicolored (variegated) forms also exist, and textures range from fine to coarse, and soft to rough.

## Material and Environmental Benefits of Ground Covers.

Reduced maintenance expense (in comparison to turf grass) is the primary financial advantage ground covers have to offer. Generally speaking, turf is less expensive at first, but considering its ongoing maintenance needs (frequent mowing, edging, fertilization, irrigation, disease and weed control, etc.), it proves to be more expensive in the long run.

Much annual cleanup work (and expense) can be eliminated by using ground covers. In nature, a cycle exists in which microorganisms reduce organic matter (i.e. leaves, fruit, twigs and flowers) into humus. The humus, rich in nutrients, is the source of fertility that assures the continuation of life. Ironically, in our landscapes we often disrupt this cycle (with back breaking labor, usually on weekends!) by raking and vacuuming up fallen fruits, leaves, flowers, and twigs. Instead, if we were to underplant our trees and shrubs with carefully selected ground covers, such organic debris would not only be concealed, but would rot, be returned to the soil, and would furnish nutrients to the ground covers.

The environmental benefits of ground covers should not be overlooked either. Ground covers control erosion, reduce snow drifting during winter, and humidify, oxygenate, and cool the air.

## Aesthetic Benefits of Ground Covers.

Ground covers unify unrelated elements in the landscape. For example, consider a brown brick house constructed on a streamside lot. The coarse-textured, symmetrical, brick house and the clear, silvery, winding, tranquil stream have little in common. Yet, by using ground covers creatively, such as a broad sweeping bed of purple wintercreeper, the two can be joined in harmony. Similarly, by softening the sharp edges and angles of benches, drives, fences, and walks, ground covers can make such features seem at home among the living elements—trees, shrubs, and other plants.

Ground covers are indispensable for creating a rich, enjoyable, inviting atmosphere. Using sweeping beds of loosely arranged ground covers (as edgings along walkways) communicates a pleasant welcoming message to those who visit.

Additionally, ground covers function in altering perceptions. To convey the impression of spaciousness, use small leaved smooth textured ground covers in broad, curving plantings. On the other hand, use large leaved coarsely textured ground covers to create the perception of intimacy and closeness. Brightly colored or fine textured ground covers tend to lighten areas and elevate or intensify one's mood. Shades of blue, green, or gray, particularly if the leaves are large and smooth textured, tend to enhance feelings of tranquility and peacefulness.

For relieving monotony in the landscape, ground covers are paramount. Entryways, steps, decking, ornaments, and trees and shrubs are infinitely more interesting when accented with ground covers. Amazing for their intricate branch patterns, colorfully painted foliage, and sometimes attractively flaking bark, ground covers can enhance feelings of joy and light-heartedness. Evergreen ground covers exhibit year-round beauty, while many others grace us with flowers of heavenly scent and bright, beautiful spring, summer, and autumnal color. Finally, wildlife and songbirds are often attracted to their flowers and fruit—an added benefit to the environment, and to the people who benefit from the entertainment that they provide.

*Gaultheria procumbens*

The uses of ground covers are nearly endless, and are limited only by your imagination. Even so, you should always attempt to follow the four basic rules of ground cover use. Adhering to these four rules will prevent the use of inappropriate or incompatible ground covers and will insure optimal success.

**#1.** Combining too many different types of ground covers in the same landscape results in a busy, cluttered appearance. To create the most appealing landscape, use only one or a few selected varieties.

**#2.** In general, plant large-leaved ground covers when the scale is large, and small-leaved ground covers when the scale is small. By following this rule you will create a harmonious setting and your plants will always be in the proper proportion to the landscape. Doing the opposite will waste the precious little space of the smaller landscape or leave the large landscape looking naked.

**#3.** Sensitivity to companionship should be exercised when combining ground covers with other plant types, such as trees or shrubs. In other words, you should only install plants which will comfortably coexist. Such plants should possess not only similar cultural requirements, but complementary colors, textures, forms, and sizes. If plants of different compatibility (companionship) are planted together, not only will harmony be lacking, but extra maintenance will be required.

**#4.** Never combine ground covers that have incompatible growth habits. The worst offense in this regard is to combine a species of vigorous, horizontal spreading habit (such as English ivy, trailing dead nettle, goutweed, or fleece flower) with a species of diminutive or refined habit (such as stonecrop or germander). The vigorous plants will soon overrun the smaller, slower growing ones.

# Planting and Maintenance:

**Even though ground covers are unique low maintenance plants that will help you to further enjoy your landscape, in order to perform their best, they will need some help to become well established. Here is what you must do: first, plant them properly; second, give them proper care. If you do these two things, your ground covers will fill in rapidly and provide maximum enjoyment with little work or expense.**

## When to Plant:

Ground covers may be planted from spring through fall. Spring and summer are the best times, but planting in fall is also acceptable (just make sure that the soil is mulched with wood chips to provide insulation and prevent soil heaving from the cycle of freezing and thawing).

## Preparing the Planting Site:

Before planting, first remove all existing grass and weeds. This includes the roots as well as the above ground parts. There are three ways to accomplish this and they are outlined as follows:

## Method #1.

Black plastic mulch can be pinned on top of the site with rocks, bricks, or soil as a means of destroying weeds or turf. The principle behind this is that the combination of darkness and heat will destroy the underlying weeds. Darkness works by making it impossible for plants to manufacture food through photosynthesis, and the sun hitting the plastic causes the weeds and soil below to become very hot. Literally the combination of sun and black plastic creates an opaque solar oven that causes destruction of the weeds. This method works best in locations exposed to direct sunlight, and naturally works better in summer than spring or fall. In general the plastic should be left in place for 2 months. Later, the site may be rototilled or spaded to loosen and aerate the soil before planting.

## Method #2.

Herbicides may also be used to destroy existing turf or weeds. Herbicides work quickly and although there are a number of different herbicides available, those which work best are absorbed into the plant and translocated throughout its sap stream. These types of herbicides (such as Roundup) kill the root system as well as the top growth— absolutely essential to effective eradication since most weeds are capable of coming back from their roots. Once the herbicide has killed the turf or weeds, rototill or spade up the area to loosen the soil. Consult your local garden center for recommendations as to the best herbicide to use.

## Method #3.

The final method involves repeatedly rototilling or spading the planting site until all vegetation has rotted and been converted into soil (by decomposers including fungi, bacteria, and earthworms). Typically three or four turns of the site over the course of five to six weeks will accomplish this objective.

After killing the weeds and loosening the soil, spade or rototill in any necessary amendments such as leaf mold, lime, peat moss, organic compost, or topsoil. Amendments enhance the soil's fertility, change its texture, or alter its chemical properties (such as pH), so that it is suitable for a particular plant. Amendments should be worked into the top 8 to 12 inches of soil and followed by the final grading—usually performed with a hand rake.

## Planting Your Ground Covers:

When planting, the soil level at the base of the ground covers should be the same as it was in the containers prior to transplanting. Therefore, if the containers are 3 inches deep, the planting holes should also be 3 inches. If the holes are too deep, the stems will be covered with soil and may rot. On the other hand, if they are too shallow, the roots will not have enough soil contact for adequate anchoring or water absorption. Use a tool such as a spade, trowel, or hoe to dig the holes for planting. Following planting, be sure to water your plants in thoroughly, then follow by topdressing the exposed soil between them with a 1 1/2 to 2 inch layer of wood chips. This not only helps exclude weeds but reduces the amount of watering that will be needed, cools the soil, and by insulating it, prevents the ground from heaving during late fall and winter.

## Spacing the Plants:

Ground covers need to be spaced at an appropriate distance so that plantings will be easy to maintain and so that all areas of the planting fill in at the same rate. To calculate the number of plants needed, use the chart on the following page. This chart should be used with the recommendations for each plant (found next to the container size for each plant). Spacing is based upon rate of growth and mature spread. In general, these recommendations will allow your planting to fill in and become completely established in 1 1/2 growing seasons. Planting at the closest recommended distance may speed this to 1 season, and the farthest recommendation may extend it to 2 seasons. Of course the rate will vary somewhat with soil fertility, maintenance practices, irrigation, and climate.

# SPACING CHART

| Spacing | Plants needed per: | | | |
|---|---|---|---|---|
| Inches between Plants | Square Foot | 100 Square Feet | 1000 Square Feet | Square feet covered per each plant |
| 3 | 16.00 | 1,600 | 16,000 | 0.06 |
| 4 | 9.00 | 900 | 9,000 | 0.11 |
| 5 | 5.75 | 575 | 5,750 | 0.17 |
| 6 | 4.00 | 400 | 4,000 | 0.25 |
| 7 | 2.93 | 293 | 2,930 | 0.34 |
| 8 | 2.25 | 225 | 2,250 | 0.44 |
| 9 | 1.78 | 178 | 1,780 | 0.56 |
| 10 | 1.44 | 144 | 1,440 | 0.69 |
| 12 | 1.00 | 100 | 1,000 | 1.00 |
| 14 | 0.73 | 73 | 730 | 1.37 |
| 16 | 0.56 | 56 | 560 | 1.78 |
| 18 | 0.44 | 44 | 440 | 2.27 |

Also see: www.premiumplants.net for plant need calculator.

## Maintaining Ground Covers:

One of the greatest advantages of ground covers is that they require little maintenance, especially in comparison to turf grass. However, to believe that no maintenance is needed is a misconception. As with other plants, ground covers may need periodic watering, weeding (at least until established), and fertilizing.

## Watering Ground Covers:

Thoroughly watering your ground covers immediately after planting is the first item on the maintenance schedule. This reduces the degree of transplant stress to the plants. Until the roots become well established, new plantings should be watered frequently so as to keep the soil constantly moist—but not saturated. Three months is usually an adequate period for root establishment. From then on, water as follows:

Watering during the early morning so that the foliage can quickly dry. Water to the extent that the soil becomes moistened through the entire root zone (6-12 inches deep), and only when there is a genuine need, evidenced by a slight wilting of the leaves at midday.

Typically, little or no supplemental watering is necessary after the first year. If it is, it is usually only during extended hot, dry summer days. It is also a good idea to water thoroughly in late fall before the ground becomes solidly frozen. This enables the plants to better cope with winter's harshness. When plants enter winter without drought stress, they come through in much better condition.

## Controlling Weeds in Ground Cover Plantings:

The most critical step in weed control occurs before the plants are ever placed in the ground. Completely eliminating all weeds (including their roots) before you plant is essential to the rapid establishment of ground covers. Mulching after planting helps to keep weed seeds from germinating and becoming established. In time, as the ground covers fill in and outmuscle the weeds, the need for weeding will taper off, and eventually little or no weed control will be required.

During establishment, ongoing weed control can be accomplished in three ways. The first method is manual hoeing or hand pulling. Consider it an opportunity to relax and be reflective: weeding is good for your body, takes little mind power, and is a good stress reducer. The second method is through the use of preemergent and postemergent herbicides. Preemergent herbicides prevent weeds from becoming established. Postemergent herbicides kill weeds after they have come up. They must be used carefully as they may also kill your ground cover, if you happen to spray it as well. The last and most preferred method is periodic mulching around your ground covers with organic materials. Simply resupply

1 to 2 inches of wood chips or bark as the initial mulching thins and decomposes. Mulching does not kill established weeds but helps prevent weeds from becoming established. Also, as they decompose organic mulches help to supplement the soil's fertility.

## Fertilizing Ground Covers:

Many ground covers benefit from one or two annual fertilizer applications. A general fertilization program should include the use of an organic or slow-release fertilizer. Organic fertilizers are essentially those which have come from the digestive tract (organs) of animals (i.e., horse, chicken, turkey, cow, and even human manure, as in the case of Milorganite, the product which comes from the Milwaukee sewage treatment facility). Slow-release fertilizers are chemical fertilizers that gradually release nutrients to the plant. Low-grade, soluble fertilizers (non-slow release types) are less expensive but can wash through the soil before the plant can use them completely. Because of this they are more likely to contribute to groundwater contamination, and therefore should be avoided.

The ratio of nitrogen, phosphorus, and potassium in the fertilizer should be about 2-1-2, such as a 10-5-10 formulation, and it should be applied at the rate of 1 pound per 100 square feet, first in early spring and then again in early fall. A more precise custom fertilizer program can be provided by your garden center or county extension agent. This involves sampling the soil during early spring and tailoring the fertilization program to the exact needs of your particular plants and soil.

Fertilizers should only be applied when the leaves of the plants are dry, otherwise spotting or rotting may occur. Following the application, use a fast stream of water to wash off any fertilizer that has adhered to or become trapped in the leaves.

## Leaf Removal:

Leaves should only be raked up or vacuumed when they smother and mat down the ground cover. If the ground cover is of such habit that the fallen leaves slip through its canopy, then allow the leaves to remain and decompose to supplement the soil.

**Planting sedums on rooftops** is often practiced in Europe and is becoming more common in the United States. Not only does it insulate the building or home but extends the life of the roof, positively effects the environment, and lends color and textural interest.

*Matteuccia struthiopteris, Ostrich Fern*

### Ferns as Ground Covers:

Especially when used in broad sweeping beds, many species of ferns make lushly beautiful no-maintenance ground covers. And, of course, in woodland settings and naturalized landscapes, ferns are often the necessary cement for binding the other plants—trees, shrubs, and perennials—with the nonliving, physical elements of the landscape, such as the house, land, water, and rocks. Typically ferns need shade and rich moist soil, but otherwise have few limitations.

### Ornamental Grasses as Ground Covers:

Without question, some of the most exciting ground covers in use today are the ornamental grasses. Grasses, including bamboos, are quite distinct.

Ground covering type grasses are diverse. They range in size from a few inches to about 3 feet tall. Leaf color variation is also broad. Selections are available with leaves of green, blue, yellow, red, and gray. Some leaves even have combinations of these colors. Ground covering grasses of clump forming habit (nonrunning, slow spreading) may be used on a small or large scale. Those that run have extensive root systems that make them useful for binding the soil and controlling erosion.

*Pennisetum alopecuroides, Fountain Grass*

The flower clusters of ground covering grasses may be tiny or more than a foot long, and also display diversity. Although usually straw colored, some flowers are silvery, yellow, rosy, reddish, black, or purple. Some flowers are broad and fan shaped while others are shaped like a bottle brush. What's more, many grasses bloom in fall (when the flowers of many plants have faded) and persist through winter, protruding through the snow, a welcome sight when landscapes are at their least showy.

Many grasses display vertical or arching orientation, adding interest and breaking up the dominant horizontal habits of other plants and landscape elements such as water, pavement, and garden structures. Consider using grasses as a background to horizontally spreading junipers and cotoneasters, or at pondside where their beauty can be reflected off the surface of the water. In island beds of parking lots and as accent plants abreast of benches and statuary, ornamental grasses are simply marvelous.

More so than most plants, grasses respond to breezes with graceful, swaying motions. To most people, foliar and floral movement is not a momentous spectacle. But to the perceptive, they are beautiful and extremely graceful—much appreciated for their calming effect on the tired mind. For these reasons, planting grasses in areas adjoining walkways, patios, decks, and landscape borders is highly recommended.

# GROUND COVER SELECTION CHART

*Abbreviations:  X = Applicable to this plant*
*P = Partially applicable to this plant*

| NAME | Full Sun | Light Shade | Moderate Shade | Dense Shade | Large Area | Moderate Area | Small Area | Controls Erosion | Tolerates Foot Traffic | Drought Tolerant | Moisture Tolerant | Tolerates Sandy Soil | Salt Tolerant | Spring Bloom | Summer Bloom | Fall Bloom | Evergreen |
|---|---|---|---|---|---|---|---|---|---|---|---|---|---|---|---|---|---|
| *Achillea millefolium* 'Red Beauty' | X | | | | | X | X | | | X | | X | | X | | | |
| *Aegopodium podograria* 'Variegatum' | X | X | X | | X | X | | X | | | | P | | | X | | |
| *Agastache x* 'Blue Fortune' | X | X | | | X | X | | | | P | | P | | | X | | |
| *Ajuga cultivars* | | X | X | | | X | X | | P | | | P | | X | | | X |
| *Alchemilla vulgaris* | X | X | X | | | X | X | | | | | P | | X | | | |
| *Allium maximowiczii* 'Alba' | X | X | | | | X | X | P | | X | | X | P | X | | | |
| *Allium schoenoprasum* 'Forescate' | X | X | | | X | X | X | P | | X | | X | P | X | | | |
| *Allium sensecens subsp. montanum* | X | X | | | X | X | X | P | | X | | X | P | X | | | |
| *Amsonia* 'Blue Ice' | X | X | | | X | X | | | | X | | P | | X | | | |
| *Amsonia hubrichtii* | X | X | | | X | X | | | | X | | P | | X | | | |
| *Arctostaphylos uva-ursi* 'Massachusetts' | X | X | | | X | X | X | X | | X | | X | X | X | | | X |
| *Armeria maritima* 'Rubrifolia' | X | | | | | X | X | | P | P | | X | | X | X | | X |
| *Aruncus aesthusifolia* | X | X | X | | | X | X | | | P | | P | | | X | | |
| *Asarum europaeum* | | X | X | X | | X | X | X | | | | | | X | | | X |
| *Asarum splendens* 'Quick Silver' | | X | X | X | X | X | X | | | | | | | X | | | X |
| *Aster cultivars* | X | X | | | X | X | | | | X | | P | | | | X | |
| *Astilbe cultivars* | | X | X | | X | X | X | | | | | P | | | X | | |
| *Bergenia purpurascens* | X | X | X | | X | X | X | | | X | | X | | X | X | X | X |
| *Boltonia asteroides* 'Pink Beauty' | X | | | | X | X | | X | | | | X | | X | X | | |
| *Brunnera macrophylla* 'Jack Frost' | X | | | | X | X | | X | | | | X | | X | X | | |
| *Calamintha nepeta* 'Gottlieb Friedkund' | X | X | | | X | X | | X | | | | P | | X | X | X | |
| *Calamintha nepeta subsp. nepeta* | X | X | | | X | X | | X | | X | | P | | | X | X | |
| *Calamintha nepeta* 'White Cloud' | X | X | | | X | X | | X | | X | | P | | | X | X | |
| *Campanula carpatica cultivars* | X | X | | | | X | X | | | | | P | | | X | | |
| *Campanula glomerata* 'Acaulis' | X | X | | | | X | X | | | | | P | | X | X | | |
| *Campanula punctata cultivars* | X | X | | | X | X | | | | | | P | | | X | | |
| *Campanula* 'Samantha' | X | X | | | X | X | X | | | | | P | | X | X | | |
| *Campanula* 'Sarastro' | X | X | | | X | X | | | | | | P | | X | X | | |
| *Caryopteris x clandonensis cultivars* | X | X | | | X | X | | X | | X | | X | | | X | | |
| *Ceratostigma plumbaginoides* | X | X | X | | X | X | | X | | | | P | | | X | X | |
| *Chamaemelum nobile* 'Trenague' | X | X | | | | X | X | | X | P | | P | | X | | | |
| *Chelone lyonii* 'Hot Lips' | X | X | | | X | X | | X | | | P | | | | X | X | |
| *Chelone obliqua* 'Rosea' | X | X | | | X | X | | X | | | P | | | | X | X | |
| *Conoclinium coelestinum* 'Wayside' | X | X | | | X | X | | X | | | | X | | | | X | |
| *Convallaria majalis* | | X | X | X | | X | X | | | X | | X | | X | | | |
| *Coreopsis* 'Limerock Ruby' | X | X | | | | X | X | | | | | | | | X | P | |
| *Coreopsis rosea cultivars* | X | X | | | | X | X | | | | X | | | | X | | |
| *Coreopsis verticillata cultivars* | X | X | | | X | X | X | | | X | | X | | | X | | |
| *Cornus canadensis* | | X | X | | | X | X | | | | X | | | X | | | |
| *Coronilla varia* | X | X | | | X | X | | X | | X | P | X | | | X | X | |
| *Corydalis lutea* | | X | X | X | | X | X | | | P | | P | | | X | | |
| *Crocosmia x* 'Lucifer' | X | X | | | X | X | X | | | | | | | | X | | |
| *Cymbalaria aequitriloba* | | X | X | | | | X | | X | | | | | | X | | |
| *Delosperma* 'John Proffitt' | X | | | | | X | X | | | X | | X | | X | | | X |
| *Delosperma nubigena* | X | | | | | X | X | | | X | | X | | X | | | X |
| *Deutzia gracilis* 'Nikko' | X | X | | | X | X | | | | X | | | | X | | | |
| *Dianthus x allwoodii* 'Little Bobby' | X | | | | | X | X | | | P | | P | | | X | P | X |
| *Dianthus* 'Candy Dish' | X | | | | | X | X | | | P | | P | | | X | | X |
| *Dianthus* 'Firewitch' | X | | | | | X | X | | | P | | P | | | X | | X |
| *Dianthus gratianopolitanus* 'Tiny Rubies' | X | | | | | | X | | | P | | P | | X | X | | X |
| *Dicentra* 'King of Hearts' | | X | X | X | X | X | X | | | | | P | | X | X | X | |
| *Dicentra spectabilis cultivars* | | X | X | X | | X | X | | | | | P | | X | | | |
| *Disporum sessile* 'Variegatum' | | X | X | X | | X | X | X | | | | P | | X | | | |
| *Echinacea purpurea cultivars* | X | X | | | X | X | | | | X | | X | | | X | X | |
| *Epimedium cultivars* | | X | X | X | X | X | X | | | X | | X | | X | | | |
| *Erica carnea cultivars* | X | X | | | | X | X | | | X | | X | | X | | | X |
| *Euonymus fortunei* 'Coloratus' | X | X | X | X | X | X | | X | | X | | X | X | | | | X |
| *Euonymus fortunei* 'Kewensis' | X | X | X | X | X | X | | X | | X | | X | X | | | | X |
| *Eupatorium cannabinum* 'Plenum' | X | X | | | X | X | | X | | | X | P | | | X | X | |
| *Eupatorium dubium* 'Little Joe' | X | X | | | X | X | X | X | | | X | P | | | X | X | |
| *Eupatorium fistulosum* 'Gateway' | X | X | X | | X | | | X | | | X | | | | | | |
| *Eupatorium rugosum* 'Chocolate' | X | X | X | | X | X | | X | | | X | X | | | | X | |
| *Euphorbia amygdaloides var. robbiae* | X | X | | | | X | X | X | | X | | P | | X | X | | X |

# GROUND COVER SELECTION CHART

Abbreviations: X = Applicable to this plant
P = Partially applicable to this plant

| NAME | Full Sun | Light Shade | Moderate Shade | Dense Shade | Large Area | Moderate Area | Small Area | Controls Erosion | Tolerates Foot Traffic | Drought Tolerant | Moisture Tolerant | Tolerates Sandy Soil | Salt Tolerant | Spring Bloom | Summer Bloom | Fall Bloom | Evergreen |
|---|---|---|---|---|---|---|---|---|---|---|---|---|---|---|---|---|---|
| Euphorbia cyparissias 'Fens Ruby' | X | X | | | | X | X | | | X | | X | | X | X | | |
| Fallopia japoncia 'Compacta' | X | X | | | X | X | | X | | X | | X | | | X | X | |
| Fallopia japoncia 'Variegata' | X | X | X | | X | X | | X | | X | | X | | | X | X | |
| Fragaria x 'Lipstick' | X | X | | | | X | X | X | X | | | P | | X | P | X | X |
| Gaillardia x grandiflora 'Fanfare' | X | | | | | X | X | | | | | P | | X | X | X | |
| Galium odoratum | | X | X | X | X | X | X | | | | | P | | X | | | X |
| Gaultheria procumbens | X | X | X | X | | X | X | | P | P | | X | | X | | | X |
| Gaura lindheimeri cultivars | X | | | | X | X | | | | | | P | | | | X | |
| Geranium x cantabrigiense cultivars | X | X | | | X | X | X | P | | X | | P | | X | | | X |
| Geranium cinereum cultivars | X | X | | | | X | X | P | | | | P | | | X | | X |
| Geranium 'Dily's' | X | X | | | X | X | | X | | X | | X | | | X | X | |
| Geranium 'Johnson's Blue' | X | X | | | X | X | | X | | X | | x | | X | X | | P |
| Geranium macrorrhizum cultivars | X | X | X | | X | X | X | | | X | | X | | | X | | X |
| Geranium x magnificum | X | X | | | X | X | | P | | X | | X | | | X | | P |
| Geranium phaeum 'Samobor' | X | X | | | X | X | X | X | | X | | P | | X | | | |
| Geranium sanguineum 'Alpenglow' | X | X | | | X | X | | P | | X | | X | | X | | | P |
| Geranium sanguineum 'Striatum' | X | X | | | X | X | | P | | X | | X | | | X | | P |
| Hedera colchica cultivars | X | X | X | X | X | X | | X | P | X | | X | | | | | X |
| Hedera helix cultivars | X | X | X | X | X | X | | X | P | X | | X | | | | | X |
| Helleborus x hybridus | | X | X | X | | X | X | | | X | | X | | X | | | X |
| Hemerocallis 'Big Smile' | X | X | | | X | X | | X | | X | | X | | | X | | |
| Hemerocallis 'Catherine Woodbury' | X | X | | | X | X | | X | | X | | X | | | X | | |
| Hemerocallis 'Chicago Apache' | X | X | | | X | X | | X | | X | | X | | | X | | |
| Hemerocallis 'Custard Candy' | X | X | | | X | X | X | X | | X | | X | | | X | | |
| Hemerocallis 'Fairy Tale Pink' | X | X | | | X | X | X | X | | X | | X | | | X | | |
| Hemerocallis 'Forgotten Dreams' | X | X | | | X | X | X | X | | X | | X | | | X | | |
| Hemerocallis 'Gentle Shepherd' | X | X | | | X | X | | X | | X | | X | | | X | | |
| Hemerocallis 'Happy Returns' | X | X | | | X | X | | X | | X | | X | | | X | | |
| Hemerocallis 'Little Business' | X | X | | | X | X | X | X | | X | | X | | | X | | |
| Hemerocallis 'Little Grapette' | X | X | | | X | X | X | X | | X | | X | | | X | | |
| Hemerocallis 'Mary's Gold' | X | X | | | X | X | | X | | X | | X | | | X | | |
| Hemerocallis 'Mary Todd' | X | X | | | X | X | | X | | X | | X | | | X | | |
| Hemerocallis 'Pardon Me' | X | X | | | X | X | X | X | | X | | X | | | X | | |
| Hemerocallis 'Piano Man' | X | X | | | X | X | | X | | X | | X | | | X | | |
| Hemerocallis 'Siloam Double Classic' | x | x | | | | X | X | X | | X | | X | | | X | | |
| Hemerocallis 'Stella de' Oro' | X | X | | | X | X | X | X | | X | | X | | X | X | X | |
| Hemerocallis 'Strawberry Candy' | X | X | | | X | X | X | X | | X | | X | | | X | | |
| Hemerocallis 'Sue Rothbauer' | X | X | | | X | X | X | X | X | X | | X | | | X | X | |
| Hemerocallis 'Summer Wine' | X | X | | | X | X | | X | | X | | X | | | X | | |
| Hemerocallis 'Rocket City' | X | X | X | | X | X | | | | X | | X | | | X | | |
| Herniaria glabra | X | X | | | X | X | X | X | X | | | X | | | X | | X |
| Heuchera 'Amber Waves' | | X | X | X | | X | X | | | | | P | | X | X | | X |
| Heuchera 'Frosted Jade' | | X | X | X | | X | X | | | | | P | | X | X | | X |
| Heuchera 'Green Spice' | X | X | X | | | X | X | | | P | | | | X | | | X |
| Heuchera 'Obsidian' | X | X | X | | | | X | | | P | | P | | | X | | X |
| Heuchera x 'Palace Purple' | X | X | | | | X | X | | | P | | P | | X | | | X |
| Heuchera sanguinea 'Snow Angel' | X | X | | | | | X | | | P | | P | | X | | | X |
| Heuchera 'Silver Scrolls' | X | X | | | | X | X | | | P | | P | | X | | | X |
| Heuchera 'Stormy Seas' | X | X | | | | X | X | | | P | | P | | | X | | X |
| Heucherella 'Sunspot' | | X | | | | X | X | | | | | P | | | X | | X |
| Hosta 'Allan P. McConnell' | X | X | X | X | | X | X | X | | X | | P | | | X | X | |
| Hosta 'Blue Angel' | | X | X | X | | X | X | X | | X | | P | | | X | | |
| Hosta 'Cherry Berry' | | X | X | | | X | X | X | | X | | P | | | X | | |
| Hosta 'Crowned Imperial' | | X | X | | X | X | | X | | X | | P | | | X | | |
| Hosta 'Daybreak' | | X | X | | X | X | | X | | X | | P | | | X | | |
| Hosta 'Diamond Tiara' | | X | X | | | X | X | X | | X | | P | | | X | | |
| Hosta 'Fire and Ice' | | X | X | | X | X | | X | | X | | P | | | X | | |
| Hosta fortunei 'Gold Standard' | | X | X | X | X | X | | X | | X | | P | | | X | | |
| Hosta fortunei 'Moerheim' | X | X | X | X | X | X | | X | | X | | P | | | X | | |
| Hosta 'Fragrant Blue' | | X | X | | X | X | X | | | X | | P | | | X | | |
| Hosta 'Fragrant Bouquet' | | X | X | | X | X | X | | | X | | P | | | X | | |
| Hosta 'Francee' | X | X | X | X | X | X | | X | | X | | P | | | X | | |
| Hosta 'Frosted Jade' | | X | X | | X | X | | X | | X | | P | | | X | | |

# GROUND COVER SELECTION CHART

Abbreviations: X = Applicable to this plant
P = Partially applicable to this plant

| NAME | Full Sun | Light Shade | Moderate Shade | Dense Shade | Large Area | Moderate Area | Small Area | Controls Erosion | Tolerates Foot Traffic | Drought Tolerant | Moisture Tolerant | Tolerates Sandy Soil | Salt Tolerant | Spring Bloom | Summer Bloom | Fall Bloom | Evergreen |
|---|---|---|---|---|---|---|---|---|---|---|---|---|---|---|---|---|---|
| Hosta 'Golden Tiara' | | X | X | X | | X | X | X | | X | | P | | X | | | |
| Hosta 'Great Expectations' | | X | X | X | X | X | | X | | X | | P | | X | | | |
| Hosta 'Guacamole' | | X | X | X | X | X | | X | | X | | P | | X | X | | |
| Hosta 'Halcyon' | | X | X | X | X | X | | X | | X | | P | | X | | | |
| Hosta 'June' | | X | X | X | | X | X | X | | X | | P | | X | | | |
| Hosta 'Krossa Regal' | | X | X | X | | X | | X | | X | | P | | X | | | |
| Hosta montana 'Aureo-Marginata' | | X | X | X | | X | | X | | X | | P | | X | | | |
| Hosta 'On Stage' | | X | X | | | X | X | | | X | | P | | X | | | |
| Hosta 'Patriot' | X | X | X | X | | X | | X | | X | | P | | X | | | |
| Hosta plantaginea 'Grandiflora' | | X | X | | | X | X | | | X | | P | | X | | | |
| Hosta 'Regal Splendor' | | X | X | | | X | X | | | X | | P | | X | | | |
| Hosta 'Royal Standard' | | X | X | X | | X | | X | | X | | P | | X | | | |
| Hosta 'Sagae' | | X | X | X | | X | | X | | X | | P | | X | | | |
| Hosta sieboldiana 'Elegans' | | X | X | X | X | X | | X | | X | | P | | X | X | | |
| Hosta sieboldiana 'Francis Williams' | | X | X | X | X | X | | X | | X | | P | | X | | | |
| Hosta sieboldiana 'Northern Exposure' | | X | X | X | X | X | X | | | X | | P | | X | | | |
| Hosta 'Striptease' | | X | X | | | X | X | | | X | | P | | X | | | |
| Hosta 'Sum and Substance' | | X | X | X | X | X | | X | | X | | P | | X | | | |
| Hosta 'Summer Fragrance' | X | X | X | X | X | X | | X | | X | | P | | X | X | | |
| Hosta 'Touch of Class' | | X | X | | | X | X | | | X | | P | | X | | | |
| Hosta undulata 'Albo-marginata' | | X | X | X | X | X | X | X | | X | | P | | X | | | |
| Hosta 'Wide Brim' | | X | X | X | X | X | X | X | | X | | P | | X | | | |
| Houttuynia cordata 'Variegata' | X | X | | | X | X | X | X | | | X | P | | X | | | |
| Hypericum androsaemum 'Albury Purple' | X | X | | | X | X | | X | | P | | P | | X | | | P |
| Hypericum patulum 'Hidcote' | X | X | | | X | X | | X | | P | | P | | X | | | P |
| Iberis sempervirens 'Snowflake' | X | | | | | X | X | | | X | | X | | X | | | X |
| Iris cristata | | X | X | | | X | X | | | | P | | | X | | | |
| Iris ensata cultivars | X | X | | | X | X | X | | | | X | P | | X | | | |
| Iris pseudacorus cultivars | X | X | | | X | X | X | X | | | X | X | | X | | | |
| Iris siberica cultivars | X | X | | | | X | X | P | | | | P | | X | | | |
| Iris verna | | X | X | | | X | X | | | | | P | | X | | | |
| Iris versicolor 'Gerald Darby' | X | X | X | | X | X | X | | | | X | P | | X | | | |
| Iris virginica | X | X | X | | | X | X | X | | | X | P | | X | | | |
| Isotoma fluviatilis | X | X | X | | | X | X | | X | | | P | | X | X | P | X |
| Kalimeris pinnatifida var. hortensis | X | X | X | | X | X | | X | | P | | X | | | X | X | |
| Kalimeris yomena 'Shogun' | X | X | | | X | X | | X | | P | | P | | | X | X | |
| Lamiastrum galeobdolon 'Herman's Pride' | | X | X | X | | X | X | | | | | P | | X | | | X |
| Lamiastrum galeobdolon 'Variegatum' | X | X | X | X | X | X | X | X | | | | P | | X | | | X |
| Lamium maculatum cultivars | X | X | X | | | X | X | | | | | P | | X | | | X |
| Lavandula angustifolia cultivars | X | X | | | | X | X | | | X | | X | | | X | | P |
| Lavandula x intermedia 'Grosso' | X | X | | | X | X | | | | X | | X | | | X | | P |
| Leptinella minor | X | X | X | | | | X | | X | | | P | | | X | | X |
| Leptinella squalida 'Platt's Black' | X | X | X | | | | X | | X | | | P | | | X | | X |
| Leucanthemum maximum 'Crazy Daisy' | X | X | | | | X | X | | | P | | P | | | X | X | |
| Leucanthemum x superbum 'Becky' | X | X | | | X | X | | | | P | | P | | | X | | |
| Leucanthemum x superbum 'Snowcap' | X | X | | | | X | X | | | P | | P | | | X | X | |
| Liatris spicata 'Kobold' | X | X | | | X | X | | | | P | | P | | | X | | |
| Liriope muscari 'Big Blue' | X | X | X | | X | X | X | | X | X | | X | | | X | X | X |
| Liriope muscari 'Silvery Sunproof' | X | X | X | | X | X | X | | X | X | | X | | | X | X | X |
| Liriope spicata | X | X | X | | X | X | X | | X | X | | X | | | | X | X |
| Liriope spicata 'Silver Dragon' | X | X | X | | X | X | X | | X | X | | X | | | | X | P |
| Lotus corniculatus 'Pleniflorus' | X | X | | | | X | X | X | X | X | | X | | | X | | P |
| Lysimachia clethroides | X | X | | | | X | X | X | | | X | X | | | X | | |
| Lysimachia nummularia | X | X | X | | | X | X | | X | | X | | | | X | | X |
| Lysimachia nummularia 'Aurea' | X | X | X | | | X | X | | X | | X | | | | X | | X |
| Mazus reptans | X | X | X | | | X | X | | X | | | P | | X | P | P | P |
| Mentha requienii | X | X | | | | | X | | | | P | | | X | | | X |
| Mitchella repens | | X | X | X | | X | X | P | X | X | | X | | X | | | X |
| Monarda didyma 'Petite Delight' | X | X | | | | X | X | | | P | | | P | | X | P | |
| Nepeta x faassenii 'Blue Wonder' | X | X | | | X | X | X | P | | X | | X | | X | X | | P |
| Nepeta x faassenii 'Six Hills Giant' | X | X | | | X | X | | P | | X | | X | | X | X | | P |
| Nepeta x faassenii 'Walker's Low' | X | X | X | | X | X | | X | X | X | | X | | | | X | P |
| Nepeta racemoa 'Blue Ice' | X | X | | | | X | X | P | | X | | X | | X | X | | P |

# GROUND COVER SELECTION CHART

Abbreviations:  X = Applicable to this plant
P = Partially applicable to this plant

| NAME | Full Sun | Light Shade | Moderate Shade | Dense Shade | Large Area | Moderate Area | Small Area | Controls Erosion | Tolerates Foot Traffic | Drought Tolerant | Moisture Tolerant | Tolerates Sandy Soil | Salt Tolerant | Spring Bloom | Summer Bloom | Fall Bloom | Evergreen |
|---|---|---|---|---|---|---|---|---|---|---|---|---|---|---|---|---|---|
| Nepeta subsessilus 'Sweet Dreams' | X | X | X | | X | X | | X | X | X | | X | | | | X | |
| Nepeta yunanensis | X | X | | | X | X | | P | | X | | X | | X | X | | |
| Oenothera berlandieri 'Siskiyou' | X | X | | | X | X | X | P | | | | P | | | X | | |
| Ophiopogon planiscapus 'Nigrescens' | X | X | X | | | X | X | X | | X | | X | | | X | | X |
| Origanum laevigatum 'Herrenhausen' | X | X | | | X | X | | P | | X | | P | | | X | X | X |
| Origanum x 'Rosenkuppel' | X | X | | | X | X | | P | | X | | P | | | X | X | X |
| Oxalis crassipes 'Rosea' | | X | X | X | X | X | X | | | | | P | | X | X | X | |
| Pachysandra procumbens | | X | X | X | X | X | X | P | P | X | | X | | X | | | P |
| Pachysandra terminalis and cultivars | | X | X | X | X | X | X | X | P | | | P | | X | | | X |
| Perovskia atriplicifolia cultivars | X | X | | | X | X | | X | | X | | X | X | | X | X | |
| Persicaria filiformis cultivars | X | X | X | | X | X | | X | | P | | P | | | X | X | |
| Persicaria microcephala 'Red Dragon' | X | X | X | | X | X | | X | | P | | P | | | X | | |
| Persicaria virginiana 'Lance Corporal' | X | X | X | | X | X | | X | | P | | P | | | X | | |
| Petasites japonicus cultivars | | X | X | X | X | X | | X | | | X | X | | X | | | |
| Phlox paniculata 'Laura' | X | | | | X | X | | | | | | P | | | X | X | |
| Physostegia virginiana 'Vivid' | X | X | | | X | X | X | | | | P | | | | X | X | |
| Polemonium caeruleum 'Snow and Sapphires' | | X | X | | | X | X | | | | | P | | | X | | P |
| Polygonatum humile 'Fred Case' | | X | X | | | X | X | | | X | | X | | X | X | | |
| Polygonatum odoratum 'Variegatum' | | X | X | X | X | X | X | P | | X | | | | X | | | |
| Pulmonaria longifolia ssp. cevennensis | | X | X | | X | X | X | | | | | P | | X | | | |
| Pulmonaria longifolia 'Diana Clare' | | X | X | | X | X | X | X | | | | P | | X | | | X |
| Rhus aromatica 'Grow Low' | X | X | | | X | X | | X | | X | | X | X | X | | | |
| Rodgersia aesculifolia | | X | X | X | | X | X | | | | | P | | X | | | |
| Rosa x 'Nearly Wild' | X | X | | | X | X | | | | X | | P | | | X | X | |
| Rubus calycinoides | X | X | X | | | X | X | X | | X | | X | | | X | | X |
| Rudbeckia fulgida 'Goldsturm' | X | X | | | X | X | X | X | | P | | X | | | X | X | |
| Rudbeckia laciniata 'Goldquelle' | X | X | | | X | X | X | X | | P | | P | | | X | X | |
| Rudbeckia speciosa 'Viette's Little Suzy' | X | X | | | X | X | X | X | | P | | P | | | X | X | |
| Sagina subulata and 'Aurea' | | X | X | | | | X | | X | | | P | | | X | | P |
| Salvia nemorosa cultivars | X | X | | | | X | X | | | X | | P | | | X | | |
| Saponaria lempergii 'Max Frei' | X | X | | | X | X | X | | | X | | X | | | X | X | |
| Scabiosa columbaria cultivars | X | X | | | | X | X | | | | | P | | | X | | P |
| Sedum 'Autumn Fire' | X | X | | | X | X | | P | | X | | X | | | X | X | |
| Sedum 'Autumn Joy' | X | X | | | X | X | | P | | X | | X | | | X | X | |
| Sedum cautacola 'Bertram Anderson' | X | X | | | | X | X | | | X | | X | | | X | X | |
| Sedum dasyphyllum 'Major' | X | | | | | | X | P | | X | | X | | | X | | X |
| Sedum ellacombianum | X | X | | | X | X | X | P | | X | | X | | | X | | |
| Sedum hispanicum 'Minus' | X | X | | | | | X | X | | X | | X | | | X | | X |
| Sedum kamtschaticum 'Tekaridake' | X | X | | | X | X | X | P | | X | | X | | | X | | |
| Sedum kamtschaticum 'Variegatum' | X | X | | | X | X | X | P | | X | | X | | | X | | X |
| Sedum 'Matrona' | X | X | | | X | X | | P | | X | | X | | | X | X | |
| Sedum middendorfianum var. diffusum | X | X | | | X | X | X | X | | X | | X | | | X | | X |
| Sedum 'Purple Emperor' | X | X | | | X | X | | P | | X | | X | | | X | X | |
| Sedum rupestre 'Angelina' | X | X | | | X | X | X | X | | X | | X | | X | X | | X |
| Sedum spectabile 'Brilliant' | X | X | | | X | X | | P | | X | | X | | | X | X | |
| Sedum spectabile 'Neon' | X | X | | | X | X | | P | | X | | X | | | X | X | |
| Sedum spectabile 'Pink Chablis' | X | X | | | X | X | | P | | X | | X | | | X | X | |
| Sedum spurium cultivars | X | X | | | X | X | X | P | | X | | X | | | X | | X |
| Sedum x 'Vera Jameson' | X | X | | | X | X | X | P | | X | | X | | | X | | |
| Sempervivum cultivars | X | X | | | | X | X | | | X | | X | | | X | | X |
| Sisyrinchium angustifolium 'Lucerne' | X | X | | | | X | X | | | X | | P | | X | X | | |
| Smilacina racemosa | | X | X | | X | X | X | X | | P | | P | | X | | | |
| Solidago rugosa 'Fireworks' | X | X | | | X | X | | P | | X | | X | | | X | X | |
| Stachys byzantina 'Silver Carpet' | X | X | | | X | X | X | P | | X | | X | | | P | | P |
| Stylophorum diphyllum | | X | X | X | X | X | | P | | P | | P | | X | X | | |
| Thymus x citriodorus 'Doone Valley' | X | X | | | | X | X | P | X | X | | X | | | X | | X |
| Thymus nitens | X | X | | | | X | X | | X | X | | X | | | X | | X |
| Thymus pseudolanuginosus | X | X | | | | X | X | P | X | X | | X | | | X | | X |
| Thymus serpyllum and cultivars | X | X | | | | X | X | P | X | X | | X | | | X | X | X |
| Tiarella cordifolia 'Eco Running Tapestry' | X | X | X | X | X | X | X | X | X | P | | P | | X | | | X |
| Tiarella 'Ink Blot' | X | X | X | X | | X | X | | | P | | P | | X | | | X |
| Tiarella 'Pink Bouquet' | | X | X | X | | X | X | | | P | | X | | X | | | X |
| Tiarella wherryi | | X | X | X | X | X | X | | | P | | P | | | X | | X |

# GROUND COVER SELECTION CHART

Abbreviations: X = Applicable to this plant
P = Partially applicable to this plant

| NAME | Full Sun | Light Shade | Moderate Shade | Dense Shade | Large Area | Moderate Area | Small Area | Controls Erosion | Tolerates Foot Traffic | Drought Tolerant | Moisture Tolerant | Tolerates Sandy Soil | Salt Tolerant | Spring Bloom | Summer Bloom | Fall Bloom | Evergreen |
|---|---|---|---|---|---|---|---|---|---|---|---|---|---|---|---|---|---|
| *Tradescantia cultivars* | X | X | | | X | X | | X | | X | | X | | X | | | |
| *Tricyrtis cultivars* | | X | X | | | X | X | | | P | | P | | | X | X | |
| *Trifolium repens* 'Atropurpureum' | X | X | X | | | | X | | P | | | P | | X | | | |
| *Veronica oltensis* | X | X | | | | | X | | X | P | | P | | | X | | X |
| *Veronica spicata* 'Red Fox' | X | X | | | X | X | X | | | | | P | | | X | X | X |
| *Veronica spicata* 'Royal Candles' | X | X | | | X | X | X | | | | | P | | | X | X | |
| *Vernonica* 'Waterperry Blue' | X | X | | | | X | X | X | X | P | | P | | X | | X | X |
| *Vinca minor and cultivars* | X | X | X | X | X | X | X | X | P | X | | P | | X | | P | X |
| *Viola coreana* 'Syletta' | X | X | X | | | X | X | | X | P | | P | | X | | | P |
| *Viola* 'Purple Showers' | X | X | | | | X | X | | | | | P | | X | X | X | X |
| *Waldsteinia ternata* | X | X | X | | X | X | X | X | X | P | | P | | X | | | X |

# Perpetually underused, Ceratostigma plumbaginoides, Dwarf Plumbago, is among the finest ground covers for small to large-scale use. It is always handsome, reliable, and easy to care for.

# GROUND COVERS
## *For dependable, low maintenance landscaping*

### Achillea millefolium 'Red Beauty' (a-kil-<u>lee</u>-a mil-le-<u>foe</u>-lee-um)
('Red Beauty' Yarrow)..................................................Zone 3

1 1/2'-2'; full sun to light shade. 'Red Beauty' is exceptional in foliage and flower, and compact and nonflopping—unlike many taller selections, which may lay over as they mature. It is clothed in fine fern-textured, fragrant blue green foliage which changes to beautiful shades of yellow and burgundy in fall, and is even more beautiful when covered, midsummer to fall, with its impressive display of intensely crimson red flowers. Grow 'Red Beauty' alone on a moderate to large scale or as a companion plant.
Rec. Size: #1 pot (8/flat)    Space: (14"-18")

### Aegopodium podograria 'Variegatum' (ee-go-<u>poe</u>-dee-um poe-da-grare-<u>ee</u>-a)
(Snow-on-the Mountain)..................................................Zone 3

6"; full sun to moderate shade. A fast growing herbaceous ground cover, the leaves of variegated goutweed are light green and edged with white. Its white carrot-like umbels are borne in June on 12-18 inch stems. This is a high contrast plant for brightening up shady settings. It is good planted enmass and combines well with tall ferns and large blue leaved hosta selections.
Rec. Size: 3 1/4" (18/flat)    Space: (6"-8")

### Agastache x 'Blue Fortune' (a-<u>gah</u>-sta-kee or ah-guh-<u>stach</u>-ee)
('Blue Fortune' Anise Hyssop)..................................................Zone 5

2 1/2'-3'; full sun to light shade. An exceptional cultivar, 'Blue Fortune' was bred and selected by Gert Fortgens of the Arboretum Trompenberg in Rotterdam. Fortgens created one magnificently florifierous, drought and heat tolerant, large scale ground cover. Nice smelling, like anise candy, the rich green foliage of 'Blue Fortune' is lovely during spring and early summer. By midsummer, however, it all but disappears under a cloud of blue violet flower spikes. Suitable companions are Amsonia, ornamental grasses, asters, Solidago, and countless others.
Rec. Size: #1 pot (8/flat)    Space: (1 1/2'-2')

### Agastache foeniculum 'Golden Jubilee' (a-<u>gah</u>-sta-kee fee-<u>nik</u>-you-lum)
('Golden Jubilee' Fennel)..................................................Zone 5/6

16"-20"; full sun to light shade. Named to commemorate the 50 year reign of Queen Elizabeth II, this fine selection, displays striking chartreuse golden mint scented foliage with dense spikes of lavender-blue summerborne flowers. Great for high contrast, excellent companions include purple pennisetums, 'Catlin's Giant' ajuga, 'Palace Purple' heuchera, blue leaved ajugas, and 'Chocolate' Joe-Pye.
Rec. Size: #1 pot (8/flat)    Space: (16"-24")

### Ajuga 'Chocolate Chip' (a-<u>jew</u>-ga)
('Chocolate Chip' Ajuga)..................................................Zone 3

3"; light to moderate shade. With tiny tear-drop-shaped, deep chocolate bronze, evergreen foliage, this dwarf creeping ajuga is attractive in any season. In spring, however, it hits its peak, bearing many spikes of bright blue, hummingbird attracting tubular flowers. Nice in combination with golden, blue, or variegated hostas, colorful sedges, and Lamium selections, 'Chocolate Chip' is a fine addition to any landscape.
Rec. Size: 3 1/4" (18/flat)    Space: (6"-10")

## Ajuga reptans 'Bronze Beauty' (a-jew-ga   rep-tanz)
(Bronze Ajuga)................................................................Zone 3

2"-3"; light to moderate shade. Bronze ajuga is an extremely popular mat forming perennial that blankets the ground (spreading like a strawberry) with rich bronze colored evergreen leaves. Valued also for its suberb springtime floral display, bronze ajuga sends up copious masses of blue flowered, hummingbird attracting floral spikes.
Rec. Size: 38 cell flat   Space: (8"-12")

## Ajuga reptans 'Burgundy Glow' (a-jew-ga   rep-tanz)
('Burgundy Glow' Ajuga) ........................................Zone 5

2"-3"; light to moderate shade. Burgundy glow ajuga is prized for its multicolored white, pink, rose, and green foliage. Its flowers of bluish purple arise in early spring. Be sure to plant it in rich, well drained soil. Use for accent or small scale general cover, but avoid planting large masses as reversion to the purple leaved parent is common and maintenance tends to be high.
Rec. Size: 38 cell flat   Space: (10"-14")

## Ajuga reptans 'Catlin's Giant' (a-jew-ga   rep-tanz)
(Catlin's Giant Ajuga) ............................................Zone 4

3"-5"; light to moderate shade. The largest bronze ajuga cultivar, 'Catlin's Giant' reaches 10 inches tall when in bloom. Its enormous, bronzy purple, cabbagelike leaves are superb for color contrast and its flowers of blue are a welcome sight in early spring. Companions include large white/green variegated and blue leaved hostas, variegated iris, Pulmonaria, variegated Solomon's seal, dwarf grasses, and many types of ferns.
Rec. Size: 3 1/4" (18/flat)   Space: (12"-18")

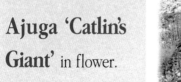

### Ajuga 'Catlin's Giant' in flower.

## Ajuga reptans 'Mahogany' (a-jew-ga   rep-tanz)
('Mahogany' Ajuga) ................................................Zone 3

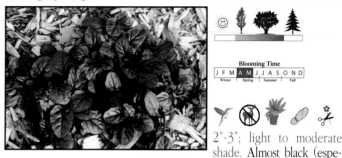

2"-3"; light to moderate shade. Almost black (especially during spring and fall) this is the most deeply purple-leaved of all ajugas. 'Mahogany', not surprisingly, is superior for high contrast and becomes a spectacle during spring when decorated with bright blue flowers. Companions include showy ginger and other ajugas, as well as selections of Allium, Campanula, Dicentra, epimedium, Heuchera, hosta, crested iris, Lamium, Sagina, Tricyrtis, Waldsteinia, and Carex.
Rec. Size: 3 1/4" (18/flat)   Space: (8"-12")

## Alchemilla vulgaris (al-ke-mil-a   vul-gay-ris)
(Lady's Mantle) ......................................................Zone 3

6"-12"; full sun to moderate shade. Said to have been worn as an adornment by the Virgin Mary, lady's mantle is soft textured, clump forming, and a plant of charm and grace. Among its unique features is its lovely soft gray-green velvet covered, 2 to 4 inch wide, multilobed foliage. In youth the leaves are pleated, and later display glistening beads of water about their edges during early morning (from a process known as guttation). The curious chartreuse green flowers of lady's mantle are borne in good quantity mid to late spring and lend an element of subtle contrast.
Rec. Size: #1 pot (8/flat)   Space: (8"-12")

## Allium maximowiczii 'Alba' (ale-ee-um maks-i-moe-witz-ee-ee)
(White Flowered Ornamental Chive)................................Zone 4

6"-10"; full sun to light shade. This Allium is vigorous, crisp, and vibrant green during early spring when other plants are still sound asleep. By May it is decorated with spire shaped pale yellow flower heads which by late May open to reveal masses of snow white flowers that all but smother the foliage. White flowered ornamental chive is a tough, drought resistant plant excellent for small scale landscape use, edging, and accent. It is a great companion to 'Forescate' chive and works well with Dianthus and sedum selections as well.
Rec. Size: #1 pot (8/flat)   Space: (8"-12")

## Allium schoenoprasum 'Forescate' (<u>ale</u>-ee-um   skoyn-oh-prah-sum)
('Forescate' Chive) ...................................................Zone 3

12"-18"; full sun to light shade. This remarkable ground cover fills the need for a plant that gives long running early season color in full sun. Super hardy, drought resistant, and durable, 'Forescate' chive leafs out early during spring with attractive bluish green foliage. Above it, carried upon stout stems, are numerous pointed clusters of intensely rose pink springborne flowers that intensify to bluish purple as they age. Both colors are present at the same time giving a cheerful confetti-like appearance. Great as an edging or general ground cover and excellent in combination with mountain garlic, hardy geraniums, daylilies, and sedums.
Rec. Size: #1 pot (8/flat)   Space: (8"-12")

## Allium senescens subsp. montanum (<u>ale</u>-ee-um   si-<u>ness</u>-enz mon-<u>tay</u>-num)
(Mountain Garlic) ...................................................Zone 5

8"-12"; full sun to light shade. Amazingly easy to grow, this durable allium is neat, tidy, and trouble free. As a foliage plant it displays blemish free, vibrant medium green, leathery textured, vertically oriented, 10 inch long elliptical (in cross section) straplike leaves. Held in tight clusters, the attractive foliage, all by itself, makes this a worthy garden specimen. But couple this with dozens of 2 inch clusters of vibrant pink-purple florets, carried mid to late summer in balloonlike fashion (8 inches above the foliage) and you have a plant that's just plain fun.
Rec. Size: #1 pot (8/flat)   Space: (10"-14")

## Amsonia 'Blue Ice' (am-<u>sone</u>-ee-a)
('Blue Ice' Blue Star) NATIVE CULTIVAR.....................Zone 5

12"-15"; full sun to light shade. Compact growing and long blooming, this fine selection (from White Flower Farm) is extraordinary. It is very tough and

drought resistant, and its foliage is deep green and clean throughout the year. But, what is most remarkable is its deep gentian blue flower buds which are effective for weeks prior to opening to deep blue petaled flowers, and lasting another 4 to 5 weeks. Both in flower and foliage, this is an exceptionally pleasing ground cover for small to large scale massing (when planted in drifts) or for accent or along borders and walkways as a dwarf edging. Alone, or in combination with such plants as ajuga, Campanula, or Sedum for companionship, this is a remarkable sure bet addition to the landscape.
Rec. Size: #1 pot (8/flat)   Space: (14"-18")

## Amsonia hubrichtii (am-<u>sone</u>-ee-a hue-<u>brek</u>-tee-eye)
(Narrow Leaf Blue Star) NATIVE SPECIES.....................Zone 4

2'-3'; full sun to light shade. Narrow leaf blue star bears its clusters of sky blue flowers during spring, and although the floral display is nice, this plant is about more than flowers—mainly it's a foliage plant extraordinare. Whispy and thread-narrow, its handsome willow shaped foliage is carried in horizontal fashion upon upright to arching stems. Colored a soft green during summer, by autumn it has changed to a dazzling golden hue and is carried this way well into the cold weather of autumn.
Rec. Size: #1 pot (8/flat)   Space: (1 1/2'-2')

## Arctostaphylos uva-ursi 'Massachusetts' (ark-toe-<u>staf</u>-i-los u-va-<u>er</u>-see)
(Massachusetts Bearberry) NATIVE CULTIVER.....................Zone 3

1"-3" spreading indefinitely; full sun to light shade. This florific selection of our lovely native species is a beautiful rugged trailing ground cover that is excellent in infertile sandy acidic soils. Not only is it drought tolerant and long lived but very attractive with white to pinkish urn-shaped springborne flowers which make for exceptional contrast against its deep glossy-green evergreen foliage. Later in summer, its red berry-like fruit furnishes food for wildlife and often persists through winter.
Rec. Size: #1 pot (8/flat)   Space: (12"-16")

**G R O U N D   C O V E R S**

## Armeria maritima 'Rubrifolia' (ar-mee-ree-a   ma-rit-i-ma)
(Red Leaved Maritime Thrift)..................................................Zone 4

3"-5"; full sun to light shade. With stunningly hot magenta-pink spring/early summerborne balloonlike flowers set off against burgundy-red foliage, this splendid slow spreading ground cover is super colorful. It is neat, tidy, and excellent in rock gardens. As a companion perennial or dwarf edging its grassy textured foliage lends contrast against coarser textured elements. Some of its best companions include Alchemilla, Asarum, bergenia, Delosperma, Lamium, Herniaria, Sagina, Heuchera, Thymus, and sedums. Rec. Size: #1 pot (8/flat)    Space: (10"-14")

## Aruncus aesthusifolia (ah-run-kus   eis-thus-i-foe-lee-a)
(Korean Goat's Beard)..................................................Zone 3

8"-12"; full sun to moderate shade. This compact ground cover is a great plant for getting the season started. It flushes out early with fresh green fern-textured foliage long before most plants even think about waking up. Even if this were all that Korean Goat's beard did, it would be well worth using. But, it blooms as well, and during summer produces creamy white flowers above the foliar mass. Korean Goat's Beard is one of those pleasing, easy to care for, super low maintenance plants that one plants, sits back, and enjoys. It is great for edging, small to moderate scale ground cover use, and accent. It also gets along nicely with many companions. Ajugas, Heucheras, hostas, iris, and colorful sedges are some of the best. Rec. Size: #1 pot (8/flat)    Space: (12"-16")

## Asarum europaeum (a-sah-rum   you-row-pee-um)
(European Ginger)..................................................Zone 4

3"-5"; light to dense shade. Evergreen, leathery and dark glossy green, the heart to kidney shaped foliage of this plant is exceedingly handsome. Arising from the rootstalk, the leaves are carried upon leathery petioles and often obscure the curious purple to brown bell shaped, pendant springtime flowers. A fine addition to any shady landscape, European ginger combines nicely with Dicentra, hostas, Solomon's seal, and nearly all shade loving wildflowers. Rec. Size: #1 pot (8/flat)    Space: (10"-14")

## Asarum splendens 'Quick Silver' (as-a-rum splen-denz)
('Quick Silver' Showy Ginger)..................................................Zone 5

5"-7"; light to dense shade. Slow spreading, this is an exceptional selection with huge 7 inch long, semi glossy, silver mottled, deep green arrow-shaped leaves. Under them during spring are borne burgundy colored, bell shaped flowers. Great for massing on a moderate to large scale, 'Quicksilver' is superb for brightening shady areas and lends an exotic look to the landscape. Try it alone or in combination with ferns, astilbe, 'Chocolate' Joe-Pye, Lenten rose, Heucheras, hostas, Japanese forest grass, and sedges. Rec. Size: #1 pot (8/flat)    Space: (10"-14")

## Aster x dumosus 'Nesthakchen' (as-ter   dew-moe-sus)
('Nesthakchen' Aster) NATIVE CULTIVAR..................................................Zone 4

10"; full sun to light shade. 'Nesthatchken' aster is a fine easy to grow selection with tight, neat, compact habit and lustrous dark green healthy foliage. At 10 inches tall by 3 feet wide, it makes a splendid ground cover and late summer through fall is smothered in rosy pink flowers. Excellent on hillsides as a general cover, it combines nicely with other asters as well as such classic fall bloomers as goldenrod, Kalimeris, Eupatorium, and sedums. Rec. Size:  #1 pot (8/flat)     Space: (2'-3')

**What would happen if you planted a drift of low growing asters in front of this already beautiful planting of Japanese silver grass and orange coneflower?**

G R O U N D   C O V E R S

## Aster dumosus x 'Professor Anton Kippenberg' (<u>as</u>-ter dew-moe-sus)
(Kippenberg Aster) NATIVE CULTIVAR..........................Zone 5

10"-14"; full sun to light shade. 'Professor Anton Kippenberg' is a superior cultivar that has withstood the test of time. Its compact habit of rich deep green foliage is sufficient to shut out weeds, and it looks nice all year long, especially when in bloom. Flowering comes late summer and fall and plants become loaded with lavender-blue petaled, gold-centered, semi-double daisylike flowers. Overall the effect is dramatic and is the perfect finale to another growing season. Naturally 'Professor Anton Kippenberg' is good for accent use, but it is exceptionally fine as a moderate to large scale ground cover, especially on undulating or sloping terrain.
Rec. Size: #1 pot (8/flat)    Space: (1 1/2'-2')

## Aster x frikartii 'Monch' (<u>as</u>-ter   fri-<u>kart</u>-ee-ee)
('Monch' Hybrid Aster).....................................................Zone 5

2 1/2'-3' full sun. Considered by many gardeners to be the best of the hybrid asters, 'Monch' is exceptional for its profuse show of large lavender blue late summer and fallborne flowers, robust nature (to 3 feet wide), deep green mildew resistant foliage, and ability to remain upright while other lesser cultivars flop over. Suitable companions include ornamental grasses, goldenrod, other asters, coneflowers, variegated fleeceflower, Gaura selections, Leucanthemum cultivars, variegated lilyturf, Origanum, Perovskia, Physostegia, Rudbeckia, and sedum cultivars.
Rec. Size: #1 pot (8/flat)    Space: (1 1/2'-2')

## Aster novae-belgii 'Alert' (<u>as</u>-ter   <u>no</u>-vee-bel-gee-eye)
('Alert' New York Aster) NATIVE CULTIVER................................Zone 4

15"-18"; full sun. to light shade Among the hundreds of cultivars of this fine species, 'Alert' is outstanding. An excellent container plant, it is great for edging and massing. It is compact, tolerant of moist soils, and is remarkably colorful during late summer and fall. This is when its bright rosy red flowers come into full bloom.
Rec. Size: #1 pot (8/flat)    Space: (14"-18")

## Aster 'Wood's Light Blue' (<u>as</u>-ter)
('Wood's Light Blue' Aster)..........................................Zone 5

12"; full sun to light shade. With clear soft blue, gold-centered flowers carried above deep green foliage from late summer through fall, 'Wood's Light Blue' is superb in that it does not open up, become leggy, or brown out at the base as is the case with lesser selections. Furthermore, it is attractive to butterflies, compact of habit, disease free, truly one of the finest asters on the market today.
Rec. Size: #1 pot (8/flat)    Space: (12"-16")

## Aster 'Wood's Pink' (<u>as</u>-ter)
('Wood's Pink' Aster)................................................Zone 5

16"; full sun to light shade. Clothed in handsome, disease resistant, dark blue-green foliage, 'Wood's Pink' is an excellent carefree selection. During late summer through fall, however, is when it really shines. This time of year 'Wood's Pink' produces a profusion of clear pink, gold centered, butterfly attracting flowers. Nice for edging, accent, mass planting, and as a fine container plant. 'Wood's Pink' is bound for great popularity.
Rec. Size: #1 pot (8/flat)    Space: (12"-16")

**Imagine what these flowers of Aster 'Professor Anton Kippenberg' look like to a hungry butterfly.**

*GROUND COVERS*

# Astilbe

Among the most easily cultured, most colorful, most durable, and most forgiving of ground covers, astilbes are great plants for all gardens. They typically display a low, leafy, stemless habit, nonintrusive horizontal spread, and upright floral stalks that ascend from a few inches to more than 4 feet. Alone or in combination with ferns, hostas, irises, bergenias, and many of the clump forming ornamental grasses, astilbes may be used on a small to large scale and are splendid as coarse-textured colorful turf substitutes. A small grouping of astilbes can be used as a facing to statuary, boulders, shrubs, and small trees. A broad facing of astilbes can literally transform an ordinary fence into a landscape spectacle and, when used enmasse about the entrance of a home or building, their vibrant flowers and crisp foliage can help extend a cheerful greeting to visitors. Astilbes can also be used to line garden paths, soften pool edges, and enhance stream banks. Regardless of their use, they can be counted upon for nearly foolproof performance. With their vibrant upright clusters of tiny flowers, which in some species are commercially valued as cut flowers, astilbes brighten the most dreary garden corners, and are even said to grow underneath black walnut trees.

Astilbes grow best in cool, well-drained, humus-rich, acidic soil. Their relatively shallow roots make them sensitive to drought, so make every effort to keep their soil moist. Astilbes need light to moderate shade and require little or no maintenance.

| FLOWER COLOR/TONE | PRIMARY BLOOM TIME | | |
|---|---|---|---|
| | EARLY SUMMER | MID SUMMER | LATE SUMMER |
| Red Tones | | A. x arendsii 'Fanal' | A. x arendsii 'Glut' |
| Purple/Rose | | A. chinensis 'Visions' | A. chinensis 'Pumila' |
| Pink | A. x japonica 'Mainz' | A. simplicifolia 'Bronze Elegans' | A. chinensis 'Superba' |
| White | | | A. x arendsii 'White Gloria' |

## Astilbe x arendsii 'Fanal' (a-<u>stil</u>-be  a-<u>renz</u>-ee-eye)
('Fanal' Astilbe).........................................................................Zone 4

2' in flower; light to moderate shade. With deeply cut, dark shiny green foliage and dark red early- to mid-summerborne flowers arranged in narrow, full-substance plumes.
Rec. Size: #1 pot (8/flat)    Space: (14"-18")

## Astilbe x arendsii 'Glut' (a.k.a. 'Glow') (a-<u>stil</u>-be  a-<u>renz</u>-ee-eye)
('Glut' Astilbe).........................................................................Zone 4

2 1/2' in flower; light to moderate shade. Blooming late summer, this popular "classic" astilbe produces pure dark red plumes upon long, narrow, upright panicles. Excellent as a background plant to other astilbes and many of the smaller variegated hostas, 'Glut' is reliable, florific, and an excellent addition to any landscape.
Rec. Size: #1 pot (8/flat)    Space: (14"-18")

## Astilbe x arendsii 'White Gloria' (syn. 'Weisse Gloria') (a-<u>stil</u>-be  a-<u>renz</u>-ee-eye)
('White Gloria' Astilbe)...............................................................Zone 4

2'; light to moderate shade. This mid to late summer blooming astilbe is the white flowered companion to 'Visions'. And, like 'Visions', it is unique for the thick substance of its floral plumes — making it an outstanding selection for bright showy impact, expecially in mass plantings.
Rec. Size: #1 pot (8/flat)    Space: (14"-18")

GROUND COVERS

## Astilbe chinensis 'Pumila' (a-<u>stil</u>-be  chi-<u>nen</u>-sis)
(Dwarf Chinese Astilbe)................................................Zone 4

**Blooming Time**
J F M A M J J A S O N D
Winter   Spring   Summer   Fall

8"-12" in flower; light to moderate shade. A rugged little dwarf cultivar, dwarf Chinese astilbe boasts neat, tooth edged, deep green foliage, and toward the end of summer and into fall, many showy, upright spikelets of rosy purplish flowers. Companions that work nicely with dwarf Chinese astilbe include large blue leaved and variegated hostas, 'Chocolate' Joe-pye, Crososmia x 'Lucifer', and golden leaved Japanese forest grass.
Rec. Size: #1 pot (8/flat)    Space: (12"-16")

## Astilbe chinensis 'Superba' (a-<u>stil</u>-be  chi-<u>nen</u>-sis) (syn. A. taquetii)
('Superba' Astilbe)................................................Zone 4

**Blooming Time**
J F M A M J J A S O N D
Winter   Spring   Summer   Fall

Clump forming, 2 1/2-3'; full sun to moderate shade. 'Superba' is a great backdrop ground cover, pathway edging, or facing plant—to fences, trees, and informal hedges. It is a comfortable companion to purple bergenia, European ginger, shade tolerant geraniums, purple leaved Heucheras, Allegheny pachysandra, barren strawberry, corydalis, hostas, pulmonarias, epimediums, and various wildflowers. Its flowers are carried high above the shiny green compound foliage from mid to late summer and effectively compliment these companions.
Rec. Size: #1 pot (8/flat)    Space: (14"-18")

## Astilbe chinensis 'Visions' (a-<u>stil</u>-be  chi-<u>nen</u>-sis)
('Visions' Astilbe)................................................Zone 4

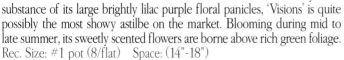

**Blooming Time**
J F M A M J J A S O N D
Winter   Spring   Summer   Fall

14"; light to moderate shade. Incredibly impressive for the extraordinarily thick substance of its large brightly lilac purple floral panicles, 'Visions' is quite possibly the most showy astilbe on the market. Blooming during mid to late summer, its sweetly scented flowers are borne above rich green foliage.
Rec. Size: #1 pot (8/flat)    Space: (14"-18")

## Astilbe x japonica 'Mainz' (a-<u>stil</u>-be  ja-<u>pon</u>-i-ka)
('Mainz' Astilbe)................................................Zone 4

**Blooming Time**
J F M A M J J A S O N D
Winter   Spring   Summer   Fall

2' in flower; light to moderate shade. With attractive dark green compound foliage 'Mainz' is a handsome clump forming foliage plant spring through fall. Yet early to mid summer, during its terrific floral display, it bears such a multitude of dark lavender rose plumes one hardly notices the leaves. Nice with other astilbes, especially pinks and whites, 'Mainz' is excellent with a host of other clump forming perennials. See premiumplants.net website for an extensive listing.
Rec. Size: #1 pot (8/flat)    Space: (14"-18")

## Astilbe simplicifolia 'Bronze Elegans' (a-<u>stil</u>-be  sim-pli-si-<u>foe</u>-lee-a)
('Bronze Elegans' Astilbe)................................................Zone 4

**Blooming Time**
J F M A M J J A S O N D
Winter   Spring   Summer   Fall

15"; light to moderate shade. An outstanding selection for both leaf and flower, 'Bronze Elegans' begins the season with a display of shiny bronze foliage—and this would be sufficient to make it worth growing. Yet, by mid July, when its foliage has turned deep green, it is smothered in heavy plumes of light pink flowers.
Rec. Size: #1 pot (8/flat)    Space: (12"-16")

## Bergenia purpurascens (ber-<u>gen</u>-ee-a  <u>per</u>-per-ay-senz)
(Purple Bergenia)................................................Zone 3

**Blooming Time**
J F M A M J J A S O N D
Winter   Spring   Summer   Fall

12"; full sun to moderate shade. Purple bergenia is durable and attractive. Originating from the Himalayas to China, its leaves are oval to elliptic, uprightly oriented, and purple underneath during the growing season. In cold weather they become reddish purple and mahogany on top as well. Flowering during spring, its nodding purplish pink flowers are held upon purple red stems and carried well above the foliage.
Rec. Size: #1 pot (8/flat)    Space: (14"-18")

GROUND COVERS

**Boltonia asteroides 'Pink Beauty' (bowl-<u>tone</u>-ee-a  ass-ter-oide-ees)**

('Pink Beauty' Boltonia) NATIVE CULTIVAR...............................Zone 4

3'-3 1/2'; full sun. Durable and easy to grow and maintain, 'Pink Beauty' is one of the finest and most functional of the eastern North American natives. 'Pink Beauty' graces the landscape from spring through summer with neat, attractive, lance shaped, blue green foliage. Then during late August, as if to welcome fall, it bursts forth with thousands of pink petaled, yellow-centered, 1 1/2 inch wide daisylike flowers. These are carried atop the foliage in such quantities as to give a pink cloudlike appearance that lasts until the first killing frost. Use 'Pink Beauty' in small groups, as a dwarf hedge, or to magnificent effect in mass plantings. Suitable companions include ornamental grasses, asters, Coreopsis, Echinacea, Eupatorium, Kalimeris, Origanum, Perovskia, sedums, and Solidago.
Rec. Size: #1 pot (8/flat)    Space: (2 1/2'-3')

**Brunnera macrophylla 'Jack Frost' (brun-<u>nee</u>-ra  mak-row-<u>fil</u>-a)**

('Jack Frost' Brunnera) ...............................................Zone 3

12"-15" tall; light to moderate shade. Selected at Walters Gardens as a sport of the cultivar 'Langtrees', 'Jack Frost' is an award winner with large silver frosted foliage and attractive green veins. 'Jack Frost' blooms during spring with whispy forget-me-not blue flowers and serves to brighten up the shade garden. It is a refined yet surprisingly quick-to-mature specimen plant and serves well as an edging or companion to dark leaved forms of Heuchera, ajuga, and bergenia as well as Dicentra, blue leaved hostas, geraniums, crested iris, and black mondo grass.
Rec. Size: #1 pot (8/flat)    Space: (1 1/2'-2')

**Calamintha nepeta subsp. nepeta (kal-a-<u>min</u>-tha  ne-pe-ta)**

(Pink Flowered Calamint Savory) ...........................................Zone 5

10"-14"; full sun to light shade. Pink flowered calamint savory, a member of the mint family, is a durable, drought resistant, disease free plant

with super fragrant, highly attractive shiny soft green foliage. This makes it a great choice for planting along sidewalks and pathways (where its beauty and fragrance can most easily be appreciated). But one should not hesitate to use it in rock walls or in broad sweeping drifts along hillsides or background areas. It is here perhaps that its floral characteristics are best displayed and this is significant because for the duration of summer, and the first part of fall, its leaves all but disappear under a billowy cloud of lilac pink flowers. Viewed up close or from a distance, this creates a pleasing, soft, rich, comforting sight. Pink flowered calamint savory tolerates dry sandy or rocky soils, and no matter what the soil type, prefers good drainage.
Rec. Size: #1 pot (8/flat)    Space: (14"-18")

**Calamintha nepeta 'White Cloud' (kal-a-<u>min</u>-thea  ne-pe-ta)**

('White Cloud' Calamint Savory).............................................Zone 5

1'-1 1/2'; full sun to light shade. 'White Cloud' calamint savory is a superb landscape plant. It is tough, resistant to disease, and immensely useful. As a general cover or edging plant it works beautifully and combines nicely with a host of other sun loving ground covers (Liatris, daylilies, sedums, Salvia, and Scabiosa to name a few). Clothed in tiny, light green, highly fragrant foliage, 'White Cloud' is also exceptional in flower, blooming several weeks from mid summer to fall with thousands of soft white, whispy, mintlike flowers.
Rec. Size: #1 pot (8/flat)    Space: (14"-18")

**Campanula carpatica 'Blue Clips' (kam-pan-you-la  kar-pat-i-ka)**

('Blue Clips' Carpathian Bellflower)..................................................Zone 3

6"-9"; full sun to light shade. A staple ingredient of the mixed perennial border, 'Blue Clips' bellflower is terrific mass planted on a small to moderate scale as a florific ground cover. 'Blue Clips' displays compact habit and spreads to 12 inches. Its triangular, tooth-edged, medium to dark green deciduous foliage makes a lovely backdrop to the masses of vibrant blue, bell-shaped, 2-to-3-inch wide, long-blooming, summerborne flowers.
Rec. Size: #1 pot (8/flat)    Space: (12"-14")

## Campanula carpatica 'Pearl Deep Blue' (kam-<u>pan</u>-you-la kar-<u>pat</u>-i-ka)
('Pearl Deep Blue' Carpathian Bellflower)......................Zone 3

6"-9"; full sun to light shade. Compared to the classic selection 'Blue Clips', 'Pearl Deep Blue' flowers earlier, its flowers are darker blue and more upright, and its habit is more rounded than sprawling. These features make 'Pearl Deep Blue' a high contrast plant for edging, accent, or general cover. It is also quite nice tucked in the cracks of retaining walls and in planter boxes and containers. Suitable companions are numerous with some of the finest being other campanulas of contrasting flower color and texture, coreopsis, sedums, and dwarf ornamental grasses.
Rec. Size: #1 pot (8/flat)    Space: (12"-14")

## Campanula carpatica 'White Clips' (<u>kam</u>-pan-you-la    kar-<u>pat</u>-i-ka)
('White Clips' Carpathian Bellflower)......................Zone 3

6"-9"; full sun to light shade. The white flowered equivalent of 'Blue Clips' (see above), this summer blooming selection combines nicely with C. 'Blue Clips' and C. 'Pearl Deep Blue', and also is excellent for use as a small scale ground cover or specimen for the perennial border.
Rec. Size: #1 pot (8/flat)    Space: (12"-14")

## Campanula glomerata 'Acaulis' (kam-pan-<u>you</u>-la    glom-er-aye-ta)
('Acaulis' Clustered Bellflower)......................Zone 4

2"-4"; full sun to light shade. With easy growing clump-forming/shy spreading habit and lovely deep green basal leaves, this well behaved bell flower is wonderful for use as a border edging, companion, or general cover. The specific epithet glomerata (clustered) refers to its rich deep blue, high-impact flowers which are borne in clusters during late spring/early summer. Companions are easy and many, some of the finest including cultivars of lady fern, Dianthus, Dicentra, Gaura, Heuchera, Iris cristata, Lamiastrum 'Herman's Pride', Liriope 'Silvery Sunproof', Ophiopogon 'Nigrescens', sedums, and sedges.
Rec. Size: #1 pot (8/flat)    Space: (10"-16")

## Campanula punctata 'Cherry Bells' (kam-pan-<u>you</u>-la punk-<u>tay</u>-ta)
('Cherry Bells' Spotted Bellflower)......................Zone 4.

1 1/2'-2'; full sun to light shade. Quick spreading, this richly textured, medium green durable ground cover is exceptional for its eye-popping summertime display of sturdy, pendulous, cherry-red, white edged, bell shaped flowers. Excellent for cutting, and for growing in containers, 'Cherry Bells' is good on a moderate to large scale and nice with ornamental grasses.
Rec. Size: #1 pot (8/flat)    Space: (10"-14")

## Campanula 'Samantha' (kam-pan-<u>you</u>-la)
('Samantha' Bellflower)......................Zone 3.

6"-8", full sun to light shade. With a slow expanding habit like 'Blue Clips', this is a very low maintenance ground cover. 'Samantha' is also very attractive with vibrant green foliage and amazing reblooming, iridescent blue violet, pale blue centered, prolifically borne, fragrant, long blooming flowers. This all points to 'Samantha' being one of those extraordinary introductions which will become a staple for decades to come. It is clean, non seeding, durable, and is an easy companion to countless other ground covers.
Rec. Size: #1 pot (8/flat)    Space: (12"-16")

**Campanula 'Sarastro', 'Sarastro' Bellflower,** is one of the most amazing ground covers when it comes to flower appeal.

*GROUND COVERS*

**GROUND COVERS**

## Campanula 'Sarastro' (kam-pan-<u>you</u>-la)
('Sarastro' Bellflower).....................................................Zone 5

**Blooming Time**
J F M A M J J A S O N D
Winter | Spring | Summer | Fall

14"-20"; full sun to light shade. With glossy, deep violet-blue, 2 1/2 to 3 inch long summerborne bells, this compact slow spreading ground cover densely blankets the soil with rich green foliage. 'Sarastro', from the Austrian nursery by the same name, is the compact version of the popular cultivar 'Kent Belle'. The compactness is a welcome feature in a ground cover which is destined to become immensely popular. Grow 'Sarastro' enmasse and in combination with such grasses as variegated Miscanthus and Calamagrostis 'Overdam'. And, pair it with Amsonia, Eupatorium, Crocosmia, or Echinacea. Either way, you will be rewarded with great variety of color and texture.
Rec. Size: #1 pot (8/flat)    Space: (14"-18")

## Caryopteris x clandonenis 'Blue Mist' (kar-i-<u>op</u>-ter-is klan-de-<u>nen</u>-sis)
('Blue Mist' Bluebeard)...............................................Zone 4

**Blooming Time**
J F M A M J J A S O N D
Winter | Spring | Summer | Fall

3'-3 1/2'; full sun to light shade. Displaying large quantities of powder blue flowers above silvery green foliage (during late summer), 'Blue Mist' bluebeard makes a lovely companion to the variegated selections of Miscanthus (maiden grass) as well as a host of late blooming perennials such as 'Brilliant' and 'Neon' sedum, black eyed Susan, and purple coneflower. Easy to care for and attractive to hummingbirds and butterflies, this wonderful selection deserves a home in every landscape.
Rec. Size: 2 gal.    Space: (3'-3 1/2')

## Caryopteris x clandonensis 'First Choice' (kar-i-<u>op</u>-ter-is klan-de-<u>nen</u>-sis)
('First Choice' Bluebeard).............................................Zone 5

**Blooming Time**
J F M A M J J A S O N D
Winter | Spring | Summer | Fall

2'-2 1/2'; full sun to light shade. With super compact habit, 'First Choice' is tidy and easy to care for. It is also unique for its intensely deep green super shiny foliage. Staying lustrous well into fall, the foliage contrasts beautifully with the deep lilac blue late summer and fallborne flowers. 'First Choice'

is drought tolerant, performs well in any well drained soil, and is a comfortable companion with such popular and florific ground covers as coreopsis, Rudbeckia, daylily, hardy ageratum, Russian sage, sedum cultivars, and countless ornamental grasses.
Rec. Size: 2 gal.    Space: (2 1/2'-3')

## Ceratostigma plumbaginoides (sir-at-oh-<u>stig</u>-ma plum-baj-i-<u>noy</u>-deez)
(Dwarf Plumbago)......................................................Zone 5

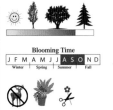

**Blooming Time**
J F M A M J J A S O N D
Winter | Spring | Summer | Fall

6"-10"; full sun to moderate shade. An excellent deciduous or semievergreen ground cover, the metallic glossy-green leaves of plumbago are carried by trailing, wiry, zig zagging stems. Deep blue flowers begin blooming in early August and persist until the first frost. Plumbago is a bit slow to leaf out in spring and therefore is the perfect companion to spring blooming bulbs which come up, flower, and just as they fade away are covered up by the new foliage of the plumbago.
Rec. Size: 3 1/4" (18/flat)    Space: (6"-10")

## Chamaemelum nobile 'Treneague' (kam-e-<u>mel</u>-um noe-bi-lee)
('Treneague' Roman Chamomile) .......................................Zone 5

**Blooming Time**
J F M A M J J A S O N D
Winter | Spring | Summer | Fall

2"-3"; full sun to light shade. This low, horizontal spreading, dense-growing, herbaceous ground cover may be used on a small or large scale as a substitute for turf or filler for between stepping stones. Colored bright green, evergreen, and finely divided, its fernlike foliage is strongly apple scented, and exudes its fine fragrance when walked upon. 'Treneague' seldom flowers and when it does, it throws up a few yellow centered white petaled daisies. Growing best in sandy or gravelly well-drained acidic to slightly alkaline soils, it is deep rooted and tolerates a fair amount of drought. If you choose to mow your chamomile, set your mower on the highest setting.
Rec. Size: 3 1/4" (18/flat)    Space: (10"-14")

## Chelone lyonii 'Hot Lips' (kee-<u>low</u>-nee li-<u>on</u>-ee-ee)
('Hot Lips' Turtle-head) NATIVE CULTIVAR.....................Zone 3

**2'-3'; full sun to light shade.** Bearing rose-pink, turtle-head-shaped, 1-inch-long midsummer to fallborne flowers, this very hardy native (of Virginia to North Carolina westward to Tennessee and Georgia) is also lovely for its rich glossy green, 3 to 7 inch long, sharply pointed foliage. An excellent perennial for massing as a ground cover or for accent in a perennial border, 'Hot Lips' is a superb selection that tolerates moist soils and can be counted upon for years of reliable service.
Rec. Size: 3 1/4" (18/flat)   Space: (1 1/2'-2 1/2')

## Chelone obliqua 'Rosea' (kee-<u>low</u>-nee o-<u>blee</u>-kwa)
(Pink Flowered Turtle-head) NATIVE CULTIVAR....................Zone 5

2'; full sun to light shade. Pink flowered turtle-head blooms late summer and fall with exceptional, two-tone cream and pink, turtle-head shaped flowers. These are borne in such quantity and substance that they stand out from quite a distance. Even so, when viewed up close, as when plants are sited along walkways and near home or building entrances, one can most fully appreciate this unique plant. Slow spreading to form a broad clump, pink flowered turtle-head is a great companion to 'Hot Lips' turtle-head, being a bit more compact and with the same fantastic deep green glossy foliage. Like 'Hot Lips', pink flowered turtle-head is durable, care-free, and comfortably combines with sedums, daylilies, Eupatorium, Solidago, coreopsis, and ornamental grasses.
Rec. Size: 3 1/4" (18/flat)   Space: (1 1/2'-2')

## Conoclinium coelestinum 'Wayside' (kon-oh-<u>klin</u>-ee-um koy-les-<u>teen</u>-um)
('Wayside' Hardy Ageratum) NATIVE CULTIVAR.....................Zone 5

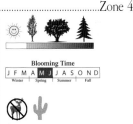

15"; full sun to light shade. With handsome, deep green, triangular deciduous foliage this rhizomatous spreader makes a nice leafy ground cover. Even so, it is also a superb flowering plant. Beginning to bloom late summer and fall, the foliage disappears under masses of flat topped panicles of azure blue flowers. 'Wayside' is superb in combination with sedums such as 'Autumn Joy', Brilliant', 'Meteor', and 'Pink Chablis' and is a welcome addition to the late season landscape.
Rec. Size: #1 pot (8/flat)   Space: (10"-14")

## Convallaria majalis (con-va-<u>lay</u>-ree-a ma-<u>jay</u>-lis)
(Lily Of The Valley)....................Zone 4

6"-8"; light to dense shade. A classic rhizomatous species that spreads at a moderate pace, lily of the valley displays attractive dark green deciduous foliage and nodding, waxy white, 1/4 inch wide, pleasantly fragrant mid- to late springborne flowers. Followed by orange-red, 1/4 inch wide berries, the fruit, however, is nonedible and thus lily of the valley should be sited in areas unlikely to be used by small children.
Rec. Size: 3 1/4" (18/flat)   Space: (8"-12")

**Convallaria majalis, Lily of the Valley,** is an heirloom plant steeped in nostalgia and folk tradition. The sweet fragrance of its flowers is unparalled.

*GROUND COVERS*

## Coreopsis 'Limerock Ruby' (koe-ree-op-sis)

('Limerock Ruby' Coreopsis). TENDER—USE FOR ANNUAL COLOR

12"-18"; full sun to light shade. 'Limerock Ruby' represents a breakthrough in coreopsis—flowers hot ruby red with yellow centers (heretofore, pastel pinks and yellows have prevailed). Because of this, and its summer through early-fall bloom period, 'Limerock Ruby' can be used to brighten the landscape as an annual, as it typically dies out during winter. 'Limerock Ruby' makes an exciting companion to other plants with white, purple, yellow and blue flowers.

Rec. Size: #1 pot (8/flat)    Space: (14"-18")

## Coreopsis rosea 'American Dream' (koe-ree-op-sis  roe-zee-a)

('American Dream' Pink Flowered Coreopsis) NATIVE CULTIVAR.Zone 4

8"-10"; full sun to light shade. Although not as drought tolerant as the cultivars of C. verticillata listed below, this colorful species will do just fine in ordinary garden settings, provided the soil is kept moist during extended periods of hot dry weather. Beginning in July, the 1/2 to 1 inch wide, yellow centered, pink-petaled, daisylike flowers begin a long procession of petite floral splendor which lasts into the first weeks of September. Plant of the Year in the Neatherlands 1993

Rec. Size: #1 pot (8/flat)    Space: (12"-18")

## Coreopsis rosea 'Sweet Dreams' (koe-ree-op-sis  roe-zee-a)
## Patent Applied For

('Sweet Dreams' Pink Flowered Coreopsis) NATIVE CULTIVARZone 4

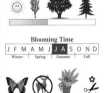

12"-16"; full sun to light shade. From Blooms of Bressingham, this is a ground breaking selection with big 1 1/2 inch wide, bicolor, summerborne flowers of white tipped, raspberry based petals surrounding golden yellow centers. A vigorous grower with attractive mounding habit, 'Sweet Dreams' is one of the most exciting introductions of the 21st century.

Rec. Size: #1 pot (8/flat)    Space: (12"-18")

## Coreopsis verticillata 'Golden Showers' (a.k.a. 'Grandiflora')
## (koe-ree-op-sis  ver-ti-si-lay-ta)

(Large Flowered Threadleaf Coreopsis) ............................................Zone 3

14"-20"; full sun to light shade. The grandaddy of threadleaf coreopsis, 'Golden Showers' is not only the tallest selection but, among the yellows, the most florific and largest flowering. A clump former, 'Golden Showers' displays durable attractive foliage in a compact upright mounded habit. During summer, it bears a long running succession of bright golden yellow flowers. As would be expected, 'Golden Showers' is excellent for edging and general ground cover use—especially when planted enmasse in broad sweeping drifts. It has several comfortable companions with ornamental grasses, asters, Agastache, Allium, Amsonia, Echinacea, Eupatorium, Leucanthemum, and Liatris all being excellent.

Rec. Size: #1 pot (8/flat)    Space: (1 1/2'-2')

## Coreopsis 'Moonbeam' being used effectively in the Tornonto Music Garden.

## Coreopsis verticillata 'Moonbeam' (koe-ree-op-sis ver-ti-si-lay-ta)
('Moonbeam' Threadleaf Coreopsis) ......................Zone 3

12"-18"; full sun to light shade. The neat-as-a-pin deciduous foliage of this fine selection is medium green, narrow and fernlike. Borne on vertical stems, it serves as a superb backdrop to the multitude of delicate, sulfur yellow, daisylike summerborne flowers. Use single plants or clumps as specimens or accent plants in the perennial border, or for a really bold statement, plant masses in beds of over 300 square feet. Perennial Plant of the Year 1992
Rec. Size: #1 pot (8/flat)   Space: (12"-18")

## Coreopsis verticillata 'Zagreb' (koe-ree-op-sis ver-ti-si-lay-ta)
('Zagreb' Threadleaf Coreopsis) ......................Zone 3

12"-18"; full sun to light shade. Very much like the cultivar 'Moonbeam' which was described above, 'Zagreb' is another "classic" but this time with dense habit and vibrant golden yellow summerborne flowers. This hue of yellow is a bit hotter which creates a sharper, more contrasting effect when planted against shades of green, burgundy, and red.
Rec. Size: #1 pot (8/flat)   Space: (12"-18")

## Cornus canadensis (kore-nus kan-a-den-sis)
(Bunchberry) NATIVE SPECIES......................Zone 2

4"-6" tall, spreading slowly; light to moderate shade. Bunchberry is fussy and must have its roots in a cool, organically rich, moisture retentive soil of acidic pH. Its deciduous, prominently veined foliage is first lime green before changing to dark glossy green. By midspring the foliage is topped by tiny yellow flowers made showy by their large white bracts. Later, toward the end of summer, clusters of prominent bright red fruit mature, and finally, during fall, the foliage turns deep reddish purple before it goes to sleep for the winter.
Rec. Size: 3 1/4" (18/flat)   Space: (6"-10")

## Coronilla varia (kore-oh-nil-a vare-ee-a)
(Crownvetch) ......................Zone 4

2'; full sun to light shade. Crownvetch is an excellent ground cover for erosion control on steep banks or any large areas where rapid cover is desired. Pink and white flowers appear in June and continue until frost. Good companions include tall forms of Japanese silver grass, switch grasses, and species of beach grass.
Rec. Size: 3 1/4" (18/flat)   Space: (10"-12")

## Corydalis lutea (ko-rid-a-lis lew-tee-a)
(Yellow Corydalis)......................Zone 5

9"-15"; light to dense shade. With soft, lacy, fern-textured, blue green, semi-succulent foliage, this colonizing/self sowing ground cover is a welcome addition to the shade garden. Here it fits nicely with native wildflowers, bulbs, ferns, and shade loving perennials—always complimentary and never overpowering. And corydalis is good for more than just foliage. Flowering nonstop all summer with a succession of soft sulfur yellow, dainty, spurred flowers (much like fringed bleeding heart, Dicentra eximia), corydalis is a bloomer extraordinare.
Rec. Size: #1 pot (8/flat)   Space: (12"-16")

## Crocosmia x 'Lucifer' (krow-koz-mee-a)
('Lucifer' Hybrid African Lily)......................Zone 5

3'-3 1/2'; full sun to light shade. 'Lucifer' is easy to grow and thrives in organically rich, slightly moist soils. Slowly increasing by bulbous offsets, 'Lucifer' will not get out of bounds. It will, however, amaze you with its lovely light-to-medium-green, vertically oriented, irislike foliage and horizontal chains of rich scarlet-red, hummingbird attracting, nodding, gladiolus-like midsummerborne blossoms.
Rec. Size: #1 pot (8/flat)   Space: (12"-18")

GROUND COVERS

## Cymbalaria aequitriloba (cym-ba-<u>lay</u>-ree-a   ee-kwee-try-<u>lo</u>-ba)
(Toadflax Ivy).............................................................Zone 4

1/2"-1"; light to moderate shade. A whole lot more hardy than originally published (many books list it at Zone 7 or 8), this charming Foot Friendly creeper has withstood several winters in Michigan in Zone 5 and 6. The key is to have a soil that is well drained. Great along pathways in courtyards and around and between stepping stones, toadflax ivy has charming light lime green foliage and during summer a continuous bloom of tiny snapdragonlike purple flowers. Interesting companions include crested iris, black mondo grass, colorful sedges, and various wildflowers.
Rec. Size: 3 1/4" (18/flat)    Space: (8"-12")

## Delosperma 'John Proffitt' (del-<u>oh</u>-sper-ma)
('John Profitt' Iceplant)...............................................Zone 5

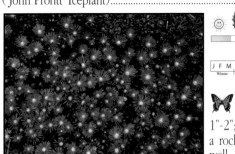

1"-2"; full sun. Excelling as a rock garden specimen as well as general cover and container plant, 'John Proffitt' is a remarkable selection of hardy ice plant. Not only is 'John Proffitt' clothed in semievergreen, rich green, succulent foliage (often tinged purple in fall and winter), it is an exceptional bloomer. Budding during May and blooming June and much of July, its hundreds of shiny 1 1/2" wide, fuchsia, daisylike flowers all but smother its foliage. 'John Proffitt' is a good companion to boulders and large stones, as well as other plants such as daylilies, dwarf clump forming ornamental grasses, and tall sedums like Sedum 'Brilliant', and 'Neon'. Best performance is in well drained soils.
Rec. Size: 3 1/4" (18/flat)    Space: (8"-12")

## Delosperma nubigena (del-<u>oh</u>-sper-ma   new-bi-<u>geen</u>-a)
(Hardy Ice Plant).......................................................Zone 5

1"-2"; full sun. A low growing creeper, this import from South Africa is exceptional among the "ice plants" as, with heavy snow cover and good drainage, it has been found to tolerate temperatures to -25°F. Its foliage is triangular in cross section, succulent, and brilliant shiny-lime green. Useful as a general cover and facer to shrubs, it is well adapted to withstand drought and infertility. Blooming mid-spring with daisylike, yellow flowers.
Rec. Size: 3 1/4" (18/flat)    Space: (12"-16")

## Deutzia gracilis 'Nikko' (dewt-see-a   gras-i-lis   nee-koe)
(Dwarf Slender Deutzia)...............................................Zone 5

1 1/2'-2' tall by 3'-5' across; full sun to moderate shade. Dwarf slender deutzia is an exceptionally compact shrublet that functions beautifully as a moderate to large scale general cover or accent plant. Its narrow, tooth-edged deciduous leaves are colored a splendid rich green and for a while, during mid to late spring, they almost disappear behind masses of nearly pure white, 1/2 inch wide fragrant flowers. Then, signaling the end of the season, during mid September the foliage transitions to deep burgundy.
Rec. Size: 2 gal.  Space: (3'-3 1/2')

## Dianthus x allwoodii 'Little Bobby' (di-<u>an</u>-thus   al-wood-ee-eye)
('Little Bobby' Carnation)..............................................Zone 4

6"-8" tall by 1-1/2' wide; full sun. Not only is 'Little Bobby' compact with clean blue-gray foliage, but it resists crown rot — unlike many cultivars of dianthus. The flowers are equally if not more impressive. Beginning during mid to late spring they burst forth in such quantity as to nearly obscure the leaves. Colored brilliant raspberry-pink with dark maroon centers and frilled edges, they are a true spectacle. Even so, it is no exaggeration to say that their fragrance is every bit as superb.
Rec. Size: #1 pot (8/flat)    Space: (10"-14")

## Dianthus 'Candy Dish' (di-<u>an</u>-thus)
('Candy Dish' Carnation)..............................................Zone 5

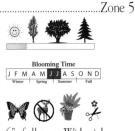

6"; full sun. With rich powdery blue, semievergreen foliage, 'Candy Dish' makes a pleasing carpet during late winter and spring. But, it is during June and early July that this plant really sets itself apart. This is when its multitude of fully double, watermelon pink, one-inch-wide flowers are borne. Standing a full 6 inches above the foliage, the flowers are the same shape as florists carnations, and naturally are excellent for cutting.
Rec. Size: #1 pot (8/flat)    Space: (10"-14")

GROUND COVERS

## Dianthus 'Firewitch' (die-an-thus)
('Firewitch' Carnation)........................................................Zone 4

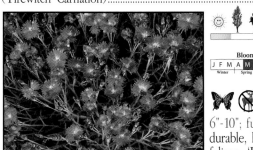

6"-10"; full sun. Clothed in durable, healthy, deep blue foliage, 'Firewitch' makes a nice blue pincushionlike mat when not in flower. But in bloom, which lasts for several weeks during mid spring and early summer, the foliage all but disappears under masses of bright raspberry magenta flowers. Eye-catching and trouble free, 'Firewitch' is a nice colorful addition to the rock garden, perennial garden, or any sunny landscape when mass-planted as an edging or general ground cover.
Rec. Size: #1 pot (8/flat)    Space: (10"-14")

## Dianthus gratianopolitanus 'Tiny Rubies' (di-an-thus gra-tee-aye-no-poe-li-tay-nus)
('Tiny Rubies' Carnation)........................................................Zone 5

1"; full sun. Attractive in every respect, 'Tiny Rubies' reaches 1 inch tall and resembles blue-green velvet. And, from spring well into summer, is topped with numerous petite, soft pink, fragrant, 3/4 inch wide flowers. Noteworthy for its resistance to opening up in the center, 'Tiny Rubies' is very popular and requires little maintenance.
Rec. Size: #1 pot (8/flat)    Space: (10"-14")

## Dicentra 'King of Hearts' (die-sen-tra)
('King of Hearts' Bleeding Heart)........................................................Zone 5

12"-15"; light to dense shade. This superb hybrid displays strong hybrid vigor and many admirable traits. It is clothed in finely divided soft grayish green foliage that holds up nicely throughout the growing season (as opposed to many ephemeral species that fade in the heat of summer). And it is a big bloomer, actually an incredibly big bloomer. Flowering nonstop through summer, 'King of Hearts', goes and goes with loads of soft rosy pink, heart-shaped blooms carried attractively above the foliar mass.
Rec. Size: #1 pot (8/flat)    Space: (12"-16")

## Dicentra spectabilis (die-sen-tra spek-tab-i-lis)
(Bleeding Heart)........................................................Zone 2

1 1/2'-2'; light to dense shade. The classic bleeding heart, this fabulous spring bloomer bears numerous large, pendant, heart shaped flowers. Dangling in a single row under the lovely green foliage, each flower is composed of rosy outer petals with a cap of white inner petals. Bleeding heart is a superb companion to ferns, gingers, ajuga, plumbago, bunchberry, corydalis, variegated fairy bells, variegated Solomon's seal, epimediums, geraniums, and other shade lovers. Bleeding heart grows well in a range of sandy to heavy soils provided drainage is good.
Rec. Size: #1 pot (8/flat)    Space: (12"-16")

## Dicentra spectabilis 'Gold Heart' (die-sen-tra spek-tab-i-lis)
('Gold Heart' Bleeding Heart)........................................................Zone 4

1 1/2'-2' tall by 3' across; light to moderate shade. Like a bright beacon in the springtime shade garden, the electric golden yellow foliage of 'Gold Heart' bleeding heart is attractively carried upon soft peach colored, succulent stems. For foliage alone 'Gold Heart' is a worthy small scale ground cover or accent plant, but its merits don't stop with foliage. During spring it bears exquisitely rich rose-pink, pendant, heart shaped flowers, which contrast with the foliage in absolutely perfect fashion.
Rec. Size: #1 pot (8/flat)    Space: (1 1/2'-2 1/2')

## Disporum sessile 'Variegatum' (die-spore-um ses-i-lee)
(Variegated Fairy Bells)........................................................Zone 5

14"-18"; light to dense shade. Japanese fairy bells displays a graceful arching habit of sturdy green stems. These carry artistically painted, deep green and creamy white-striped, narrowly oval, 3 inch long deciduous leaves. During spring, bell-shaped, six-parted, creamy white flowers hang from the nodes of the leaves. Followed by round green berries, the flowers are exquisite. Variegated fairy bells is a slow rhizomatous spreader and makes a nice small to moderate scale ground cover.
Rec. Size: #1 pot (8/flat)    Space: (12"-16")

GROUND COVERS

## Echinacea purpurea 'Double Decker' (ek-i-nay-see-a per-per-ree-a)

('Double Decker' Purple Coneflower) NATIVE CULTIVAR ........Zone 3

2 1/2'; full sun to light shade. 'Double Decker' is a spectacular coneflower with a second set of pinkish purple petals (like a flowery bonnet) carried atop each vivid orange central cone. It is one of those "must have" oddball plants that every enthusiast must include (in a highly visible place) in his/her garden. Companions are countless and include various low growing sedums, dwarf ornamental grasses and Coreopsis 'Moonbeam.'
Rec. Size: # 1 pot (8/flat) Space: (12"-16")

## Echinacea purpurea 'Kim's Knee High' (ek-i-nay-see-a per-per-ree-a)

('Kim's Knee High' Purple Coneflower)...............................Zone 3

1 1/2'-2'; full sun to light shade. Selected by Kim Hawks, this fabulous dwarf coneflower is smothered in clear pink, droopy petals during mid to late summer. Excellent for mass planting in small to large areas, 'Kim's Knee High' is as tough as it is attractive. Naturally, it combines well with Allium, Amsonia, Calamintha, Campanula, coreopsis, other Echinaceas, Eupatorium, Heuchera, daylilies, lavender, Liatris, and sedums.
Rec. Size: #1 pot (8/flat) Space: (12"-16")

## Echinacea purpurea 'Kim's Mop Head' (ek-i-nay-see-a per-per-ree-a) NATIVE CULTIVAR

('Kim's Mop Head' White Flowered Coneflower) ..........................Zone 3

12"-15'; full sun to light shade. A true dwarf, this white petaled sport of 'Kim's Knee High' was discovered by Pierre Bennerup and named for Kim Hawkes. Like its predecessor it is compact and florific. Blooming midsummer with massive golden cones surrounded by creamy white petals, 'Kim's Mop Head' is a great companion to other coneflowers, coreopsis, daylilies, and Liatris. It is fantastic mass planted as a moderate scale ground cover, and is excellent as an edging. It is also wonderful for cuttings, and a magnet for butterflies.
Rec. Size: # 1 pot (8/flat) Space: (12"-16")

## Echinacea purpurea 'Magnus' (ek-i-nay-see-a per-per-ree-a)

('Magnus' Purple Coneflower) NATIVE CULTIVAR
PERENNIAL PLANT OF THE YEAR 1998...............................Zone 3

2 1/2'-3'; full sun to light shade. Among the most popular perennials, 'Magnus' is sturdy, drought tolerant, and florific. It combines marvelously with ornamental grasses such as Calamagrostis, Miscanthus, and Pennisetum. Or, it can be massed as a ground cover for dramatic effect. During spring, 'Magnus' coneflower sports dark green, coarse textured leaves and by mid summer is decorated with masses of large purple orange brown centered cones.
Rec. Size: #1 pot (8/flat) Space: (12"-16")

## Echinacea purpurea 'Rubinstern' (a.k.a. 'Ruby Star') (ek-i-nay-see-a per-per-ree-a)

(Ruby Star Purple Coneflower) NATIVE CULTIVAR.....................Zone 3

2 1/2'-3'; full sun to light shade. Similar to 'Magnus' (see above) in habit, size, and growth characteristics, 'Rubinstern' (ruby star in English) blooms during summer with intensely carmine-red horizontally held petals surrounding a magenta hazed golden yellow cone.
Rec. Size: #1 pot (8/flat) Space: (12"-16")

## Echinacea purpurea 'White Swan' (ek-i-nay-see-a per-per-ree-a)

(White Flowered Coneflower) NATIVE CULTIVAR.....................Zone 3

2 1/2'-3'; full sun to light shade. Flowering mid to late summer and beautifully named, 'White Swan' is the superb white-flowered counterpart to 'Magnus', mentioned above. The two make lovely companions and 'White Swan', in addition to combining nicely with grasses, makes a wonderful companion to tall sedums such as 'Autumn Joy', 'Brilliant', and 'Meteor', and such outstanding ground covers as the hardy geraniums, Dianthus selections, and dwarf spireas.
Rec. Size: #1 pot (8/flat) Space: (12"-16")

GROUND COVERS

# EPIMEDIUMS

*Among the finest ground covers for shade, epimediums are plants that densely cover the ground, fill in at a steady pace, and yet never become weedy. Decorated with neatly arranged deciduous or semievergreen leaves, epimediums rival pachysandra for the pleasantness of their foliage. But they are also plants of remarkable floral appeal. Ranging from white to yellow, pink, purple, and red, during early spring they bear a multitude of 4-pointed starlike florets.*

*Consider using epimediums for edging walkways and garden paths, alongside steps, and around the periphery of perennial borders. Single clumps or small groupings make excellent accent plants along shady borders, and mass plantings are superb for reducing maintenance when used as a living mulch around trees, foundations, shrubs, garden ornaments, and statuary. Epimediums, the ultimate companion plants, are complimentary to ferns, astilbes, hostas, spring blooming bulbs, and wildflowers.*

## Epimedium grandiflorum 'Lilafee' (ep-i-<u>mee</u>-dee-um gran-di-<u>floe</u>-rum)
(Lilac Fairy Epimedium)........................................................Zone 5

**Blooming Time**
J F M **A M** J J A S O N D
Winter  Spring  Summer  Fall

10"; light to dense shade. Selected by Ernst Pagel, this fabulous deciduous-leaved, fast maturing selection sports compact habit and bright green foliage. Flowering profusely, during early spring it bears a multitude of large violet-purple flowers (with lighter spurs) held slightly above the new foliage—which at this time of year is glossy green.
Rec. Size: #1 pot (8/flat)   Space: (10"-14")

## Epimedium x 'Rubrum' (ep-i-<u>mee</u>-dee-um <u>rew</u>-brum)
(Red Flowered Epimedium).....................................................Zone 5

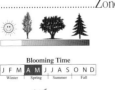

**Blooming Time**
J F M **A M** J J A S O N D
Winter  Spring  Summer  Fall

8"-14"; light to dense shade. A must for the shade garden, 'Rubrum' is simply superb—easy to care for, long lived, and attractive in leaf and bloom. A deciduous plant in the Midwest, its lovely heart shaped leaves emerge coppery green with hints of burgundy during spring, mature to deep green, then become bronzy in fall. Carried atop thin wiry stems, the foliage alone is sufficient to merit the use of this plant. Even so, 'Rubrum' also bears a multitude of bright pinkish crimson sepaled, creamy white petaled, 1/2 inch wide, springtime flowers.
Rec. Size: #1 pot (8/flat)   Space: (10"-14")

## Epimedium x versicolor 'Sulphureum' (ep-i-<u>mee</u>-dee-um <u>ver</u>-si-cul-er)
(Yellow Flowered Epimedium)................................................Zone 5

**Blooming Time**
J F M **A M** J J A S O N D
Winter  Spring  Summer  Fall

12"-15"; light to dense shade. Originating from the cross of E. pinnatum and E. grandiflorum, this medium green selection is attractive spring through fall. And, its lovely pale sulfur yellow flowers, arriving during mid spring, are borne in good numbers and make for a very pleasing display. Rugged and drought tolerant, yellow flowered epimedium is a plant you can depend upon for long life with little or no maintenance.
Rec. Size: #1 pot (8/flat)   Space: (10"-14")

*GROUND COVERS* (vertical, right margin)

**GROUND COVERS**

**Epimedium x youngianum 'Niveum' (ep-i-<u>mee</u>-dee-um yung-ee-<u>aye</u>-num)**
(White Flowered Epimedium)...........................................Zone 5

8"-10"; light to dense shade. Compact in habit with dainty light to medium green leaves, this refined selection is adorned with masses of pure white, star-shaped springborne flowers. Its foliage, borne upon wiry red stems and grouped in threes, is small (1 1/2" to 2 1/2" long by 1" wide) compared to other epimediums, colored an attractive medium green, and makes a clean attractive foil throughout the growing season.
Rec. Size: #1 pot (8/flat)   Space: (8"-12")

**Epimedium x youngianum 'Roseum' (ep-i-<u>mee</u>-dee-um yung-ee-<u>aye</u>-num)**
(Pink Flowered Epimedium)...........................................Zone 5

8"-10"; light to moderate shade. Pink flowered epimedium is an excellent, popular, very beautiful selection with vibrant green (red-streaked in spring, burgundy-red in fall) variable leaves of 2-, 6-, or 7-segments. Like the cultivar 'Niveum', it is compact in habit but during spring bears rose to lilac colored, 3/4 inch wide pendulous flowers – carried 4 to 12 together in loose inflorescences.
Rec. Size: #1 pot (8/flat)   Space: (10"-14")

**Erica carnea 'Springwood Pink' (<u>air</u>-i-ka   <u>kar</u>-nee-a)**
('Springwood Pink' Spring Heath)...........................................Zone 5

8" high by 2' wide; full sun to light shade. Spring heaths are charming rhododendron relatives that thrive in well drained acidic soil. What makes them so interesting is their habit of flowering during February, March, and April (and anytime before if there is an unseasonable warm-up). 'Springwood Pink' is known for clear pink urn-shaped flowers and deep green foliage. It may be used in small- to large-scale ground cover plantings, is particularly nice on sloping sandy or gravelly terrain, and makes an exceptional companion to other cultivars of Erica, heathers, bearberry, and dwarf azaleas and rhododendrons. Such combinations can cover large areas and slopes and serve as brilliantly colorful, multitextured ground covers.
Rec. Size: #1 pot (8/flat)   Space: (14"-20")

**Erica carnea 'Springwood White' (<u>air</u>-i-ka   <u>kar</u>-nee-a)**
('Springwood White' Spring Heath)...........................................Zone 5

8 inches by 2 feet wide; full sun to light shade. 'Springwood White' is the snow white flowered equivalent of 'Springwood Pink'. Predictably, it too is a highly popular "classic" selection which requires well drained, gravelly, acidic soil. Use 'Springwood White' alone, in small groups, or most impressively in drifts, by itself or with other varieties of spring heath. It looks particularly impressive when planted atop or in the cracks of retaining walls or planters and allowed to cascade over.
Rec. Size: #1 pot (8/flat)   Space: (14"-20")

**Erica carnea 'Winter Beauty' (<u>air</u>-i-ka   <u>kar</u>-nee-a)**
('Winter Beauty' Spring Heath)...........................................Zone 5

8 inches by 2 feet wide; full sun to light shade. 'Winter Beauty' is one of the most impressive spring heath selections in existence. Clothed in deep green foliage, it sets a perfect backdrop to the multitude of deep bright rose, densely set sprays of urn shaped florets. Borne late winter through mid-spring, it flowers often begin before the snow mlets, contrast beautifully with the snow, and bring hope that warmer weather is at hand. Good uses include trailing over walls and planters, and as a specimen, companion, or accent in rock gardens.
Rec. Size: #1 pot (8/flat)   Space: (14"-20")

**Euonymus fortunei 'Coloratus' (you-<u>on</u>-i-mus   fore-<u>too</u>-nee-eye)**
(Purple Leaf Wintercreeper) ...........................................Zone 4

12"-15"; full sun to dense shade. A popular evergreen vine, 'Coloratus' is an excellent drought tolerant moderate to large scale ground cover. Dark green, its leathery evergreen leaves turn reddish-purple in autumn. 'Coloratus' is nonblooming in its juvenile state (as a ground cover) and is outstanding for erosion control.
Rec. Size: 50 cell flat   Space: (8"-12")
Rec. Size: 38 cell flat   Space: (10"-14")
Rec. Size: 1 gal.   Space: (1 1/2'-2')
Generally nonbloombing

*G R O U N D   C O V E R S*

## Euonymus fortunei 'Kewensis' (you-<u>on</u>-i-mus   fore-<u>tew</u>-nee-eye)
('Kewensis' Wintercreeper) ..........................................Zone 4

1"-2"; full sun to dense shade. The absolute most miniature of the winter-creepers, this tiny teardrop leaved selection is ideal for use around stepping stones, along pathways, and trailing over rocks and retaining walls especially in areas next to stairs so that its uniqueness may best be appreciated. 'Kewensis' may be tiny, but it is very tough and has pretty good vigor. It may be combined with such clump formers as hostas, Helleborus, Tricyrtis, and 'Silvery Sunproof' lily-turf to add vertical dimension and color contrast.
Rec. Size 6-pack (18/flat)    Space: (10"-14")

## Eupatorium cannabinum 'Plenum' (you-pa-<u>tore</u>-ee-um can-a-<u>bie</u>-num)
(Double Flowered Agrimony) ..........................................Zone 5

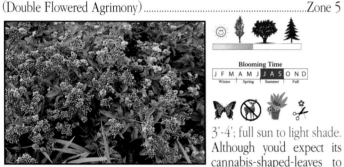

3'-4'; full sun to light shade. Although you'd expect its cannabis-shaped-leaves to attract attention, the foliage of double flowered agrimony hardly gets noticed—at least when the plant is in flower, which turns out to be most of the time. Beginning during mid summer, double flowered agrimony bears a never pausing succession of pleasing mauve flowers (carried on purple stems)—until the first hard frost in the fall. This is a bloomer extraordinaire, and a tough, durable, trouble free plant to boot. Adapted to normal garden settings, 'Plenum' also does nicely at pond- and streambank and in ditches where it tolerates a good deal of moisture.
Rec. Size: #1 pot (8/flat)    Space: (2'-2 1/2')

## Eupatorium dubium 'Little Joe' (you-pa-<u>tore</u>-ee-um <u>dew</u>-bee-um)
('Little Joe' Joe-Pye) NATIVE CULTIVAR..........................Zone 4

4'; full sun to light shade. Selected for its compact 4 foot height, this tidy cultivar is everything that the taller super popular selection 'Gateway' is, just in compact form. Its sturdy habit is upright, its flowers rugged rich green, and during July and August the entire plant is crowned in big rich mauve colored flower heads. These dry nicely and are carried well through the winter months.
Rec. Size:  2 gal.    Space: (2 1/2'-3 1/2')

## Eupatorium fistulosum 'Gateway' (you-pa-<u>tore</u>-ee-um   fist-you-low-sum)
('Gateway' Joe-Pye) NATIVE CULTIVAR..........................Zone 3

**Blooming Time**
| J | F | M | A | M | J | J | A | S | O | N | D |
| Winter | | Spring | | Summer | | | | Fall | | | |

5'-7'; full sun to moderate shade. Derived from our native Joe-Pye, this compact, florific, easy to maintain selection is exceptional for its massive, dusky rose, summer to fall-borne flower heads carried atop rich purple, stout, upright stems. Attractive to butterflies and swallowtails, its flowers are superb and once finished blooming dry to rich brown for late season interest. The colorful stems, clothed in deep green elliptical leaves, contribute to making this a superior companion to porcupine grass, selections of sunflower, Liatris, 'Chocolate' Joe-pye, and goldenrod.
Rec. Size: 2 gal.    Space: (2'-2 1/2')

## Eupatorium rugosum 'Chocolate' (you-pa-<u>tore</u>-ee-um rew-go-sum)
('Chocolate' Joe-Pye) NATIVE CULTIVAR..........................Zone 4

**Blooming Time**
| J | F | M | A | M | J | J | A | S | O | N | D |
| Winter | | Spring | | Summer | | | | Fall | | | |

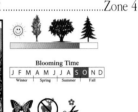

2 1/2'-3'; full sun to moderate shade. A lovely selection of our native Joe-Pye, 'Chocolate', as you might expect, displays pleasingly chocolate colored foliage carried upon shiny purple stems. It is a slow colonizing ground cover valued for contrast, yet stands well on its own with additional color provided by masses of bright white late summer- and fall-borne flowers. 'Chocolate' is a plant that needs a fair amount of moisture if grown in full sun. It is nice for cut flowers, is an excellent foreground plant to vibrunums, tall grasses, and perennials, and is a great moderate to large scale ground cover.
Rec. Size:  #1 pot (8/flat)    Space: (1 1/2'-2')

## Euphorbia amygdaloides var. robbiae (you-fore-bee-a a-<u>mig</u>-da-loy-deez   <u>rob</u>-ee-aye)
(Wood Spurge)..........................................Zone 5

**Blooming Time**
| J | F | M | A | M | J | J | A | S | O | N | D |
| Winter | | Spring | | Summer | | | | Fall | | | |

10"-16"; full sun to dense shade. A fabulous foliage plant, wood spurge is clothed in shiny deep dark green evergreen leaves and looks a bit tropical. And, during early spring, it bears numerous yellow bracted flowers held well above the foliage upon thin wiry stems. Very versatile, wood spurge is tolerant of both drought and moisture, sun and shade. It works nicely as a pathway edging and general cover, and combines with such popular plants as sedges, ferns, hostas, Heucheras, and variegated cultivars of lily-turf.
Rec. Size: #1 pot (8/flat)    Space: (12"-16")

**Blooming Time**
| J | F | M | A | M | J | J | A | S | O | N | D |
| Winter | | Spring | | Summer | | | | Fall | | | |

*G R O U N D   C O V E R S*

**Euphorbia cyparissias 'Fens Ruby' (you-fore-bee-a sy-pa-ris-ee-as)**
('Fens Ruby' Cypress Spurge)......................................................Zone 5

8"-12", full sun to light shade. An absolutely fantastic ground cover for hot or cool and even dry conditions, 'Fens Ruby' is super fine textured with one inch long nearly hair-thin foliage. During spring the leaves are ruby-red then change to blue green and during late spring and summer are topped with chartreuse bracted flowers. Use 'Fens Ruby' enmasse to good effect around rocks and coarse textured garden ornaments and sculpture. Companion plants include cone flowers, Heuchera, hostas, rodgersia, sedges, and tall sedum selections.
#1 pot (8/flat)    Space (12"-16")

**Fallopia japonica 'Compacta' (a.k.a. Polygonum cuspidatum 'Compactum' ) (fa-low-pee-a ja-pon-i-pa)**
(Compact Japanese Fleeceflower).......................................Zone 3

2'-3'; full sun to light shade. When planted around parking areas or sidewalks where reflected light and physical abuse are common, this ground cover has few

equals. It may be used as an edging or general cover and knits the soil together by rhizomes to control erosion. Its foliage emerges burgundy, changes to green, then turns reddish during fall. Floral and fruit display begins in late summer with red buds which open to pink sepals, followed later by pink to reddish winged apparently sterile fruit.
Rec. Size: 3 1/4" (18/flat)    Space: (10"-14")

**Fallopia japonica 'Variegata' (fa-lope-ee-a ja-pon-i-pa)**
(Variegated Japanese Fleeceflower)....................................Zone 3

3'-4'; full sun to moderate shade. This colorful selection is prized for its attractive, white dappled, medium green foliage and tiny white, fallborne, sweet scented florets. Carried in neat parallel rows upon prominently jointed, pink tinged bamboolike stems, variegated fleeceflower is rugged, drought tolerant, and accepting of any well drained soil. It is excellent in perennial borders, as a specimen, in containers, and as a large-scale low maintenance ground cover, and is exceptional for brightening up shady areas..
Rec. Size: #1 pot (8/flat)    Space: (2'-2 1/2')

**Fallopia japonica 'Compacta', Compact Japanese Fleeceflower,**

is tough/drought resistant, and extremely effective for erosion control.

## Fragaria x 'Lipstick' (fra-gay-ree-a)
('Lipstick' Strawberry)..................................................Zone 3

3"-5"; full sun to light shade. What makes 'Lipstick' unique is that it displays numerous rich deep rose-pink flowers for several weeks during spring, then intermittently all summer, and finally numerously again in early fall. To top this off it often produces sweet edible fruit, and its attractive deep shiny green leaves are evergreen. 'Lipstick' forms a thick, weed impenetrable blanket in no time at all. It tolerates sandy soils, and in addition to being a good small to large scale general cover, it grows well in planters and containers.
Rec. Size: 3 1/4' (18/pot)   Space: (10"-14")

## Gaillardia x grandiflora 'Fanfare' (gay-lard-ee-a grand-i-floe-a)
('Fanfare' Blanket Flower)..........................................Zone 5

12"-15"; full sun. Certainly the most exciting blanket flower ever introduced, 'Fanfare' arose as a seedling sport of the popular cultivar 'Goblin'. The differences are stunning and begin with the super compact habit of this plant. It is rich green leaved and stays in a tight globe shape without flopping over or opening up. The flowers, however, are what make 'Fanfare' a standout. Borne from spring until frost in the fall, 'Fanfare' is appropriately named for its multitude of flower heads of brilliant scarlet trumpets that flare out and become bright yellow at their ends. 'Fanfare' is great as a small to moderate scale ground cover, edging, or accent plant, alone or in combination with such fine companions as dwarf selections of fountain grass, Deschampsia, asters, lavender, and many others.
Rec. Size: #1 pot (8/flat)   Space: (12"-16")

## Galium odoratum (gay-lee-um oh-doe-ray-tum)
(Sweet Woodruff)......................................................Zone 4

6"; light to dense shade. A longtime favorite, sweet woodruff thrives in dense shade and can be used for accent under such plants as rhododendron and azalea. Subtly fragrant, its numerous, tiny, four-pointed, white, star-shaped flowers are borne during early spring and persist for many weeks.
Rec. Size: 3 1/4" (18/flat)   Space: (10"-14")

## Gaultheria procumbens (gaul-thee-ree-a pro-kum-benz)
(Wintergreen) NATIVE SPECIES.................................Zone 3

3"-5", spreading indefinitely; full sun to dense shade. Evergreen and preferring moist acidic soils, this is a slow creeper that is tough enough to withstand limited foot traffic. This makes wintergreen a good choice for use along woodland paths and between stepping stones in shady landscapes. In addition to being utilitarian, wintergreen is quite attractive. During spring it blooms with tiny, white, bell shaped flowers which in short order make lovely, edible red fruit. Wintergreen also displays superb leaves which in youth are either red or lime green, mature to dark jade green, and later turn reddish purple in fall and winter.
Rec. Size: 3 1/4" (18/flat)   Space: (8"-10")

## Gaura lindheimeri 'Siskiyou Pink' (gaw-ra lind-hyme-er-eye)
('Siskiyou Pink' Gaura) NATIVE CULTIVAR ...............Zone 5

2'-2 1/2'; full sun. When not in bloom, 'Siskiyou Pink' displays lance shaped medium green leaves upon numerous slender stems. But in bloom, from midsummer to frost, it sprouts a bouquet of wiry stems each holding dozens of butterfly shaped, wind responsive, deep pink veined, pink petaled flowers. 'Siskiyou Pink' is a plant that looks terrific for a long time in the garden center and the landscape. It is easy to grow, tolerates heat and humidity, and is dependable year after year.
Rec. Size: #1 pot (8/flat)   Space: (8"-12")

## Gaura lindheimeri 'Whirling Butterflies' (gaw-ra lind-hyme-er-eye)
('Whirling Butterflies' Gaura) NATIVE CULTIVAR...........Zone 5

2'-2 1/2'; full sun. The white flowered counterpart of 'Siskiyou Pink', this superb selection bears snowy white "butterflies" waving about on the slightest breeze atop wiry stems from midsummer to frost. It combines nicely with tall sedums, coneflowers, goldenrod, and of course, Gaura 'Siskiyou Pink'.
Rec. Size: #1 pot (8/flat)   Space: (8"-12")

G R O U N D   C O V E R S

## Geranium x cantabrigiense 'Biokovo' (je-ray-nee-um kan-ti-brig-ee-en-see)
('Biokovo' Geranium)..................................................Zone 5

10"-12"; full sun to light shade. Originating in the Biokovo Mountains of Yugoslavia as a mutation of G. x cantabrigiense (itself a natural hybrid of G. dalmaticum x G. macrorrhizum), 'Biokovo' is drought tolerant and spreads slowly to form attractive mats of shiny, pleasantly fragrant, nearly evergreen medium green foliage. Its attractive light pink flowers, arising during mid spring to early summer, are borne in profusion.
Rec. Size: #1 pot (8/flat)   Space: (10"-16")

## Geranium x cantabrigiense 'Biokovo Karmina' (je-ray-nee-um kan-ti-brig-ee-en-see)
(Carmine 'Biokovo' Geranium)..................................Zone 5

10"-12"; full sun to light shade. Like 'Biokovo', this wonderful selection is drought tolerant and spreads slowly to form attractive mats of shiny, pleasantly fragrant, nearly evergreen medium green foliage. Its mid spring to early summerborne flowers, however, are colored a lovely carmine purple.
Rec. Size: #1 pot (8/flat)   Space: (10"-16")

## Geranium cinereum 'Ballerina' (je-ray-nee-um sin-air-ee-um)
('Ballerina' Grayleaf Geranium) ................................Zone 5

3"-5", full sun to light shade. Petite, florific, and shy spreading, 'Ballerina' is one of the most desirable of the hardy geraniums. From England — there a recipient of numerous awards, 'Ballerina' is clothed in neat gray-green, pleasantly fragrant leaves which lend subtle contrast to the 2 inch diameter, lilac-pink, dark pink-centered, purple-veined flowers borne throughout the summer months.
Rec. Size: #1 pot (8/flat)   Space: (10"-14")

## Geranium cinereum 'Splendens' (je-ray-nee-um sin-air-eee-um)
('Splendens' Grayleaf Geranium)................................Zone 5

2"-4"; full sun to light shade. With dark blackish-red centered, dark veined, large luminous magenta-pink flowers, this gray green leaved selection is a real eye catcher. Neat and tidy, with clumping habit, 'Splendens' is a good edger, accent, or small scale ground cover. It combines nicely with such plants as 'Lady in Red' lady fern, Bergenia purpurascens, Gaillardia 'Fanfare', Heucheras, sedums, sedges, and dwarf cultivars of fountain grass.
Rec. Size: #1 pot (8/flat)   Space: (10"-14")

## Geranium 'Dily's' (je-ray-nee-um)
('Dily's' Geranium)..................................................Zone 5

10"-12"; full sun to moderate shade. A vigorous carefree incredibly strong and healthy ground cover that flowers all summer, 'Dily's' is one of the very best ground covering geraniums. From a cross involving G. procurrens (a strong growing rambler) and G. sanguineum (a brightly flowered species) 'Dily's' smothers the ground with very clean, attractive, vibrant green foliage topped early summer to fall with a succession of cheerfully bright, perfume scented, rich reddish-magenta 1-inch-wide flowers. Use this plant liberally as a moderate or large scale ground cover, let it drape over sidewalks and terraces, and combine it with such fine grasses as Calamagrostis 'Karl Foerster', Miscanthus selections 'Morning Light', 'Silver Arrow', and 'Silver Feather', and Pennisetum japonicum.
Rec. Size: #1 pot (8/flat)   Space: (16"-20")

## Geranium 'Johnson's Blue' (je-ray-nee-um)
(Johnson's Blue' Geranium) ....................................Zone 4

12"-18"; full sun to light shade. 'Johnson's Blue' displays dense mounds of finely divided medium green leaves, but early summer is when it really takes off. This is when it gets smothered in masses of long lived, clear iridescent blue, 2-inch-wide paper-thin flowers. Carried upon thin stems, they move about gracefully in the slightest breeze. 'Johnson's Blue' is an excellent choice for moderate to large scale commercial and residential use—its floral display significant enough to be seen from a distance.
Rec. Size: #1 pot (8/flat)   Space: (14"-18")

## Geranium macrorrhizum 'Ingwersen's Variety' (je-_ray_-nee-um  mak-roe-_rhiz_-um)
(Ingwersen's Bigroot Geranium)....................................................Zone 3

1'- 1 1/2'; full sun to moderate shade. Like the parent species, Ingwersen's bigroot geranium is drought and shade tolerant and has attractive pleasantly scented foliage. Named after Walter Ingwersen, the popular English horticulturist, this fine selection displays magenta pink summerborne flowers and somewhat glossier leaves.
Rec. Size: #1 pot (8/flat)    Space: (10"-16")

## Geranium x magnificum (je-_ray_-nee-um mag-_nif_-i-kum)
(Showy Geranium)....................................................Zone 4

10"-14"; full sun to light shade. A sterile hybrid (between G. ibericum and G. platypetalum), this loftily named plant is _appropriately_ named—it is magnificent, in bloom and otherwise. Otherwise known as showy geranium, G. x magnificum matures quickly and displays a full robust habit composed of rich silvery- to jade-green leaves. Above these, during early to mid summer, are borne masses of double 1 1/2 inch wide, saucer-shaped deep violet-blue, dark blue veined long-lived flowers. Finally, during autumn, the foliage picks up intense tones of red and yellow.
Rec. Size: #1 pot (8/flat)    Space: (14"-18")

## Geranium sanguineum 'Alpenglow' (je-_ray_-nee-um  san-_gwin_-ee-um)
('Alpenglow' Geranium)....................................................Zone 3

9"-12"; full sun to light shade. 'Alpenglow' gives an attractive display of 1 to 1 1/2 inch wide vibrant rose-red flowers during late spring and summer. Quite vigorous, 'Alpenglow' forms neat mounds of attractive, deep green, shallowly divided palm-shaped leaves which turn crimson in fall. Additionally it tolerates drought and heat, and in the landscape may be used as a specimen, accent plant, or massed as a very colorful general purpose ground cover.
Rec. Size: #1 pot (8/flat)    Space: (10"-16")

## Geranium sanguineum 'Striatum' (a.k.a. 'Lancastriense') (je-_ray_-nee-um san-_gwin_-ee-um)
(Striped Bloody Geranium)....................................................Zone 3

6"-10"; full sun to light shade. 'Striatum' is a lovely sprawling cultivar with pink, crimson-veined, summerborne flowers. Drought tolerant, vigorous, and quite florific, this is a remarkable ground cover which looks exceptionally nice on sloping soil and fantastic creeping over terraces, retaining walls, and boulders.
Rec. Size: #1 pot (8/flat)    Space: (10"-16")

## Herniaria glabra, Rupturewort,

infuses a cool green mossy feel to Steve Windamuller's amazing waterfall garden at Frederick Meijer Gardens in Grand Rapids, Michigan.

GROUND COVERS

**Echinacea purpurea 'Magnus', Purple Coneflower,** is a "must have" plant for those interested in wildlife gardening.

GROUND COVERS

## Hardy Ivies

6"

1. Hedera colchica 'Dentata'
2. H. colchica 'Sulfur Heart'
3. H. colchica 'Variegata'
4. H. helix
5. H. helix 'Baltica'
6. H. helix 'Thorndale'
7. H. helix 'Walthamensis'

*Among the most versatile, useful, and reliable plants, ivies flourish throughout North America and are valued for their shiny evergreen leaves, durability, and long term effectiveness as ground covers. Ivies are dimorphic, meaning that they have two forms, juvenile and adult. In the juvenile stage they are vinelike—trailing along the ground, nonflowering, with three-lobed or five-lobed leaves. In the adult form, the foliage becomes leathery, unlobed, and darker green. The adult form blooms and bears fruit, but the seed does not seem to readily germinate. The transition to adult form rarely occurs—only when the ivy has been allowed to climb upward (usually up a tree), and even then flowering may take decades or longer. The ivy that is on the ground does not make the transition to adult form, and always trails along dutifully doing its job as a ground cover.*

*There are two species of ivy that perform well in the Great Lakes region. They are Hedera helix, English ivy, which is immensely popular, and H. colchica, Persian ivy, an exceptional up and comer. The picture above shows a variety of superior forms of ivy. They vary from small leaved selections of H. helix to the massive H. colchica 'Dentata', often exceeding six inches in length.*

*In the landscape ivies are used to blanket the soil with their trailing stems and evergreen foliage. As these spread they root in and effectively bind the soil in place. They are excellent for erosion control and because of this are frequently used on steep slopes where mowing would be too dangerous. In addition, because ivies are trailers, they are one of the best choices to plant under shallowly rooted trees where it would be too difficult to dig holes and plant other types of ground covers.*

*Established ivy is a strong grower, but when one plants ivy for the first time, it often comes as a bit of a surprise that it doesn't just take off and start spreading. Indeed, ivy may take two to three growing seasons (varies with soil, irrigation, etc.) to completely cover up the ground. This property has led to the saying that during year one ivy sleeps (it's building a root system), year two it creeps, and year three it leaps. Generally speaking, this holds true.*

*Because ivy is a strong and dense grower, one must choose appropriate companions, those that have enough muscle to compete with ivy. Some of the best shady-site companions to ivies are large hostas like 'Francis Williams', 'Francee', 'Krossa Regal', 'Summer Fragrance', and sieboldiana 'Elegans'. In the sun, effective vertical dimension can be found by adding such extraordinary grasses as Arundo donax 'Variegata', Pennisetum 'Japonicum', and such exceptional forms of Japanese silver grass as 'Cosmopolitan', 'Grosse Fontane', 'Morning Light', 'Silver Arrow', 'Undine', and 'Variegatus'.*

*Regardless of how you use ivy; protecting a hillside from erosion, edging walkways, blanketing the soil under trees, or large scale use to reduce maintenance, one thing is for sure. Ivies are aristocratic and classy. Possibly more than any other plant, they create a rich, warm, inviting, established look to the landscape. They are dependable plants that will outlive their owners. And, they are classic easy to care for plants that will never go out of style.*

GROUND COVERS

**G R O U N D   C O V E R S**

**Hedera colchica 'Dentata'** (<u>hed</u>-er-a   <u>kole</u>-chi-ka   den-<u>tay</u>-ta)
(Persian Ivy)............................................................Zone 5

4"-6" tall, spreading indefinitely; full sun to dense shade. With massive rich green leaves, this is our cold weather equivalent of Canary Island ivy (H. canariensis), so prevalent and impressive in California. Now, we too, can develop landscapes around a coarse textured ivy suitable for moderate to large scale use and capable of giving our landscapes that vibrant, unique, up to the minute look. This is a plant that will become one of your favorites. Not only is it lush and reliable, but pleasingly fragrant (somewhat like celery), resistant to disease, and easy on the eye.
Rec. Size: 38 cell flat   Space: (12"-14")

**Hedera colchica 'Sulfur Heart'** (<u>hed</u>-er-a   <u>kole</u>-chi-ka)
('Sulfur Heart' Persian Ivy)...............................Zone 5

4"-6" tall, spreading indifinitely; full sun to dense shade. Like the species, H. colchica, 'Sulfur Heart' (a.k.a. Paddy's Pride' and 'Gold Leaf') is durable, attractive, and coarse textured. In this case, however, its leaves are colored deep jade green with yellow central variegation.
Rec. Size: 38 cell flat   Space: (12"-14")

**Hedera colchica 'Variegata'** (<u>hed</u>-er-a   <u>kole</u>-chi-ka)
(Variegated Persian Ivy)..................................Zone 5/6

4"-6" tall, spreading indefinitely; light to dense shade. A remarkable large-leaved Persian ivy, 'Variegata' is beautifully clothed in leathery, light green leaves attractively streaked gray-green and edged with broad, creamy green margins. Although it is quite hardy, it definitely does better with winter protection from sun and wind.
Rec. Size: 38 cell flat   Space: (12"-14")

**Hedera helix** (<u>hed</u>-er-a   <u>he</u>-licks)
(English Ivy)............................................................Zone 5

Reaching a height of 3"-5" as a ground cover; climbing to 50'; full sun to dense shade. Exceptionally versatile and popular, this trailing evergreen ground cover is one of the finest for large plantings where a lush, low maintenance evergreen cover is desired. Leaves are typically 3 or 5-lobed, dark shiny green, and 2 to 3 inches long. Stems root as they spread, and with support (such as a brick wall or coarse textured tree trunk) produce aireal root-like projections which allow it to climb. Planting after Sept. 1st, or in wind exposed locations, is not recommended for any ivy.
Rec. Size: 50 cell flat   Space: (8"-10")
Rec. Size: 38 cell flat   Space: (10"-12")
Rec. Size: #1 pot (8/flat)   Space: (1 1/2'-2')

**Hedera helix 'Baltica'** (<u>hed</u>-er-a   <u>he</u>-licks)
(Baltic Ivy)............................................................Zone 5

3"-5"; climbing to 50'; full sun to dense shade. A very popular selection of English ivy, 'Baltica' is unique in that its leaves are smaller than the species and colored deep dark green.
Rec. Size: 50 cell flat   Space: (8"-10")
Rec. Size: 38 cell flat   Space: (10"-12")

**Hedera helix 'Thorndale'** (<u>hed</u>-er-a   <u>he</u>-licks)
(Thorndale' Ivy)....................................................Zone 5

3"-5" tall and spreading indefinitely, climbing to 50'; full sun to dense shade. Like the parent species, Hedera helix, this is an evergreen ground cover. Compared to H. helix its atrractive dark green leaves are a bit smaller, have a more prominent central lobe, and display creamy white veins. Slow growing until rooted it later spreads at a moderate pace and makes a thick attractive mat.
Rec. Size: 50 cell flat   Space: (8"-10")
Rec. Size: 38 cell flat   Space: (10"-12")
Rec. Size: 6-pack (18/flat)   Space: (14"-16")

## Hedera helix 'Walthamensis' (hed-er-a  he-licks)
('Walthamensis' Ivy) ...............................................Zone 5

2"-3" as a ground cover, climbing to 25'; full sun to dense shade. The foliage of this vigorous small-leaved form is medium green with white veins, and might best be described as a miniature version of 'Thorndale' (see above). Because of its small foliage, this is the selection of choice for areas where a fine texture is desirable.
Rec. Size: 50 cell flat    Space: (6"-10")

## Helleborus x hybridus (hell-e-bore-is  hy-brid-us)
(Lenten Rose) ...............................................Zone 4

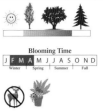

**Blooming Time**

| J | F | M | A | M | J | J | A | S | O | N | D |
|---|---|---|---|---|---|---|---|---|---|---|---|
| Winter | | | Spring | | | Summer | | | Fall | | |

15"-18"; light to moderate shade. Lenten rose is a stemless herbaceous ground cover that blooms very early; usually beginning February and lasting into April. It is a rugged, coarse textured, leathery salt with shiny green foliage that remains attractive year-round. Ideally suited for use on a moderate scale in naturalistic woodland landscapes, Lenten rose is best employed near the house to increase visibility, especially of its flowers, during cold weather when one is less likely to be outdoors.
Rec. Size: #1 pot (8/flat)    Space: (1 1/2'-2')

# Hedera helix, English Ivy, is surely one of the most versatile of all ground covers. Here it creates a low maintenance alternatiave to turf and transforms this long boring sidewalk into a rich inviting passagway.

GROUND COVERS

# HEMEROCALLIS/DAYLILY

*Hemerocallis 'Strawberry Candy'*

Daylilies are among the most useful ground covers for small, moderate, or large areas. Nearly indestructible, they are often excellent choices for use as accent and specimen plants. Daylily flowers come in all sorts of colors, shapes, and sizes. Each blooms only for one day, but a succession of buds brings continual color for several weeks or even months — as is the case with the rebloomers. Placed atop a retaining wall, on sloping terrain, or in beds paralleling steps brings daylilies up to eye level where they can be appreciated to the fullest. Along walkways they are exceptional edgings and at building entrances they present a pleasing, colorful, welcoming appearance. Frequently they are employed as effective foundation plants or as erosion-controlling soil binders. Planted at the edge of a pond or stream, they stabilize the soil and promote a tranquil atmosphere.

**Heavy 2-Season Plants**

Daylilies adapt to almost any soil, preferring moist, rich, acidic, well-drained loam. Because of their fleshy, water-storing roots and rhizomes, they are particularly well suited to withstand drought; for mere survival, they seldom require watering other than provided by nature, but to maximize flower production an occasional deep watering, sufficient to keep the soil slightly moist at all times, is beneficial throughout the flowering season.

## Hemerocallis 'Big Smile' (hem-er-oh-<u>kal</u>-is)
('Big Smile' Daylily)............................................................Zone 4

**Blooming Time**
| J | F | M | A | M | J | J | A | S | O | N | D |
|---|---|---|---|---|---|---|---|---|---|---|---|
| Winter | | Spring | | | Summer | | | Fall | | | |

2 1/2'; full sun to light shade. Bred by Darrel Apps, this robust daylily is perfectly named. That's because its sunny-yellow, fragrant, 7-inch-wide flowers, with their ruffled blush-pink edges, look like a great big smile. 'Big Smile' not only bears superior flowers, but loads of them, which makes it not only good in the home landscape but also suitable for use on a commercial scale. It may be used in conjunction with other daylilies, mass planted as a ground cover, or combined with such staples as bell flower cultivars, coreopsis selections, Gaillardia 'Fanfare', Nepeta selections, and various ornamental grasses.
Rec. Size: #1 pot (8/flat)    Space: (14"-18")

## Hemerocallis 'Catherine Woodbury' (hem-er-oh-<u>kal</u>-is)
('Catherine Woodbury' Daylily)...................................Zone 4

**Blooming Time**
| J | F | M | A | M | J | J | A | S | O | N | D |
|---|---|---|---|---|---|---|---|---|---|---|---|
| Winter | | Spring | | | Summer | | | Fall | | | |

2'-2 1/2'; full sun to light shade. A lovely mid to late summer bloomer, 'Catherine

Woodbury' displays 6 inch wide soft salmon pink, highly fragrant flowers. A soft pastel, the flowers of 'Catherine Woodbury' combine comfortably with other tones of pink, yellow, white, and purple.
Rec. Size: #1 pot (8/flat)    Space: (10"-14")

## Hemerocallis 'Chicago Apache' (hem-er-oh-<u>kal</u>-is)
('Chicago Apache' Daylily))...........................................Zone 4

**Blooming Time**
| J | F | M | A | M | J | J | A | S | O | N | D |
|---|---|---|---|---|---|---|---|---|---|---|---|
| Winter | | Spring | | | Summer | | | Fall | | | |

2 1/2'; full sun to light shade. With large (7 inch wide) intensely scarlet red ruffle-edged flowers, 'Chicago Apache' adds an element of excitement to the late summer landscape. Clearly a hot color, this is not a plant for subtle effect. Rather, with its sturdy leaves and flower stalks and flowers of thick substance and deep color (owed to its tetraploid chromosome count),. 'Chicago Apache' commands attention and is superb for edging borders and walks as well as for mass planting.
Rec. Size: #1 pot (8/flat)    Space: (10"-14")

**GROUND COVERS** (vertical, left margin)

## Hemerocallis 'Custard Candy' (hem-er-oh-<u>kal</u>-is)
('Custard Candy' Daylily)..................................................Zone 4

2'; full sun to light shade. Highly popular, 'Custard Candy' is an exceptionally attractive daylily with super clean foliage, robust habit, and loads of mid-summer borne, sturdy, attractively creamy-peach petaled, rich maroon centered, 4 1/2 inch wide flowers. Easy to design with, 'Custard Candy' combines well with other daylilies and summer bloomers especially those with blue and violet flowers. Great companions include Salvias, Russian sage, Agastache 'Blue Fortune', Campanula 'Blue Clips' and 'Sarastro', and numerous ornamental grasses.
Rec. Size: #1 pot (8/flat)   Space: (14"-18")

## Hemerocallis 'Fairy Tale Pink' (hem-er-oh-<u>kal</u>-is)
('Fairy Tale Pink' Daylily).................................................Zone 4

2'; full sun to light shade. Perpetually high in the Popularity Poll of the American Hemerocallis Society, 'Fairy Tale Pink' is unique for its ruffled, iridescent pink, green throated, mid to late summer flowers of heavy substance. Like 'Stella de Oro', 'Fairy Tale Pink' has been a winner of the Stout Silver Medal (top award of the American Hemerocallis Society), testimony that this repeat bloomer is one of the very finest.
Rec. Size: #1 pot (8/flat)   Space: (10"-14")

## Hemerocallis 'Forgotten Dreams' (hem-er-oh-<u>kal</u>-is)
('Forgotten Dreams' Daylily)............................................Zone 4

2'; full sun to light shade. 'Forgotten Dream's' is a magnificent super high impact daylily with huge 6 1/2 inch wide, fragrant, cream-purple, maroon-purple-centered flowers. Unusually large, especially for this color pattern, the blooms of 'Forgotten Dreams' are of heavy substance with ruffled edges. They hold up well throughout the day, and do a terrific job of brightening up the midsummer landscape.
Rec. Size: #1 pot (8/flat)   Space: (14"-18")

## Hemerocallis 'Gentle Shepherd' (hem-er-oh-<u>kal</u>-is)
('Gentle Shepherd' Daylily)..............................................Zone 4

2 1/2'; full sun to light shade. Thick and full in substance, its lovely 5 inch wide, ruffled, creamy white flowers have made this early to mid summer daylily a very popular selection. Among the very best of the "near white" daylilies, the flowers of 'Gentle Shepherd' combine nicely with those of other daylilies as well as many other summer blooming perennials.
Rec. Size: #1 pot (8/flat)   Space: (10"-14")

## Hemerocallis 'Happy Returns' (hem-er-oh-<u>kal</u>-is)
('Happy Returns' Daylily).................................................Zone 4

16"; full sun to light shade. Bred by the accomplished hybridizer Daryl Apps, 'Happy Returns', a descendent of 'Stella de Oro', demonstrates a very long blooming season (late spring through fall), superb heat tolerance, and fragrant canary yellow 3 1/2 inch wide flowers that go nicely with other colors in the landscape. 'Happy Returns' is known for filling out rapidly and making a bold visual statement. It has won numerous awards and is extremely popular.
Rec. Size: #1 pot (8/flat)   Space: (10"-14")

## Hemerocallis 'Little Business' (hem-er-oh-<u>kal</u>-is)
('Little Business' Daylily)..................................................Zone 4

15"; full sun to light shade. One of the most promising daylilies to come along in years, 'Little Business' is a repeat bloomer providing colorful 3 inch wide, fragrant, green throated, rich pinkish red flowers early summer through July. With heavy bud count, the floral impact of 'Little Business' is substantial and suitable for commercial applications as well as home landscaping.
Rec. Size: #1 pot (8/flat)   Space: (10"-14")

**GROUND COVERS**

## Hemerocallis 'Little Grapette' (hem-er-oh-kal-is)
('Little Grapette' Daylily)..............................................Zone 4

**Blooming Time**
J F M A M J J A S O N D
Winter  Spring  Summer  Fall

12"; full sun to light shade. A unique new introduction that features a neat tidy habit of medium green deciduous foliage, 'Little Grapette' is a splendid repeat bloomer. Beginning early summer, 'Little Grapette' bears a tremendous quantity of 2 inch wide, purple-grape, heavy substanced, semi-fragrant flowers with contrasting yellow halo and green throat.
Rec. Size: #1 pot (8/flat)    Space: (10"-14")

## Hemerocallis 'Mardi Gras Parade' (hem-er-oh-kal-is)
('Mardi Gras Parade' Daylily)..............................Zone 4

**Blooming Time**
J F M A M J J A S O N D
Winter  Spring  Summer  Fall

2'; full sun to light shade. 'Mardi Gras Parade' is a lovely, charming, super neat, highly attractive, very sough after variety with long summer blooming season. Reaching 4 inches wide, its fabulous bicolor flowers are cheerful rose pink with rich burgundy eyezones and chartreuse centers. Ruffled about their edges, the flowers are rich in substance, borne in great quantity, and among the best of all daylilies.
Rec. Size: #1 pot (8/flat)    Space: (14"-18")

## Hemerocallis 'Mary's Gold' (hem-er-oh-kal-is)
('Mary's Gold' Daylily)..............................................Zone 4

**Blooming Time**
J F M A M J J A S O N D
Winter  Spring  Summer  Fall

2 1/2'-3'; full sun to light shade. Perpetually ranked high in the American Daylily Society Popularity Poll, this award winner is incomparable for sheer brightness. Flowering July and early August, 'Mary's Gold' brings a blast of color with its huge 6 1/2 inch wide flowers that can be seen from a mile away. Naturally, 'Mary's Gold' is a great plant for curb appeal (visible at 55 miles an hour or higher) and for high contrast with other daylilies and summer bloomers of all types.
Rec. Size: #1 pot (8/flat)    Space: (14"-18")

## Hemerocallis 'Mary Todd' (hem-er-oh-kal-is)
('Mary Todd' Daylily)..............................................Zone 4

**Blooming Time**
J F M A M J J A S O N D
Winter  Spring  Summer  Fall

2' in flower; full sun to light shade. Recipient of many awards, including the highest award — the Stout Silver Medal (1978), this "classic" early summer blooming tetraploid bears striking 6 inch wide, heavily ruffled, heavy textured buff yellow flowers above semievergreen foliage.
Rec. Size: #1 pot (8/flat)    Space: (10"-14")

## Hemerocallis 'Pardon Me' (hem-er-oh-kal-is)
('Pardon Me' Daylily)..............................................Zone 4

**Blooming Time**
J F M A M J J A S O N D
Winter  Spring  Summer  Fall

1 1/2'; full sun to light shade. An exceptional daylily, 'Pardon Me' is a fragrant repeat bloomer that combines neat deciduous foliage with a striking floral show. Beginning mid June and lasting for several weeks, 'Pardon Me' bears copious 2 3/4 inch wide bright red, yellow/green-throated flowers of heavy substance.
Rec. Size: #1 pot (8/flat)    Space: (10"-14")

## Hemerocallis 'Piano Man' (hem-er-oh-kal-is)
('Piano Man' Daylily)..............................................Zone 4

**Blooming Time**
J F M A M J J A S O N D
Winter  Spring  Summer  Fall

2'-2 1/2'; full sun to light shade. 'Piano Man' is a very catchy daylily with strong growth habit and showy mid season bloom time. Bearing many flower stalks each laden with a high bud count, 'Piano Man' bears sturdy 4 1/2 inch wide flowers of heavy substance with lovely richly ruffled edges. Colored creamy peach with deep ruby maroon purple centers, its flowers are outstanding in every way.
Rec. Size: #1 pot (8/flat)    Space: (14"-18")

GROUND COVERS

## Hemerocallis 'Rocket City' (hem-er-oh-<u>kal</u>-is)
('Rocket City' Daylily)................................................Zone 4

30"-36"; full sun to light shade. A commanding selection, 'Rocket City' is popular and florific. Blooming mid summer above attractive medium green deciduous foliage, this strong growing tetraploid bears many 6 inch wide, vibrant orange petaled, burnt-orange centered flowers. An award winner, 'Rocket City' is a classic selection which has proven itself over the years as a sturdy ground cover in both the home and commercial landscape. It is excellent for edging and accent use and combines nicely with other daylilies, cone flowers, Liatris, ornamental grasses, and a host of other ground covers and perennials.
Rec. Size: #1 pot (8/flat)     Space: (1 1/2'-2 1/2')

## Hemerocallis 'Siloam Double Classic'
('Siloam Double Classic' Daylily)................................Zone 5

1 1/2'; full sun to light shade. Popular since its introduction, 'Siloam Double Classic', like 'Stella de Oro', is a Stout Silver Medal winner (the highest award of the American Hemerocallis Society). This fabulous selection is a treasure in the daylily world. A midsummer bloomer with lovely fully double, rich pink, fragrant five-inch-wide blossoms, 'Siloam Double Classic' imparts an aristocratic look upon the landscape. Its foliage is a clean rich green even after flowering, and in every way it is neat, tidy, and attractive.
Rec. Size: #1 pot (8/flat)     Space: (12"-16")

## Hemerocallis x 'Stella de 'Oro' (hem-er-oh-<u>kal</u>-lis)
('Stella de 'Oro' Daylily)..........................................Zone 4

1 1/2'-2'; full sun to light shade. Without a doubt this cultivar is the most significant daylily introduction of the century. Flowers are fragrant, pure golden orange, and reliably and numerously borne from mid spring to early fall. Its foliage is so tough as to last the entire season without becoming tattered, and its compact habit and pleasant green color make an ideal backdrop for the outstanding flowers.
Rec. Size: #1 pot (8/flat)     Space: (8"-12")

## Hemerocallis 'Strawberry Candy' (hem-er-oh-<u>kal</u>-is)
('Strawberry Candy' Daylily)....................................Zone 4

2'; full sun to light shade. A Stamile, 1989 introduction, this exceptional daylily was the recipient of the daylily society's top award, the Stout Silver Medal in 1998 (previously won by 'Stella de Oro'). To say the least, it is a very good daylily. Its bud count is high, it blooms early summer well into fall (considered a rebloomer), and its 4 1/2 inch wide flowers are a lovely strawberry pink with a rich rose-red eyezone and golden green throat. Heavy of substance, this tetraploid has good foliar qualities and is good for both residential and commercial use.
Rec. Size: #1 pot (8/flat)     Space: (10"-14")

## Hemerocallis 'Sue Rothbauer' (hem-er-oh-<u>kal</u>-is)
('Sue Rothbauer' Daylily)........................................Zone 3

2'; full sun to light shade. It's hard to imagine that among 40,000+ daylily varieties, 'Sue Rothbauer' could be that much different, but it really is. What makes 'Sue Rothbauer' so great is the combination of its propensity to rebloom along with 5 1/2-inch-wide, exquisite rose pink petaled, greenish yellow centered, pleasantly fragrant flowers. Beginning to bloom during July, 'Sue Rothbauer' has been known to rebloom until frost. Moreover, its foliage is a pleasing mid green with the ability to stay clean throughout the entire growing season.
Rec. Size: #1 pot (8/flat)     Space: (12"-16")

## Hemerocallis 'Summer Wine' (hem-er-oh-<u>kal</u>-is)
('Summer Wine' Daylily)..........................................Zone 4

2'-2 1/2'; full sun to light shade. Simply pleasing, 'Summer Wine' is one of those easy going plants that is easy to take in all respects. Its foliage stays clean, it flowers well, and it requires about zero maintenance. 'Summer Wine' is aptly named for its rich wine red, yellow throated, 5 1/2-inch-wide midsummer flowers which are lightly ruffled about their edges.
Rec. Size: #1 pot (8/flat)     Space: (10"-14")

GROUND COVERS

## Herniaria glabra (her-nee-<u>air</u>-ee-a  <u>glay</u>-bra)
(Rupturewort) ................................................................Zone 5

1"-2"; full sun to light shade. OK, maybe this isn't the most exciting ground cover—tiny green summerborne flowers and fruit almost unnoticable against miniature evergreen foliage. But, it can be used for exciting (ground smothering) things. A trailer, rupturewort dutifully blankets the ground, excludes weeds, and makes a nice carpetlike cover that accepts a good degree of foot traffic. Use rupturewort on a small to large scale as a lawn substitute or filler for sidewalk cracks and between stepping stones. Colorful bulbs, hostas, and other perennials can be interplanted to add textural and color contrast.
Rec. Size: 6- pack (18/flat)   Space: (10"-14")

## Herniaria glabra 'Sea Foam' (her-nee-<u>air</u>-ee-a  <u>glay</u>-bra)
**Patent Applied For**
('Sea Foam' Rupturewort)................................................Zone 5

1"-2"; full sun to light shade. During June 2003, while walking by a stock block of rupturewort, I noticed a stem with white leaves in the carpet of green. I made a couple of cuttings, rooted them and ended up with this lovely mosslike, heretofore never seen, shade brightening, foot friendly ground cover. So far it has proven to be disease free, tolerant of foot traffic, not bothered by humidity, or heat, and effective in both sun and light shade. 'Sea Foam' displays a soft textured habit and cheerful color which combine to make it a fine small to moderate scale general cover, filler for between stepping stones, and an excellent companion to Alliums, heucheras, hostas, Nepetas, Persicaria 'Red Dragon', tall sedums, sedges, and dwarf ornamental grasses.
Rec. Size: 6- pack (18/flat)   Space: (8"-12")

## Heuchera 'Amber Waves' (<u>hew</u>-ker-a)
('Amber Waves' Coral Bells)..........................................Zone 4

8"-10"; light to moderate shade. This stunning award winning selection represents a significant color breakthrough. In a world of purple-dominated coral bells selections, 'Amber Waves' is clothed in ruffled golden-amber foliage. It is a great designer plant which combines nicely with nearly every other color—especially purples, greens, and blues, and can find a home in near-

ly every landscape. During early summer it brings even greater interest when topped with light rose-colored flowers.
Rec. Size: #1 pot (8/flat)   Space: (12"-16")

## Heuchera 'Frosted Violet' (<u>hew</u>-ker-a)
('Frosted Violet' Coral Bells)..........................................Zone 4

12"-15"; full sun to moderate shade. Bred by Charles and Martha Oliver, this superb Heuchera selection is vigorous and sturdy, but also exceptionally attractive. Burgundy violet colored, its foliage is velvety soft, rich purple, and carried in an upright bouquetlike fashion. During late spring/early summer, the splendid foliage is accented sprays of soft pink flowers carried as high as 15 inches above the foliage. As with other Heucheras, it benefits from afternoon shade.
Rec. Size: #1 pot (8/flat)   Space: (14"-18")

## Heuchera 'Green Spice' (<u>hew</u>-ker-a)
('Green Spice' Coral Bells)..............................................Zone 4

9"; full sun to moderate shade. With great big, dark gray edged, purple veined, silvery frosted leaves, 'Green Spice' is a good ground cover for small to moderate scale general cover or accent use. Blooming during summer, 'Green Spice' bears creamy flowers upon leafy upright spikes. It looks nice in a container, and makes a superb companion to purple leaved forms of Heuchera, hostas, and ferns.
Rec. Size: #1 pot (8/flat)   Space: (12"-16")

## Heuchera 'Obsidian' (<u>hew</u>-ker-a)
('Obsidian' Coral Bells)..................................................Zone 4

10"; full sun to light shade. This is perhaps the darkest purple (nearly black) of any Heuchera. Spreading 16 inches across, 'Obsidian' can be used to create contrast against bright colored Heucheras such as 'Green Spice', 'Snow Angel', and 'Silver Scrolls', Heucherellas like 'Sunspot', sedges like 'Evergold' and 'Bowles Golden', golden leaved Japanese forest grass, golden hostas, or golden creeping moneywort—the possibilities are endless. One thing is for sure, this plant adds interest to any garden. Small white flowers arise during summer.
Rec. Size:  #1 pot (8/flat)   Space: (12"-16")

## Heuchera x 'Palace Purple' (<u>hew</u>-ker-a)

('Palace Purple' Coral Bells)..................................Zone 4

10"-14"; full sun to dense shade. Introduced from Europe by Alan Bush of North Carolina, the intensity of the purple of its rugged maple-like leaves must be seen to be believed. It is outstanding when used as a backdrop for low growing hostas, and combines well with many non-invasive shade loving perennials. Flowers are tiny wisps of yellowish white that arise above the foliage during spring.
Perennial Plant of the Year 1991
Rec. Size: #1 pot (8/flat)   Space: (10"-14")

## Heuchera sanguinea 'Snow Angel' (<u>hew</u>-ker-a  a-mare-i-<u>kay</u>-na)

('Snow Angel' Coral Bells) NATIVE CULTIVAR ...................Zone 3

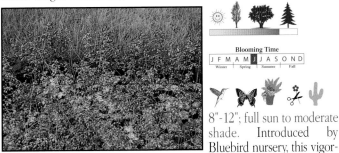

8"-12"; full sun to moderate shade. Introduced by Bluebird nursery, this vigorous, highly colorful selection is uniquely patterned with creamy white mottling over light green, attractively lobe-edged foliage. A superb choice for brightening up the shade garden, 'Snow Angel' also bears rich pink bell-shaped florets in late spring. Not only do these enhance its ornamental effect, but they also act as a magnet to hummingbirds.
Rec. Size: #1 pot (8/flat)   Space: (10"-14")

## Heuchera 'Silver Scrolls' (<u>hew</u>-ker-a)

('Silver Scrolls' Coral Bells)..................................Zone 5

8"-12"; full sun to moderate shade. Among the many Heuchera selections, 'Silver Scrolls' is a standout with rich purple leaves beautifully overlaid with an intense veil of silver. This coupled with a deep purple scrollwork of veination creates an exceptionally dazzling mosaic of color. Further enhancing this fine cultivar is the intensely plum purple underside to the leaves and the pink tinged, tiny white flowers of late spring. Good companions include smaller varieties of lady fern, black wood fern, Asarum, Bergenia, Dicentra, epimedium, Helleborus, hostas, Japanese forest grass, prairie dropseed, and many others.
Rec. Size: #1 pot (8/flat)   Space: (10"-16")

## Heuchera 'Stormy Seas' (<u>hew</u>-ker-a)

('Stormy Seas' Coral Bells)..................................Zone 3

8"-12"; full sun to moderate shade. Considered the strongest grower among the fancy leaved purple heucheras, 'Stormy Seas' matures quickly and is long lived. In addition, it is one of the most stunning cultivars. Its foliage is rich purple, ruffle-edged, and overlaid in shiny silver. On its undersides it is stained rich wine-purple. Forming a neat mounding habit, 'Stormy Seas' may be the best heuchera for large scale landscape use—especially when planted in sweeping drifts where it creates a classy rich feel. Sprays of tiny white flowers further decorate it during summer.
Rec. Size: #1 pot (8/flat)   Space: (12"-16")

## x Heucheralla 'Sunspot' (<u>hew</u>-ker-a) Patent Applied For

('Sunspot' Foamy Bells) ..................................Zone 4

8"; light to moderate shade. This fascinating selection makes a bright splash in the shade garden. Reaching 1 1/2 feet across, its electric yellow foliage is decorated with bright blood red central splotches. In early to mid summer it produces a good quantity of rich pink flowers atop upright floral spikes. About this time its leaves change to straw yellow and look nice this way throughout the rest of the growing season until covered by snow. Consider this plant as a bright accent or light reflecting ground cover. Companions are endless with purple leaved heucheras, blue leaved hostas, and rich green ferns being the best.
Rec. Size: #1 pot (8/flat)   Space: (12"-18")

GROUND COVERS

# Lily-turf — Unlimited potential for low maintenance landscaping

*Liriope spicata*

*Liriope spicata*

*Liriope spicata*

## Lawns that need mowing only once per year.

*Liriope muscari 'Big Blue' and L. spicata*

*Liriope spicata*

*Ophiopogon planiscapus nigrescens*

*Liriope spicata*

*Liriope spicata*

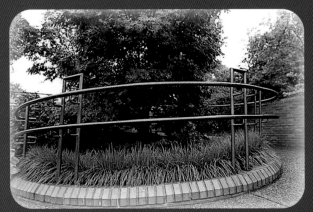
*Liriope spicata*

# Ultimate Edging

*Liriope spicata*

*Liriope muscari 'Silvery Sunproof'*

*Liriope muscari 'Silvery Sunproof'*

*Liriope spicata*

*Liriope spicata*

# Superb surrounding trees

*Liriope muscari 'Silvery Sunproof'*

**Earth Friendly**

# Earth Friendly Plants are Grown Using Biological Methods

### What this Means

* Healthy, vigorous, quick establishing plants.
* Reduced use of synthetic pesticides.
* Less risk to the environment.

### How We Do It

* Helpful predatory insects to control harmful pest insects.
* Predatory mites to control harmful mites.
* Soaps and oils to control pest insects and their eggs.
* Helpful bacteria and nematodes to control harmful bacteria and insects.
* Organic mulches for weed control.
* Slow release and organic fertilizers.
* Growing media made from organic by-products.
* "Hands On" culture by professionals trained in Integrated Pest Management (as opposed to "factory" growing with indiscriminate use of fertilizers and pesticides).

### Environmentally Friendly Alternatives to Turf Grass

* Less fertilizer use.
* Less water consumption.
* Eliminate the noise and air pollution of lawn mowing.

### Environmentally Appropriate Plant Selections

* Premium Plants are test grown in our trial garden. We believe them to be NONINVASIVE to natural areas in Growing Zones 4, 5, 6, of the Great Lakes States.
* What this means is that it is our opinion that these plants do not "by natural means" (wind, birds, currents, animals) jump across spacial gaps to invade natural areas.

*GROUND COVERS*

# SPECIAL SECTION: Invasive Plants

In 1999 President Clinton signed Executive Order 13112 requiring each state to organize an Invasive Species Council for the management of existing non-native invasive species of plants and animals (at various governmental and private levels), and for the education of the public in matters related to non-native invasive species. The executive order also charges state invasive species councils with developing and implementing a plan to manage/prevent the future introduction of invasive species from other countries which may exhibit invasive qualities in the United States.

The intent of the Executive Order seems appropriate to most people; purple loosestrife (Lythrum salicaria), tree of heaven (Ailanthus altissima), zebra mussel, gypsy moth, Japanese beetle, lamprey eel, and carp are all introduced biological entities that have rapidly established themselves in environments where they were never intended (to the detriment of native species and ecosystems). It is only reasonable and appropriate to have a plan to manage such organisms.

Naturally, like most well intended endeavors, the executive order is taking some time to implement—mostly because it is prone to various perspectives on key issues, and because there is more complexity to the issues than one might first imagine. Here are some of the key elements of contention.

**Geography** Sometimes people overlook geographical (and climatological) differences and jump to inappropriate conclusions. For example, Lonicera japonica, Japanese honeysuckle vine, can grow 20 feet or more in a single year in the Midsouth (Tennessee, Kentucky, Carolinas, Georgia). There it produces copious seed which is dispersed (by birds) over spatial gaps away from its initial site of introduction. It has few biological competitors, it can out-compete other species in natural plant communities, and it is costly to eradicate.

Not surprisingly, in the Midsouthern states, most people agree that Japanese honeysuckle is an invasive plant. But, what about the same plant in hardiness Zones 4, 5, and 6a of the Great Lakes states—where it grows more slowly and where the growing season is too short for seed production, and therefore it is unable to jump over spatial gaps? Common sense would indicate that this, and every other plant, be evaluated by how it behaves in specific local climatological conditions, and not somewhere else.

**Know the Biology of the Plant (and its History)** Some people have been prone to point the finger at any non-native plant they have encountered in any natural area, and based on that alone, to call it invasive. This too, is not logical, as the plant may not have gotten there by natural means. An example of this is myrtle—which can sometimes be found in natural wooded areas.

To be sure, myrtle is a dense grower, able to out-compete less vigorous species (one reason that it is such an effective ground cover). But, since it does not effectively reproduce from seed, it can not disperse across spatial gaps. As it turns out, the reason it can sometimes be found in natural areas is that somebody, one way or another, planted it there! Usually this can be traced to its historical use as a grave site adornment, inappropriately dumped yard waste, or to it being a landscape relic from a preexisting home site (which was either torn down or burned down some time previously). Once eradicated, short of human reintroduction, myrtle will not return to the natural area.

**Properly Identify the Plant (Common Names Are Misleading)** If you are talking about purple loosestrife, it is important to indicate that you mean Lythrum salicaria—for there are over 30 species of Lythrum, many with purple flowers, and thus several different plants that can wear the name purple loosestrife. Not all of them are invasive and some are native. Likewise, one shouldn't talk about an invasive species simply by the genus name Lythrum or its common name loosestrife. There are actually several different genera that go by the common name loosestrife. At Hortech we once grew Decodon palustris, commonly called swamp loosestrife. The sales of that plant, a native, were ruined because people mistakenly confused it with Lythrum salicaria (because of the common name loosestrife). By the time we figured out what was going on and switched the common name to willow herb it was too late. That is a shame, because Decodon palustris offers erosion control and habitat and breeding ground for desirable fish and bird species, not to mention nectar for hummingbirds and butterflies. Few plants can stabilize shorelines like Decodon palustris, and one has to wonder how many feet of shoreline have been lined with concrete or steel because of unawareness of plant species which could do the job and also contribute positively to the environment.

**Communicate Accurately** The above scenario indicates why you should always communicate exactly which plant you are talking about. To do this you must know the scientific name of the plant in question—as most plants go by several common names, and there is a good degree of duplicate use of common names. Similarly, realize that there may be unique features to varieties and cultivars within a given species. In such case, even if the parent species were to be determined to be invasive, it is conceivable that a variety or cultivar of that species may not be invasive—due to sterility, dwarfism, or some other condition which generally limits its dispersal or reproductive effectiveness. Every plant must be evaluated individually and generalizations must be avoided.

**Expect Logical Recommendations** Often invasive species councils (state or regional) or other horticultural or ecological groups will publish a list of invasive species with plant assessments summarized in such broad and vague terms as highly, moderately, or slightly invasive, without telling the public what to do with this information. The result is a confused public and possibly the omission of some very effective plants from our landscapes.

In my opinion, every plant that is talked about as an invasive (to any degree; highly, moderately, slightly, etc.) should come with a recommendation that tells the public what to do. This may be a recommendation to avoid using a given plant, or it may be a recommendation on how to use the plant responsibly. Since the authors of information about invasives are supposed to evaluate all aspects of any plant that they write about, they should also be accountable for making such recommendations. In the case of the plants I have discussed previously one might expect to see recommendations such as:

## Lonicera japonica
(Japanese honeysuckle vine)

Recommendation: In warmer climates (Zones 7a to 10) L. japonica grows very fast and produces seed that is distributed by birds and wildlife which allows for natural movement across spacial gaps. When seed is carried to natural areas (particularly areas with disturbed soil) it can readily germinate, become established, and overrun shrubs and small trees.

In cooler northern climates, such as growing Zones 4, 5, and 6a, of Michigan, Indiana, Illinois, and Ohio, L. japonica does not seem to have sufficient growing time to produce mature seed, therefore it does not jump across spacial gaps. Also, it is slower growing in such areas. Here, Lonicera japonica has been used effectively for decades as a garden plant in parts of home and commercial landscapes that do not border natural areas. In addition, cultivars of L. japonica exist. The cultivar 'Aureo-reticulata' generally is non-flowering. 'Halliana' blooms but does not set fruit in Zones 4, 5, and 6, and 'Purpurea' blooms but does not set fruit in Zones 4, 5, and 6.

## Lythrum salicaria
(purple loosestrife)

Recommendation: Do not plant the species L. salicaria in Michigan, Indiana, Illinois, or Ohio because it is known to produce copious amounts of highly viable seed and to disperse by seed over spacial gaps by natural distribution (birds, wind, currents) into wetlands where it depletes native plant species and native waterfoul habitat. Note: Sterile hybrids may exist, and may someday be approved for safe use. Please consult your local authorities.

## Vinca minor
(lesser periwinkle, Myrtle)

Recommendation: This plant does not disperse by seed over spacial gaps. However, like other garden plants, it can establish in natural areas if it is dumped there or if it is planted alongside of a natural area and allowed to creep in. You may safely and responsibly use Vinca minor (lesser periwinkle, myrtle) as a garden plant but if your property borders a natural area, you should install an edging that prevents it from creeping into the natural area. Or, you should plant it in parts of your landscape that do not border the natural area.

**It's Not about Philosophy** The executive order was never intended to be a statement endorsing a philosophy of native plants being better than nonnative plants. But, sometimes discussions take a turn in this direction. One viewpoint is that native plants perform better (in their local area) and support wildlife better because they evolved there. My perspective, with 21 years of experience as a grower and gardener of both native and nonnative plants, is this:

> Native plants are great in natural areas and in landscape settings—in many cases. But natives are not inherently better adapted to home and commercial landscape settings, nor do they necessarily furnish more or better food or habitat for wildlife. The reason for this is that landscape settings are not the same as natural settings. They are much brighter (due to light reflected from buildings), hotter (from sunlight being absorbed by brick, and asphalt), higher in salt content (due to ice control, fertilization, and runoff), full of disturbed and/or compacted soil with altered microflora and pH (from excavation activities), more polluted (from auto exhaust, mowers, etc.), and are often windier and drier than natural settings. In other words, our landscape settings are not native.

> Because our home and commercial landscape settings are not native, it means that the native plants that have evolved in the local natural environment don't always perform (or even survive) as well as plants from other geographic regions. This must be taken on a plant by plant basis. Many natives are very adaptable to landscape settings and do just fine. Others languish, and some of our most useful plants, like Japanese yew, certain types of dogwoods and viburnums, daylilies, and hostas are not native, but they do a terrific job as landscape plants—without posing a threat to our native plant communities. As such they control erosion, beautify our constructed environments, furnish food, nectar, and nesting sites, cool and oxygenate the air, and produce organic matter which enriches the soil and perpetuates the cycle of life.

**Become Involved:** We all need to do our part to sensibly manage invasive species. Nurserymen need to test-grow new plants before marketing them to avoid introducing the next Lythrum salicaria (purple loosestrife). Gardeners need to avoid dumping garden plants (or clippings of them) in natural areas. And, invasive species councils need to follow sensible, scientifically credible criteria in evaluating plants, and then provide appropriate recommendations for responsible use or eradication of only those plants they have scientifically evaluated.

It is through each group doing its part that we can both preserve our natural ecosystems as well as maximize the positive environmental and aesthetic potential of all garden plants.

# HOSTAS

*Heavy 2-Season Plants*

*The endlessly useful clump-forming hostas rank among the most popular herbaceous ground covers. Their popularity is due in part to their ease of culture, the public's greater awareness of the value of land-scaping upon property values, and the positive effect hostas have on our ecology. Hostas require no maintenance, become larger and more valuable each year, offer food to bees and hummingbirds, and enrich the soil as they die back to earth each fall. More than this, hostas are beautiful and display a lushness that imparts an element of classinesss.*

*Hostas range from a couple of inches tall to more than 3 feet, and their spread may range from one to five times their height. They are widely employed for edging walks and perennial borders and are useful as accent plants among ornamental beds containing shrubs and low-growing trees. A dramatic lush appearance is obtained when masses of hostas are planted as bank coverings or facings to trees and foundations, and a single specimen is always very attention getting. Hostas combine well with astilbes, ferns, lilies, spring-flowering bulbs, and countless varieties of deciduous and evergreen trees and shrubs.*

| LEAF COLOR PATTERN | RELATIVE PLANT SIZE | | |
|---|---|---|---|
| | SMALL | MEDIUM | LARGE |
| Golden / Green | | H. 'Daybreak' | H. 'Sum and Substance' |
| | | | H. 'Royal Standard' |
| Green and Gold | H. 'Golden Tiara' | H. 'Great Expectations'<br>H. fortunei 'Gold Standard'<br>H. 'June'<br>H. 'Sagae'<br>H. Sieboldiana 'Francis Williams' | H. montana 'Aureo-Marginata'<br>H. 'Guacamole'<br>H. 'Wide Brim' |
| Green and White | H. 'Allan P. McConnell'<br>H. 'Cherry Berry'<br>H. 'Diamond Tiara' | H. 'Antioch'<br>H. fortunii 'Moerheim'<br>H. 'Fire and Ice'<br>H. 'Francee'<br>H. 'Fragrant Bouquet'<br>H. 'Patriot'<br>H. 'Summer Frangrance'<br>H. undulata 'Albo-marginata' | H. 'Crowned Imperial'<br>H. 'Frosted Jade' |
| Blue | | H. 'Halcyon' | H. 'Blue Angel'<br>H. 'Krossa Regal'<br>H. sieboldiana 'Elegans' |

Hosta Chart

*GROUND COVERS*

G R O U N D   C O V E R S

## Hosta 'Allan P. McConnell' (<u>hos</u>-ta)
('Allan P. McConnell' Hosta)...........................................Zone 4

8"; light to dense shade. A smaller hosta, 'Allan P. McConnell' is superb for edging, small- and moderate-scale general ground cover use, and companion planting. Flowering mid summer with attractive deep lavender trumpets, it is a charming selection that has a home in every landscape.
Rec. Size: #1 pot (8/flat)   Space: (12"-16")

## Hosta 'Blue Angel' (<u>hos</u>-ta)
('Blue Angel' Hosta)...........................................Zone 4

2' tall by 3' wide; light to dense shade. 'Blue Angel' is, in a word, breathtaking. It is a big, bold, blue, highly prized hosta. Some have proclaimed it the largest of the blue hostas (reaching 3 feet tall and 6 feet wide in very rich soil), and whether or not that is true, it has a big presence. During summer, it blooms with near-white, hummingbird attracting trumpets upon stalks that reach 4 feet tall. The effect is superb, yet if it never flowered, that would be ok too. That's because its soft blue, heart shaped leaves are so soft and pleasing, and lend such a lush, tropical, rich feel to the landscape, that as a foliage plant, 'Blue Angel' can stand on its own.
Rec. Size: #1 pot (8/flat)   Space: (2 1/2'-3')

## Hosta 'Cherry Berry' (<u>hos</u>-ta)
('Cherry Berry' Hosta)...........................................Zone 4

10" foliage height, 26" in bloom; light to moderate shade. Bred by Bill and Eleanor Lachman, this is one of the most intriguing hostas ever introduced. 'Cherry Berry' displays durable lance shaped leaves with yellowish white centers and deep green, irregular margins. This feature alone is attractive, yet, during summer, 'Cherry Berry' really sets itself apart. This is when it projects upward with deep reddish purple, snakeskin patterned flowerstalks. The flowerstalks (scapes) are so intensely colored that they become a focal point, and at night when lighted by landscape lighting or illuminated by car lights, they stand out even more. Atop the flowerstalks are carried many violet flowers which give rise to rich cherry red seed pods, hence the name 'Cherry Berry'.
Rec. Size: #1 pot (8/flat)   Space: (12"-16")

## Hosta 'Crowned Imperial' (<u>hos</u>-ta)
('Crowned Imperial' Hosta)...........................................Zone 3

1 1/2'-2' foliage height, 40" in bloom; light to moderate shade. With stately gray-green leaves edged in creamy white, this fast grower is exceptional for covering moderate and large areas as an economical ground cover. Not only is it attractive in foliage, but during summer it is decorated with pale lavender flowers. Naturally, it combines well with other hostas and cultivars of astilbe, but it is a good companion to ferns, Japanese forest grass, sedges, and clump forming perennial ground covers.
Rec. Size: #1 pot (8/flat)   Space: (2 1/2'-3')

## Hosta 'Daybreak' (<u>hos</u>-ta)
('Daybreak' Hosta)...........................................Zone 4

1 1/2'-2' tall, by up to 4'-5' wide; Light to moderate shade. This superb Paul Aden hybrid is likely the very brightest, most brilliant iridescent golden yellow of all hostas. 'Daybreak' is like a beacon in the landscape jumping out of shady settings and commanding attention. In addition to being an exceptional foliage plant, it is a fine bloomer as well. During mid to late summer is when it displays its complimentary lavender colored, fragrant flowers upon 30" scapes, well above the foliage. 'Daybreak' is also one of the very best of the ground covering hostas, and when planted in broad sweeping borders, it is magnificent.
Rec. Size: #1 pot (8/flat)   Space: (2'-2 1/2')

## Hosta 'Diamond Tiara' (<u>hos</u>-ta)
('Diamond Tiara' Hosta)...........................................Zone 4

12" tall by 20" wide; light to moderate shade. 'Diamond Tiara' is a splendid selection originating from the very popular 'Golden Tiara'. It differs in predictable fashion, having its green centered leaves edged in vibrant white. Otherwise it has the same desirable characteristics as 'Golden Tiara': robust clump forming habit, good foliar substance, superb ability to cover the ground and edge pathways, and attractive pale purple, hummingbird attracting flowers borne mid summer upon scapes to 30 inches.
Rec. Size: #1 pot (8/flat)   Space: (14"-18")

## Hosta 'Fire and Ice' (hos-ta)
('Fire and Ice' Hosta) ..................................................Zone 4

1 1/2' tall by 2 1/2' wide; light to dense shade. 'Fire and Ice', which arose from 'Patriot', is a fabulous mid-sized hosta with rugged, heart shaped, white centered leaves edged with broad deep green. During mid summer it is further decorated by soft pinkish lavender flowers carried upon purplish tinged leaf-stalks. 'Fire and Ice' shows up nicely in the landscape, due to the intensity of its colors, and is a superb edging plant as well as a plant for large scale massing. Naturally it combines well with ferns, ajuga, Waldsteinia, Heuchera selections, black mondo grass, and Tiarella selections.
Rec. Size: #1 pot (8/flat)    Space: (2'- 2 1/2')

## Hosta fortunei 'Gold Standard' (hos-ta   fore-too-nee-eye)
('Gold Standard' Hosta)..................................................Zone 4

2' tall by 2 1/2' wide; light to dense shade. The recipient of various American Hosta Society awards, this popular selection is unique for its 7 inch long, 5 inch wide springborne leaves that emerge light green with narrow dark green edges before turning chartreuse centered by mid summer — brightest if located to receive morning sun. 'Gold Standard' is an impressive selection for use as a specimen, accent plant, or large scale ground cover. By all accounts it is a superb foliage plant, and during mid to late summer it bears numerous lavender flowers atop the foliar mass.
Rec. Size: #1 pot (8/flat)    Space: (2 1/2'- 3')

## Hosta fortunei 'Moerheim' (hos-ta   fore-too-nee-eye)
('Moerheim' Hosta) ..................................................Zone 4

1 1/2' tall by 2'wide; light to moderate shade. A very pleasing medium sized hosta, 'Moerheim' displays silver margined, dark green-centered, heart shaped foliage. Slightly puckered in texture and rippled about their edges, the leaves of 'Moerheim' are among the finest and contrast nicely with its attractive violet summerborne flowers.
Rec. Size: #1 pot (8/flat)    Space: (1 1/2")

GROUND COVERS

A lot of people think pachysandra is the best ground cover for low maintenance and overall effectiveness, but why not jazz it up a bit with some specimens of **Hosta 'Krossa Regal'?**

**G R O U N D   C O V E R S**

## Hosta 'Fragrant Blue' (<u>hos</u>-ta)
('Fragrant Blue' Hosta)........................................................Zone 4

**Blooming Time**
J F M A M J **J A** S O N D
Winter   Spring   Summer   Fall

18" tall by 3 1/2' wide; light to moderate shade. Bred by Paul Aden, 'Fragrant Blue' hosta is one of the very finest hostas for its pleasing, frosty iridescent blue foliage. It is this feature, its fabulous foliage, that makes 'Fragrant Blue' such an easy companion to bergenia, bleeding heart, other hostas, ferns, sedges, Heucheras, Tiarellas, and Allegheny pachysandra. But, its flowers should not be overlooked. Blooming during mid to late summer, 'Fragrant Blue' bears numerous nearly white, pleasantly fragrant flowers upon 3 foot upright stems. 'Fragrant Blue' hosta makes a good small or moderate scale ground cover, edging, or accent plant.
Rec. Size: #1 pot (8/flat)     Space: (2 1/2'-3')

## Hosta 'Fragrant Bouquet' (<u>hos</u>-ta)
('Fragrant Bouquet' Hosta).............................................Zone 4

**Blooming Time**
J F M A M J **J A S** O N D
Winter   Spring   Summer   Fall

22" tall by 4' wide; light to moderate shade. Another great Paul Aden introduction, 'Fragrant Bouquet' is well known and popular. That's because it's a strong grower that matures quickly to form an attractive display of yellow-white margined, apple-green centered foliage. Fantastic when used on a moderate to large scale as a general ground cover, 'Fragrant Bouquet' is also a great companion plant, accent, or pathway edger. It blooms during late summer with soft pale lavender, super-fragrant, trumpet shaped flowers that measure 3 inches in length. Carried well above the foliage, the flowers are a very pleasing sight so late in the season.
Rec. Size: #1 pot (8/flat)     Space: (2 1/2'-3')

## Hosta 'Francee' (<u>hos</u>-ta)
('Francee' Hosta)..............................................................Zone 4

**Blooming Time**
J F M A M J **J** A S O N D
Winter   Spring   Summer   Fall

2' high, 2 1/2'+ wide; full sun to dense shade. This vigorous grower has large, heart-shaped, forest-green foliage with very narrow, pure white margins. The variegation holds up exceptionally well in full sun. Each leaf is 5 inches wide by 6 inches long and collectively they make a lovely backdrop to the lavender flowers that are borne atop 30 inch scapes in midsummer.
Rec. Size: #1 pot (8/flat)     Space: (2'-2 1/2')

## Hosta 'Frosted Jade' (<u>hos</u>-ta)
('Frosted Jade' hosta).......................................................Zone 4

**Blooming Time**
J F M A M J **J A** S O N D
Winter   Spring   Summer   Fall

2'-2 1/2' tall by 4'+ wide; light to moderate shade. 'Frosted Jade' is an exceptionally fine large mound forming selection with huge 14" long, 10" wide, distinctively pure-white margined, rich green centered foliage. The white margins are unique in that they often turn upward in a rippling effect which creates a unique attractive and unmistakable feature. During mid summer 'Frosted Jade' is further decorated with soft lavender, 2 1/2" long, fragrant, trumpet shaped flowers upon 2'-2 1/2' long scapes.
Rec. Size: #1 pot (8/flat)     Space: (3'-3 1/2')

## Hosta 'Golden Tiara' (<u>hos</u>-ta)
('Golden Tiara' Hosta)......................................................Zone 4

**Blooming Time**
J F M A M J **J A** S O N D
Winter   Spring   Summer   Fall

12" tall by 2' wide; light to dense shade. Displaying medium lavender summer-borne flowers above chartreuse-edged, medium green, round-shaped leaves, 'Golden Tiara' is a charming selection for edging, accent, or ground cover applications.
Rec. Size: #1 pot (8/flat)     Space: (14"-18")

**A garden of hostas is pleasing to the eye and easy on the back.**

## Hosta 'Great Expectations' (<u>hos</u>-ta)
('Great Expectations' Hosta)............................Zone 4

12" tall by 2' wide; light to moderate shade. Very popular, 'Great Expectations' is a well known mid-sized hosta with superb heart-shaped, rich blue green, irregularly-edged, creamy yellow centered, puckered foliage of superior substance. Blooming during summer with white, hummingbird attracting tubular flowers, 'Great Expectations' is relatively slow to spread, but is so fine that any expense or wait (for it to mature) is well justified.
Rec. Size: #1 pot (8/flat)    Space: (2'-2 1/2')

## Hosta 'Guacamole' (<u>hos</u>-ta)
('Guacamole' Hosta)............................Zone 4

1 1/2' tall by 2 1/2' wide; light to moderate shade. Originating as a sport of 'Fragrant Bouquet', this marvelous selection is easily distinguished from other hostas. Its chartreuse leaves are painted with swirls of avocado green, making for a unique foliar look. Then, during summer, 'Guacamole' sends up numerous stout stems, each bearing large, fragrant white flowers.
Rec. Size: #1 pot (8/flat)    Space: (2 1/2'-3')

## Hosta 'Halcyon' (<u>hos</u>-ta)
('Halcyon' Hosta)............................Zone 3

1 1/4' tall by 2 1/2'+ wide; light to dense shade. A superb foliage plant, this extraordinary selection displays deep blue, heavily ribbed, thick substanced, spear shaped foliage. Its soft lavender flowers are borne slightly above the foliage during summer upon compact stalks.
Rec. Size: #1 pot (8/flat)    Space: (24"-30")

## Hosta 'June' (<u>hos</u>-ta)
('June' Hosta)............................Zone 4

15" tall by 1 1/2' wide; light to moderate shade. The 2001 Hosta Society Growers Hosta of the Year, 'June', a sport of 'Halcyon', is a standout that is liked by all. Its golden centered leaves are attractively edged in blue green—with gentle brush strokes radiating toward the leaf base. Of heavy substance, the leaves resist slugs and hold their color and character through the season. 'June' blooms midsummer with lavender to violet, hummingbird attracting trumpets carried well above the foliage.
Rec. Size: #1 pot (8/flat)    Space: (1 1/2'-2')

## Hosta 'Krossa Regal' (<u>hos</u>-ta)
('Krossa Regal' Hosta)............................Zone 4

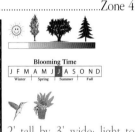

2' tall by 3' wide; light to dense shade. Relatively tall and upright growing, the frosty blue-green, wavy-edged, heart-shaped leaves of 'Krossa Regal' are oriented in such manner as to create a neat vase-shape. 'Krossa Regal' is a wonderful selection for accent and companion planting. Yet, when mass planted as a ground cover it has a unique way of brightening the landscape with its iridescent quality. Fragrant white trumpets appear during midsummer. Recipient of the American Hosta Society's Eunice Fisher Award.
Rec. Size: #1 pot (8/flat)    Space: (2 1/2'-3')
Rec. Size: 2 gal.    Space: (2 1/2'-3')

## Hosta montana 'Aureomarginata' (<u>hos</u>-ta   mon-<u>tan</u>-a)
('Aureomarginata' Mountain Hosta)............................Zone 4

2' tall by 3' wide; light to moderate shade. Slow to propagate, and thus expensive, this is a superb selection with extraordinary foliage and habit. 'Aureomarginata' is a large hosta with impressive, arching, wedge shaped green leaves with bright, irregular margins of yellow that turn creamy yellow as the season progresses. It is a hosta that makes a dramatic specimen or accent plant, and during mid-summer bears pale lavender flowers.
Rec. Size: #1 pot (8/flat)    Space: (3')

**GROUND COVERS**

G R O U N D   C O V E R S

## Hosta 'On Stage' (<u>hos</u>-ta   mon-<u>tan</u>-a)
('On Stage' Hosta)................................................Zone 4

14"-18"; by 3' wide; light to moderate shade. 'On Stage' is one of the very most spectacular hostas ever bred. Not surprisingly, it was bred by Paul Aden. Attractively layered, the magnificent foliage of 'On Stage' is lustrous golden yellow centered and edged with a jagged margin of deep green—often with streaks penetrating through the center all the way to the midrib. 'On Stage' blooms at a height of 2 feet with pale lavender trumpets during summer, and is a great choice for along a shady pathway or patio edge.
Rec. Size: #1 pot (8/flat)    Space: (2 1/2'-3')

## Hosta 'Patriot' (<u>hos</u>-ta)
('Patriot' Hosta)..............................................Zone 4

1 1/2' tall by 2'+ wide; light to moderate shade. The variegation pattern of 'Patriot', with its rich green centers surrounded by unusually broad, snow white margins is so distinct as to be easily distinguished from other white edged hostas. This is no small feat in a world of over 4,000 named selections, many with green centered, white margined leaves. 'Patriot' is not only a striking foliage plant, but gives a nice display of lavender midsummer flowers, and functions beautifully for edging, accent, or broad scale ground cover use.
Rec. Size: #1 pot (8/flat)    Space: (1 1/2')

## Hosta plantaginea 'Grandiflora' (<u>hos</u>-ta   plan-ta-<u>jin</u>-ee-a)
(Large Flowered Fragrant Hosta) ..................Zone 4

1 1/2' tall by 3' wide; light to moderate shade. With shiny soft green leaves, this is a splendid ground cover and an easy companion to other hostas, sedges, Heucheras, Tiarellas, and various ferns. More importantly, it bears what many consider to be the most valuable flowers of any hosta. These are not only huge, ivory white, and reminiscent of Easter lilies, but exude an exquisite perfumelike fragrance. The flowers come late in the season and their marvelous fragrance favors planting along pathways and walk ways, building entrances and patios, and in sweeping ground cover beds on the windward side of where people will be sitting or walking by.
Rec. Size: #1 pot (8/flat)    Space: (2'-2 1/2')

## Hosta 'Regal Splendor' (<u>hos</u>-ta)
('Regal Splendor' Hosta)...............................Zone 4

3' tall by 3' wide; light to moderate shade. Originating at Walters Gardens as a sport of 'Krossa Regal', 'Regal Splendor' displays the same exceptional upright vase shaped habit and frosty blue foliage, but this time with the leaves rimmed in creamy yellow. Its midsummerborne lavender flowers are nice also, and like 'Krossa Regal', are carried high above the foliage on scapes that reach 5 to 6 feet tall. 'Regal Splendor' makes a stately specimen or accent plant and is exceptional for edging or ground cover use. Its foliage is bright enough to lighten up shady areas and its vigor sufficient to compete with tight knit ground covers like pachysandra, myrtle, and English ivy—all of which are good companions to 'Regal Splendor'
Rec. Size: #1 pot (8/flat)    Space: (2 1/2'-3')

## Hosta 'Royal Standard' (<u>hos</u>-ta)
('Royal Standard' Hosta)................................Zone 4

2' tall by 3' wide; light to dense shade. A dependable classic with large medium-green leaves, 'Royal Standard' is relatively sun tolerant and will do quite well with 3 or 4 hours of full sun each day. Above its foliage, during late summer, 'Royal Standard' carries its perfume scented white flowers upon 36 inch tall scapes.
Rec. Size: #1 pot (8/flat)    Space: (2 1/2'-3')

## Hosta 'Sagae' (<u>hos</u>-ta) (formerly H. fluctuans 'Variegata')
('Sagae' Hosta)..............................................Zone 4

1 1/2'-2' tall by 3' wide; light to moderate shade. An exceptional selection with a reputation for being tough, drought resistant, and very colorful, 'Sagae' bears wavy edged, frosted green leaves with darkened veining and edges of creamy gold. Of heavy substance, the leaves are carried in upright fashion, collectively forming a neat compact plant with vase shaped habit. Above them on 36 inch scapes, are borne numerous pale lavender summertime flowers. 2000 American Hosta Growers, Hosta of the Year.
Rec. Size: #1 pot (8/flat)    Space: (2'-2 1/2')

## Hosta sieboldiana 'Elegans' (<u>hos</u>-ta   see-bold-ee-<u>aye</u>-na)
('Elegans' Hosta)............................................................Zone 3

2 1/2' tall by 4+ feet across; light to dense shade. With very large, deep blue green, thick substanced, prominently veined leaves, 'Elegans' is one of the most popular and time proven selections (cultivated for more than 75 years). Its mid-summerborne flowers of pale white are carried upon 30 inch scapes and are occasionally obscured by the foliage. In the landscape it combines well with tall ferns, and due to its robust stature it is especially effective as a background plant combined with other hosta selections.
Rec. Size: #1 pot (8/flat)   Space: (2 1/2'-3')

## Hosta sieboldiana 'Francis Williams' (<u>hos</u>-ta   see-bold-ee-<u>aye</u>-na)
('Francis Williams' Hosta)............................................Zone 4

1 1/2' tall by 3'+ wide; light to moderate shade. A true classic, 'Francis Williams' originated as a sport of 'Elegans', was introduced in 1986, and remains one of the very best, and most popular. This is for good reason; 'Francis Williams' is large and imposing. Its massive blue green corrugated leaves are encircled with a wide edge of rich sulphur yellow. Then, during early summer, a nice display of pure white flowers adds even more interest.
Rec. Size: #1 pot (8/flat)   Space: (3'-3 1/2')

## Hosta sieboldiana 'Northern Exposure' (<u>hos</u>-ta)
('Northern Exposure' Hosta)........................................Zone 4

2 1/2' tall by 5' wide; light to moderate shade. 'Northern Exposure' is one of the most impressive of all variegated plants. Its superb foliage, which reaches up to 13 inches long and 10 inches wide is heavily corrugated and of heavy substance, making it relatively slug resistant. Colored deep blue green in their centers, the leaves are rimmed with broad margins of white. This contrast in colors is sharp, visible from a long distance, and contributes to 'Northern Exposure's usefulness as a large scale ground cover and specimen plant. Carried in dense clusters upon 3 foot tall scapes, its flowers are near white and softly fragrant.
Rec. Size: #1 pot (8/flat)   Space: (4'-5')

## Hosta 'Striptease' (<u>hos</u>-ta)
('Striptease' Hosta)........................................................Zone 4

1 1/2' tall by 2' wide; light to moderate shade. A sport of 'Gold Standard', this selection displays a variegation pattern unlike any other. Each deep green narrowly heart shaped leaf is centered with a narrow strip of gold, and each gold center is bordered with <u>strips</u> of milky white—hence the name 'Striptease'. Still considered a "collector's" hosta, 'Striptease' is currently available in commercial quantities which makes the price reasonable. It blooms with violet trumpet shaped flowers during mid to late summer. Like all hostas, this one becomes better with age.
Rec. Size: #1 pot (8/flat)   Space: (2 1/2'-3')

## Hosta 'Sum and Substance' (<u>hos</u>-ta)
('Sum and Substance' Hosta)........................................Zone 4

1 1/2' tall by 3' wide; light to moderate shade. Likely the most recognizable of the golden hostas, 'Sum and Substance' hasn't been around all that long, yet bears 'classic' status among foliage plants. It is a hosta one never tires of seeing and always projects a stately character. Its rich golden-chartreuse, light reflecting foliage is heart-shaped, sometimes a bit puckered (especially as the plants mature) and extraordinary in its width. 'Sum and Substance' shows good slug resistance and bears many light lavender flowers on arching scapes during the summer months.
Rec. Size: #1 pot (8/flat)   Space: (2 1/2'-3')

## Hosta 'Summer Fragrance' (<u>hos</u>-ta)
('Summer Fragrance' Hosta)..........................................Zone 4

1 1/2' tall by 2 1/2' wide; full sun to dense shade. With robust habit and lovely long stalked, ovate, white margined, lime green centered leaves (shiny on the underside), this is an exceptional foliage plant. As a ground cover it is superb on a moderate to large scale for commercial and residential planting. It holds its color exceptionally well in sun or shade and bears fragrant, purple veined, violet, trumpet-shaped flowers during late summer and fall.
Rec. Size: #1 pot (8/flat)   Space: (2'-3')

GROUND COVERS

## Hosta 'Touch of Class' (<u>hos</u>-ta)
('Touch of Class' Hosta) ..................................................Zone 4

12" tall by 2' wide; light to moderate shade. Developed at Shady Oaks Nursery by Hans Hansen, this is the tetraploid version (double the normal chromosome count) of Hosta 'June'. Characterized by doubly thick, slug resistant, chartreuse-centered, extra wide, iridescent-blue margined leaves, 'Touch of Class' provides a dramatic effect in the landscape. It is great for edging, accent, and specimen use. Flowering midsummer atop 2 foot scapes, it makes a nice show of soft lavender flowers. Suggested companions include Hosta 'Daybreak', golden leaved Japanese forest grass, Imperata 'Red Baron', mid sized ferns, and brightly colored sedges such as Carex 'Evergold', 'Bowles Golden', and 'Goldband'.
Rec. Size: #1 pot (8/flat)    Space: (2 1/2'-3')

## Hosta undulata 'Albo-marginata' (<u>hos</u>-ta   un-dew-<u>lay</u>-ta)
(White Edge Wavy Leaved Hosta) ...........................Zone 3

12 inches tall, 14 to 18 inches across; light to dense shade. Vigorous growing with wavy creamy-white edged, green centered leaves, 'Albo-marginata' is a popular selection. During summer it blooms with 2 inch long, light lilac, tube-shaped flowers atop 2 to 3 feet tall slightly arching stalks.
Rec. Size: #1 pot (8/flat)    Space: (12"-16")

## Hosta 'Wide Brim' (<u>hos</u>-ta)
('Wide Brim' Hosta) ...........................................Zone 4

2' tall by 3' wide; light to moderate shade. 'Wide Brim' is an excellent large hosta with heart shaped, medium green leaves surrounded with broad irregular yellow margins that mature to creamy white. Heavy of substance, its leaves have a somewhat puckered quality that make this a unique and popular selection. Above the foliage, during summer, are borne lovely white trumpetlike flowers.
Rec. Size: #1 pot (8/flat)    Space: (2 1/2' - 3')

## Houttuynia cordata 'Variegata' (hoo-toe-<u>in</u>-ee-a   kore-<u>day</u>-ta)
(Chameleon Houttuynia) ...........................................Zone 5

6"-8"; full sun to light shade. This uncommon Japanese plant rates as one of the most unusual ground covers. Citrus scented, its variegated foliage contains hues of cream, green, purple, and gold and although blooming during June with tiny creamy white spikes, its flowers are secondary to the foliage. Chameleon houttuynia spreads at a moderate rate by rhizomes, and tolerates saturated soils. Often it is planted at pondside, or in containers placed directly in the water.
Rec. Size: #1 pot (8/flat)    Space: (10"-12")

**Iris cristata, Crested Iris,** is a dynamite little ground cover in and out of bloom.

G R O U N D   C O V E R S

**Hypericum androsaemum 'Albury Purple' (hye-pare-i-kum am-dros-a-mum)**
('Albury Purple' St. John's-wort)............................................Zone 5/6

1 1/2'-2' tall; full sun to moderate shade. 'Albury Purple' is perfectly hardy in Zone 6 and very likely hardy in Zone 5, but may benefit from a fall mulching in Zone 5 for added protection. Whatever you do, it is well worth the effort. 'Albury Purple' is an exceptionally decorative St. John's-wort with attractive purple leaves, bright yellow flowers during late spring, and green fruit that changes to red and then glowing mahogany by late summer. 'Albury Purple' is good for accent and is especially effective when used in moderate to large scale drifts as an edging or backdrop ground cover.
Rec. Size: 1 gal    Space: (1 1/2'-2')

# Hosta 'Frosted Jade' and 'On Stage' represent two of the classiest richest looking plants ever developed.

**Hypericum patulum 'Hidcote' (hye-pare-i-kum pat-tyew-lum)**
(Golden Cup St. John's-wort)............................................Zone 5

1 1/2'-3'; full sun to light shade. The most reliable bloomer among the low growing Midwest-hardy St. John's-worts, the 2"-3" wide, golden yellow summertime flowers of 'Hidcote' are particularly attractive against the backdrop of neat, gray-green, semievergreen leaves. 'Hidcote' is a dependable, deliberate spreading, moderate to large scale erosion controller that combines well with tight growing or open canopied trees such as honeylocust and Bradford pear.
Rec. Size: 1 gal    Space: (2'-2 1/2')

**Iberis sempervirens 'Snowflake' (eye-bee-ris sem-per-vie-rens)**
('Snowflake' Candytuft) ............................................Zone 5

8"-12"; full sun. Trouble free and requiring no maintenance, this slow spreading, mound forming evergreen beauty is an excellent addition to any sunny landscape—especially nice for edging or trailing over retaining walls or the sides of planters. Useful for edging, accent, or specimen planting, 'Snowflake' candytuft flowers profusely during mid spring with large, pure white, fragrant clusters.
Rec. Size: #1 pot (8/flat)    Space: (12"-18")

**Iris cristata (eye-ris kris-tay-ta)**
(Crested Iris) NATIVE SPECIES............................................Zone 3

6"; light to moderate shade. A true dwarf, crested iris is one of the most charming native ground covers. Although its height seldom exceeds 7 inches, it slowly spreads, and in time forms lush dense mats. Colored medium green, its sword shaped foliage is the perfect backdrop to a multitude of springtime flowers. The flowers, colored soft lilac, with white or yellow crests on the petals, are pleasantly fragrant and rather spectacular. Crested iris is excellent as a small scale general cover and combines nicely with dwarf hostas, variegated Japanese iris, sedges, and bergenia.
Rec. Size: 3 1/4" pot (18/flat)    Space: (6"-10")

G R O U N D   C O V E R S

## Iris ensata 'Henry's White' (<u>eye</u>-ris   en-<u>say</u>-ta)
('Henry's White' Japanese Iris)..................................Zone 4

2'-2 1/2'; full sun to light shade. A lovely selection of Japanese iris, 'Henry's White' is adorned with large, vibrant snow white, summerborne flowers. It also features neat medium green, sword shaped foliage and is a strong performer in about any soil, including moist conditions.
Rec. Size: #1 pot (8/flat)   Space: (12"-18")

## Iris ensata 'Variegata' (<u>eye</u>-ris   en-<u>say</u>-ta)
(Variegated Japanese Iris)..................................Zone 4

1 1/2'-2' tall; full sun to light shade. Like other variegated irises, this one displays lovely white and green striped foliage. It differs, however, in that its leaves remain brightly colored throughout the growing season and do not fade to green over time. This along with lovely purplish early summertime flowers and resistance to iris borer helps to make it an exceptional garden plant. Grow variegated Japanese iris alone or in small groups for accent or specimen use, and in larger groups as a colorful ground cover.
Rec. Size: #1 pot (8/flat)   Space: (14"-18")

## Iris pseudacorus 'Flore Pleno' (<u>eye</u>-ris   pseud-<u>a</u>-koe-ris)
(Double Flowered Yellow Flag Iris)..................................Zone 4

2 1/2'-4'; full sun to moderate shade. This incredible selection is the double flowered form of I. pseudacorus. It is very similar in appearance, same height, flowers look about the same—only difference is it blooms for a much longer period of time (not ceasing with pollination as pollination does not occur for it is sterile). From Europe, double flowered yellow flag is reliable, attractive, and tolerant of saturated soils. It may be used in ditches and along stream and pond banks for erosion control, and early through mid summer makes a nice display of bright yellow, brown veined flowers.
Rec. Size: #1 pot (8/flat)   Space: (1 1/2'-2')

## Iris pseudacorus 'Variegatus' (<u>eye</u>-ris   pseud-<u>a</u>-koe-ris)
(Variegated Yellow Flag Iris)..................................Zone 4

1 1/2'-2' full sun to moderate shade. Named for its appearance which closely resembles the genus Acorus (literally translated false-Acorus), the foliage of variegated yellow flag iris is attractively striped yellow and green. Excellent for planting near streams and ponds, as well as ordinary garden sites, variegated yellow flag, like the parent species, is tough and versatile. And, in addition to its colorful foliage, it bears attractive yellow flowers during early summer.
Rec. Size: #1 pot (8/flat)   Space: (1 1/2'-2')

## Iris siberica 'Ceasar's Brother' (<u>eye</u>-ris   si-<u>bir</u>-i-ka)
('Ceasar's Brother' Siberian Iris)..................................Zone 3

2 1/2'-3'; full sun to light shade. Spring blooming with dark, velvety, violet-blue flowers above narrow, lance shaped, medium green foliage, 'Ceasar's Brother' is a classic selection of Siberian Iris. Versatile in the landscape, 'Ceasar's Brother' grows well in boggy soil as well as normal garden soils (provided the soil is maintained moderately moist). It can be effectively massed as a ground cover and is an effective companion to other cultivars of iris, purple Petasites, hostas, and variegated Soloman's Seal.
Rec. Size: #1 pot (8/flat)   Space: (12"-18")

## Iris siberica 'Sparkling Rose'
('Sparkling Rose' Siberian Iris)..................................Zone 3

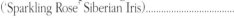

2'-2 1/2'; full sun to light shade. 'Sparkling Rose' exhibits strong vertical growth with soft bluish gray green, sword shaped foliage. Yet, it is the rich lavender-rose flowers that have a blue flush around the yellow base which draw attention to this fine Siberian iris selection. 'Sparkling Rose' brings a welcome burst of color to the spring landscape and is a good companion to other Siberian irises as well as a host of other ground covers, perennials, and ornamental grasses.
Rec. Size: #1 pot (8/flat)   Space: (12"-18")

## Iris verna (eye-ris  ver-na)
(Spring Iris) NATIVE SPECIES.........................................Zone 5

Blooming Time
J F M **A M** J J A S O N D
Winter   Spring   Summer   Fall

8"-12"; light to moderate shade. Also referred to as dwarf iris or slender blue-flag, Iris verna is a rare but lovely native species with colonizing growth habit. Colored bluish green, often with streaks of purple at their bases, the sword shaped, vertically oriented leaves are carried atop short creeping stems. During spring, violet-blue, orange-blotched, 1 1/2 inch wide flowers are borne in good quantity. Spring iris makes a good small scale ground cover, edging, or accent plant. It is a good companion to ferns, hostas, bergenia, Dicentra, and various sedges.
Rec. Size: 3 1/4" (18/flat)   Space: (6"-10")

## Iris versicolor 'Gerald Darby' (eye-ris  ver-si-ko-lor)
('Gerald Darby' Multicolored Iris) NATIVE CULTIVAR.................Zone 3

Blooming Time
J F M A M **J J** A S O N D
Winter   Spring   Summer   Fall

2 1/2'-3'; full sun to moderate shade. The common name multicolored iris actually refers to the multicolored flowers of the lovely native species Iris versicolor. In the case of this unusual selection, one might conclude that multicolor refers to the foliage--the most outstanding feature of this extraordinary plant. Emerging deep dark purple during spring, the neat sword shaped leaves of 'Gerald Darby' change to a fabulous mixture of green and purple by mid June, and by midsummer change to soft blue green. While the leaves are in the multicolored stage, 'Gerald Darby' begins to bloom and bears a good quantity of large deep purple-blue, yellow/white centered flowers.
Rec. Size: #1 pot (8/flat)   Space: (1 1/2'-2')

## Iris virginica (eye-ris  vir-jin-i-ka)
(Blue Flag Iris) NATIVE SPECIES..................................Zone 4

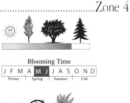

Blooming Time
J F M A **M** J J A S O N D
Winter   Spring   Summer   Fall

2'-3'; full sun to moderate shade. A lovely native iris, the blue flag is sturdy and florific. Its best uses are for accent or as ground cover in moist ditches and along the banks of ponds and streams. Flowering during late spring, the numerous blossoms of blue flag serve as stately testament to the coming warmth of summer.
Rec. Size: #1 pot (8/flat)   Space: (1 1/2'-2')

## Isotoma fluviatilis (ice-oh-toe-ma  flew-vee-at-i-lis) a.k.a. Laurentia fluviatilis or Pratia pedunculata.
(Blue-star Creeper) best in SLIGHTLY moist soil, especially during winter ..............................................Zone 5/6

Blooming Time
J F M **A M J J A S O N** D
Winter   Spring   Summer   Fall

1"-2", full sun to moderate shade. We found our plants at a nursery in Zone 5, and have grown them without too much winter stress in Zone 6. Further, we have talked to many people who have been successfully growing it in Zone 5. So, by all means try this plant. It is one of the most amazing "foot friendly" creeping/carpeting, stepping-stone-filling ground covers on the market. It is attractive for its cheerful green evergreen foliage, but what's truly amazing about blue-star creeper is that it never seems to quit blooming. Late summer to fall, it is adorned with a multitude of lilac petaled, deep-purple-veined, yellow centered flowers.
Rec. Size: #1 pot (8/flat)   Space: (10"-14")

## Kalimeris pinnatifida var. hortensis (kal-e-meer-is  pin-a-tif-i-da)
(Double Flowered Japanese Aster) ................................Zone 4

Blooming Time
J F M A M J **J A S** O N D
Winter   Spring   Summer   Fall

2 1/2'-3', full sun to moderate shade. In his book Armitage's Garden Perennials, Allan Armitage says that Kalimeris pinnatifida is a "No Brainer". I would translate this to mean that it grows in a broad range of conditions, is sturdy and disease resistant, and looks terrific in and out of bloom. In other words, it is an absolutely fantastic ground cover. Clothed in vibrant green foliage, it begins to bloom midsummer and from then until frost bears a nonstop succession of yellow centered, double white fringed flowers. Kalimeris is exceptional when mass planted or used as a dwarf hedge and it combines perfectly with asters, Boltonia, Campanulas, coreopsis, Echinacea, Eupatorium, Euphorbia, Geraniums, Hemerocallis, Heuchera, Lavandula, Liatris, Monarda, Nepeta, Origanum, Perovskia, Salvias, Saponaria, Scabiosa, sedums, Solidago, and many ornamental grasses.
Rec. Size: #1 pot (8/flat)   Space: (2'-2 1/2')

**Kalimeris yomena 'Shogun' (kal-e-meer-is yoe-meen-a)**
('Shogun' Japanese Aster)......Zone 4

14"-24"; full sun to light shade. 'Shogun' is a magnificently colorful selection of Japanese aster that brightens up the spring garden with its early emerging, bright yellow edged, deep green centered foliage. It remains a compact 14 inches tall throughout summer and retains its vibrant leaf colors even during the hottest weather. By late summer it sends up flowering shoots which become laden with large quantities of rose-purple petaled, yellow centered, daisylike flowers. 'Shogun' is a great selection for accent and specimen use, but is even better when used on a moderate to large scale as a general cover—especially in broad sweeping drifts and along high traffic areas. It is fabulous in combination with ornamental grasses like Calamagrostis 'Karl Foerster', and cultivars of Miscanthus and Panicum.
Rec. Size: #1 pot (8/flat) Space: (1 1/2'-2')

**Lamiastrum galeobdolon 'Herman's Pride' (lay-mee-as-trum ga-lee-ob-doe-lon)**
('Herman's Pride' Dead Nettle)......Zone 4

8"-12"; light to dense shade. A colorful clump former, 'Herman's Pride' is distinct for its deep silvery variegation on medium green, tooth edged leaves. Above these, during spring, are borne a multitude of sulfur yellow, highly effective flowers which are carried in leafy upright spikes. 'Herman's Pride' dead nettle is best in a cool shady site, especially with ferns and blue leaved hosta selections.
Rec. Size: #1 pot (8/flat) Space: (8"-12")

**Lamiastrum galeobdolon 'Variegatum' (lay-mee-as-trum gal-lee-ob-doe-lon)**
(Trailing Dead Nettle)......Zone 4

6"-8"; full sun to dense shade. This is a fast spreading herbaceous perennial with creeping, rooting stems. Leaves are deep green, 1 1/2"-2" long and marked with silver variegation. Flowers are yellow and appear in spring.
Rec. Size: 38 cell flat Space: (10"-14")

**Lamium maculatum 'Orchid Frost' (lay-mee-um mak-you-lay-tum)**
('Orchid Frost' Spotted Dead Nettle)......Zone 3

4"-6"; full sun to moderate shade. A lovely, highly florific selection (by Mike Bovio), 'Orchid Frost' introduces a lovely orchid pink flower to this popular species. And not only is 'Orchid Frost' a terrific flowering plant, literally loaded with clusters of mintlike flowers from April to late June and again in fall, it is also extrordinary for its bright silver and soft green variegated foliage. Great in the landscape for edging, accent, or ground cover, 'Orchard Frost' is also great in containers.
Rec. Size: #1 pot (8/flat) Space: (6"-10")

**Lamium maculatum 'Pink Pewter' (lay-mee-um mak-you-lay-tum)**
('Pink Pewter' Spotted Dead Nettle)......Zone 3

4"-5'; full sun (in moist rich soils) to moderate shade. 'Pink Pewter' spotted dead nettle is a lovely slow spreading evergreen ground cover with vibrant silvery centered, green-margined leaves. Excellent for providing brightness in shady settings, the foliage alone makes this a superb additon to the landscape. An added bonus occurs during late spring to midsummer as the luminous mass of foliage is transcended by short spikes of pink mintlike flowers.
Rec. Size: #1 pot (8/flat) Space: (6"-10")

**Lamium maculatum 'Purple Dragon' (lay-mee-um mak-you-lay-tum)**
('Purple Dragon' Spotted Dead Nettle)......Zone 3

6"-8"; full sun to moderate shade. Selected by Chris vanSanden, this exceptionally robust selection produces the largest, deepest purple snapdragon-like flowers of any Lamium. Arranged in larger, denser terminal spikes (of up to 30 flowers per spike), the spring, and fallborne flowers jump right out of the bright silvery foliage. Further decorating each flower is a bright white, V-shaped central marking.
Rec. Size: #1 pot (8/flat) Space: (10"-14")

## Lamium maculatum 'White Nancy' (<u>lay</u>-mee-um mak-<u>you</u>-lay-tum)
('White Nancy' Spotted Dead Nettle)............Zone 3

4"-6"; full sun (in moist rich soil) to moderate shade. With ivory-white, spring and summerborne mintlike flowers above evergreen, silver centered, green-edged leaves, 'White Nancy' is excellent for imparting color and contrast in perennial borders and can be used en masse on a small scale as a turf substitute.
Rec. Size: #1 pot (8/flat)   Space: (6"-10")

## Lavandula angustifolia 'Baby Blue' (la-<u>van</u>-dyu-la an-gus-ti-<u>foe</u>-lee-a)
('Baby Blue' Lavender)............Zone 5

10"-14" tall; full sun to light shade. An exceptional lavender, 'Baby Blue' is compact in habit with soft gray green, highly fragrant, densely set, evergreen foliage. During summer, atop the foliage, are borne dozens of floral spikes each smothered in soft bluish purple flowers.
Rec. Size: #1 pot (8/flat)   Space: (14"-18")

## Lavandula angustifolia 'Jean Davis' (la-<u>van</u>-dyu-la an-gus-ti-<u>foe</u>-lee-a)
('Jean Davis' Lavender)............Zone 5

15"; full sun to light shade. Flowering during summer above gray green foliage, 'Jean Davis' bears a multitude of pale pink flowers. Oriented in upright spikes, the flowers are fantastic for drying and are extremely fragrant. Great companion plants include other lavenders with differing flower colors, salvias, sedums, coreopsis, coneflowers, and Alliums.
Rec. Size: #1 pot (8/flat)   Space: (14"-18")

## Lavandula angustifolia 'Munstead Strain' (la-<u>van</u>-dyu-la an-gus-ti-<u>foe</u>-lee-a)
('Munstead' Lavender)............Zone 5

1'-2 1/2'; full sun to light shade. 'Munstead' lavender is a very popular selection with 3"-4" upright floral summerborne spikes composed of lavender blue flowers above gray-green foliage. It is superb for edging, accent, and companion planting.
Rec. Size: #1 pot (8/flat)   Space: (1'-1 1/2')

## Lavandula x intermedia 'Grosso' (la-<u>van</u>-dyu-la in-ter-<u>mee</u>-de-a)
('Grosso' Lavender)............Zone 5

2'-2 1/2' tall; full sun to light shade. An exceptional lavender, 'Grosso' is robust, uniform in habit, and clothed in soft blue green, highly fragrant, densely set, evergreen foliage. During summer, atop the foliage are borne hundreds of sturdy floral spikes, smothered in attractive purple flowers. Very fragrant and superb for drying, the flowers are attractive to butterflies and provide several weeks of interest in the landscape.
Rec. Size: #1 pot (8/flat)   Space: (2'-2 1/2')

## Lavandula x intermedia 'Provence' (la-<u>van</u>-dyu-la in-ter-<u>mee</u>-de-a)
('Provence' Lavender)............Zone 5

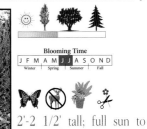

2"; full sun to light shade. Although a larger lavender, 'Provence' displays its attractive exquisitely fragrant blue gray foliage in upright stems of compact habit. Unusually clean and durable for a lavender, 'Provence' is also an exceptional bloomer. Flowering during mid summer, it bears countless upright spikes of light purple florets—upon very long stems. Naturally, it is an easy companion to daylilies, Shasta daisy, tall Phlox, coneflowers, and numerous ornamental grasses. Its flowers are also superb for cutting and for drying.
Rec. Size: #1 pot (8/flat)   Space: (2'-2 1/2')

GROUND COVERS

## Leptinella minor (lep-tin-el-a  mye-nor) (a.k.a. Cotula minor)

(Miniature Brass Buttons)..................................................Zone 5

1/2"-1", full sun to moderate shade. Relatively rare and certainly underused, this tiny creeping ground cover has been very impressive in our trial garden—super dense growth and no melting out problems. A low growing, mosslike evergreen creeper that is very "foot friendly", dwarf Cotula is ideal for tucking in between the cracks of pavers and stepping stones. On a small scale, it would even work as a turf substitute. Its tiny greenish yellow cup-shaped summerborne flowers are little more than a curiosity. But, this is a plant for function and foliar effect. If more color is needed, consider such functional companions as Iris cristata, Ophiopogon 'Nigrescens', Sempervivum cultivars, Sisyrinchium 'Lucerne', sedums, or variegated sedge selections.
Rec. Size: #1 pot (8/flat)   Space: (10"-16")

## Leptinella squalida 'Platt's Black' (lep-tin-el-a  skwol-i-da) (a.k.a. Cotula)

('Platt's Black' Brass Buttons)..................................................Zone 5

1/2"-1", full sun to moderate shade. 'Platt's Black' brass buttons is rare and choice—a real collector's plant. That's how it might have been described in 2003 (the year we began growing it). But, now it is becoming very popular. 'Platt's Black' is fascinating and functional, sure to please, and getting lots of attention. 'Platt's Black' is a tiny horizontal creeper for use around and between stepping stones and pavers. It displays unique, fern-textured, blackish purple, oftimes green-tipped, foot traffic tolerant foliage and tiny yellowish summerborne flowers. Great companions include Iris cristata, Liriope 'Silvery Sunproof', Sempervivum cultivars, Sisyrinchium 'Lucerne', sedums, and variegated sedge selections.
Rec. Size: #1 pot (8/flat)   Space: (6"-10")

## Leucanthemum maximum 'Crazy Daisy' (lew-can-the-mum max-i-mum)

('Crazy Daisy' Shasta Daisy)..................................................Zone 3

1 1/2'-2'; full sun to light shade. 'Crazy Daisy' produces multitudes of white petaled yellow-centered flowers—a high percentage being fully double. Many of these petals are of the quill type, which gives it a rather unique fluffy look. 'Crazy Daisy' blooms during spring and summer, sporadically in fall, and is the type of plant that people take notice of and talk about. Naturally it's a great specimen and accent plant, looks nice enmasse, and is great lining pathways and surrounding patios and other high traffic areas.
Rec. Size: #1 pot (8/flat)   Space: (10"-14")

## Leucanthemum x superbum 'Becky' (lew-can-the-mum sue-per-bum)

('Becky' Shasta Daisy)..................................................Zone 5

3'-3 1/2' tall; full sun to light shade. One of the longest lasting, largest, most upright, and most heat resistant of the Shasta daisies, 'Becky' is a classic mid-summer perennial. 'Becky' is also one of the most stout of stem, which means that it can hold its flowers up without flopping and therefore is super as a ground cover or accent plant. Companions include daylilies, Campanula, veronica, Salvia, soapwort, lavender, mountain garlic, and showy nepeta. Flowers are great for cutting
Rec. Size: #1 pot (8/flat)   Space: (14"-18")

## Leucanthemum x superbum 'Snowcap' (lew-can-the-mum sue-per-bum)

('Snowcap' Shasta Daisy)..................................................Zone 5

10"-12"; full sun to light shade. Blooming showily from late spring to mid-summer, 'Snowcap' is exceptional for its compact habit of dark shiny green foliage and masses of pure white petaled, yellow centered flowers—valuable as cut flowers. And, while large scale plantings are exceptional, 'Snowcap' is also a good choice for companion planting with such grasses as Pennisetum 'Hameln', dwarf forms of Miscanthus, Veronica selections, and such sedums as 'Autumn Joy'.
Rec. Size: #1 pot (8/flat)   Space: (10"-14")

G R O U N D   C O V E R S

## Liatris spicata 'Kobold' (lie-<u>aye</u>-tris  spy-<u>kay</u>-ta)
('Kobold' Spike Gayfeather) NATIVE CULTIVAR..........................Zone 3

**Blooming Time**

1 1/2'-2' tall; full sun to light shade. Not only is 'Kobold' a neat, attractive clump former with deep, shiny green leaves, from mid summer to fall it bears a multitude of upright floral spikes. Each spike contains dozens of magenta-purple flowers which have the unusual habit of maturing first at the top of the spike then progressively downward. 'Kobold' is a splendid "color" plant and may be used as a dwarf hedge, companion plant, or massed as a ground cover.
Rec. Size: #1 pot (8/flat)    Space: (12"-16")

## Liriope muscari 'Big Blue' (li-<u>rye</u>-oh-pee  mus-<u>kay</u>-ree)
('Big Blue' Lily-turf) ...................................................................Zone 5/6

**Blooming Time**

12"-15"; full sun to moderate shade. This is the classic clump forming lily-turf so common in the Midsouthern states. Here in the Great Lakes region it has been flawless in Zone 6, and reliable in Zone 5—when sited in wind protected locations. This is the case also with 'Silvery Sunproof' listed below. 'Big Blue' grows relatively tall, is quite robust, and is decorated with deep green foliage. Because it has a nonspreading habit it is superb for edging and accent, and during fall it flowers with lavender pink stars that are arranged in narrow spikes and carried above the foliage.
Rec. Size: #1 pot (8/flat)    Space: (12"-16")

## Liriope muscari 'Silvery Sunproof' (li-<u>rye</u>-oh-pee  mus-<u>kay</u>-ree)
('Silvery Sunproof' Lily-turf) ...................................................Zone 5/6

**Blooming Time**

10"-15"; full sun to moderate shade. Striped white and green, this variegated selection is colorful and attractive. It is both excellent for creating contrast in shady settings and as a colorful edging or general purpose ground cover. 'Silvery Sunproof' forms neat clumps, shows good drought tolerance, and bears light purple flowers in fall. In west Michigan, Zone 6, it easily comes through our winters. In Zone 5, however, it should be sited to protect it from winter winds.
Rec. Size: #1 pot (8/flat)    Space: (10"-14")

## Liriope spicata (li-<u>rye</u>-oh-pee  spy-<u>kay</u>-ta)
(Creeping Lily-turf)......................................................................Zone 4

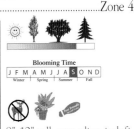

**Blooming Time**

8"-12" tall, spreading indefinitely; full sun to moderate shade. Creeping lily-turf displays the same reliability that has made pachysandra, English ivy, and purple wintercreeper so popular. In addition, it displays superior drought tolerance and is graced with attractive flowers of violet during late summer. Outstanding for edging borders and walkways, and covering vast expanses as a low maintenance turf substitute, you may walk on it, mow it (if you choose to), and generally use it as a turf grass.
Rec. Size: 38 cell    Space: (6"-8")
Rec. Size: 3 1/4" (18/flat)    Space: (8"-12")
Rec. Size: #1 pot (8/flat)    Space: (10"-14")

## Liriope spicata 'Silver Dragon' (li-<u>rye</u>-oh-pee  spy-<u>kay</u>-ta)
('Silver Dragon' Creeping Lily-turf).........................................Zone 5

**Blooming Time**

6"-10"; full sun to moderate shade. Like the species L. spicata, this is a tough, drought tolerant, rhizomatous turf-forming ground cover. Similarly, you can walk on it, mow it (if you choose), and generally use it as a turf grass. It differs, however, in that its foliage is attractively striped white and green and seldom are its fallborne violet flowers observed.
Rec. Size: 3 1/4" (18/flat)    Space: (8"-12")

## Lotus corniculatus 'Pleniflorus' (<u>low</u>-tus  kor-nik-you-<u>lay</u>-tus)
(Double Flowered Bird's-foot Trefoil)......................................Zone 5

**Blooming Time**

2"-4"; full sun to light shade. The name bird's-foot trefoil comes from the seedpods, which spread out in a the shape of a bird's foot (not relevant to this sterile cultivar). 'Pleniflorus' is, as the name would imply, a double flowered form which blooms mid summer with bright, rich yellow flowers. The flowers are nice and cheerful but the main reason this plant is grown is for its durable, reliable, matlike, foot friendly habit of growth. Its foliage is a pleasing medium green and it can be walked on quite a bit. Accordingly, it is good between stepping stones and can even be used as a substitute to conventional turf grass on a small to large scale. It is tolerant of infertile sandy soils, prefers good drainage, and because it is able to convert soilborne atmospheric nitrogen into a form it can use, it requires very little fertilizer.
Rec. Size: 6 pack (18/flat)    Space: (10"-16")

**Lysimachia clethroides (lis-i-_mak_-ee-a _cleth_-_roy_-deez)**
(Gooseneck Loosestrife) ..................................Zone 3

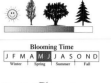

2'-3' full sun to light shade. Gooseneck loosestrife is a tenacious, fast spreading rhizomatous ground cover that thrives in well drained as well as moist to saturated soil. When in bloom, which occurs during late summer, it displays thousands of 1/2 inch wide, white fragrant blossoms. Arranged in 12 to 18 inch long, arching gooseneck-shaped inflorescences, the floral show is quite impressive, not to mention entertaining as each one looks like the head of a goose.
Rec. Size: #1 pot (8/flat)    Space: (12"-16")

**Lysimachia nummularia (lis-i-_mak_-ee-a   nem-ew-_lay_-ree-a)**
(Creeping Charley) ..................................Zone 4

1"-3"; full sun to moderate shade. A fast spreading creeper for use in moist soil, creeping Charlie displays coin-shaped light green foliage and trailing stems which root freely at the nodes. It is excellent for use between stepping stones where it tolerates foot traffic and its bright yellow flowers, 3/4" in diameter, lend interest throughout the summer.
Rec. Size: 3 1/4" (18/flat)    Space: (8"-10")

**Lysimachia nummularia 'Aurea' (lis-i-_mak_-ee-a   nem-ew-_lay_-ree-a)**
(Golden Creeping Charley) ..................................Zone 4

1"-3"; full sun to moderate shade. Like regular creeping Charlie, golden creeping Charley thrives in moist soil. Yet golden creeping Charley differs in the obvious manner by having bright golden-yellow foliage, which makes it useful for high contrast applications in lightly shaded settings. Yellow flowers arise during summer but since they are about the same color as the leaves they are not significant ornamentally. This is a plant for foliar effect and it, like green leaved Creeping Charley, tolerates foot traffic and is superb for use between stepping stones and for brightening up shady garden pathways.
Rec. Size: 3 1/4" (18/flat)    Space: (8"-10")

**Mazus reptans (_may_-zoos   _rep_-tanz)**
(Creeping Mazus) ..................................Zone 4

1"; full sun to moderate shade. Herbaceous and rooting as it spreads, creeping mazus is a charming carpet former with curious purple flowers, cheerful green foliage, and assertive spreading nature. Mazus is an effective cover for under small trees and tall single-stemmed shrubs, but maybe one of its most popular applications is as a foot friendly edging or filler between stepping stones of patios and walkways. Creeping mazus is semievergreen, light green leaved, and blooms late spring with loads of violet-blue, white and yellow lipped, purple spotted flowers.
Rec. Size: 3 1/4" (18/flat)    Space: (8"-10")

**Mentha requienii (_men_-tha   rek-wee-_en_-ee-eye)**
(Corsican Mint) ..................................Zone 5/6

1/4"-1/2"; full sun to light shade. Just plain fun to grow, Corsican mint or creeping mint is a low matlike species originally used to flavor the drink creme de menthe. In the landscape it excels as a foot friendly filler for between the cracks of stepping stones and patio blocks and its deep green, strongly aromatic foliage tolerates a fair amount of foot traffic—releasing its fine fragrance with each footfall. Its tiny flowers are colored lavender and bloom during summer.
Rec. Size: 3 1/4" (18/flat)    Space: (6"-10")

**Mitchella repens (mi-_chel_-a   _ree_-penz)**
(Partridge Berry) NATIVE SPECIES ..................................Zone 5

1"; light to dense shade. This charming evergreen is a must for every shade garden. Not only is it a functional, stand-alone, foot friendly ground cover for use on a small to moderate scale, it is also excellent between the stepping stones of a woodland path or in combination with ferns and wildflowers. Partridge berry is evergreen with pairs of deep green, white veined, coin shaped leaves. During late summer its funnel-shaped pink flowers add further interest. And, by fall, its brilliant scarlet namesake berries make a lovely show (and presumably provide food for partridges, if you happen to have any nearby).
Rec. Size: 3 1/4" (18/flat)    Space: (6"-10")

## Monarda didyma 'Petite Delight' (moe-nar-da did-i-ma)
('Petite Delight' Bee Balm) NATIVE CULTIVAR ............................Zone 2

15"-18"; full sun to light shade. From the Morden Experiment Station, Manitoba, Canada, 'Petite Delight' is the first truly dwarf, highly mildew resistant selection of bee balm. A fine foliage plant, with deep glossy green crinkled foliage, it is also an outstanding bloomer—during mid to late summer adorned with many whorls of lavender-rose, tubular, hummingbird attracting, pleasantly scented flowers. Use 'Pink Delight' in groups as a general cover and consider it for planting at the front of the border in combination with such perennials as Ajuga 'Burgundy Glow', asters, Allium, Alchemilla, bergenia, coreopsis selections, hostas, Rudbeckia, Lamium, dwarf Pennisetum, and variegated feather reed grass.
Rec. Size: #1 pot (8/flat)    Space: (10"-16")

## Nepeta x faassenii 'Blue Wonder' (nep-i-ta fah-sen-ee-ee)
('Blue Wonder' Hybrid Nepeta) ..........................................Zone 3

12"-15"; full sun to light shade. A truly excellent herbaceous, mound forming, compact growing ground cover, 'Blue Wonder' hybrid Nepeta is very hardy and trouble free. Used as a specimen or mass planted as a low maintenance ground cover, this pleasantly aromatic, gray green, heart-leaved cultivar easily combines with a multitude of other herbs and shrubs. During spring its 6-inch-tall spikes of 1/2 inch long dark blue flowers decorate the landscape, and often do so again in fall if the flowers are cut back toward the end of the spring bloom.
Rec. Size: 1 gal.    Space: (1 1/2'-2')

## Nepeta x faassenii 'Six Hills Giant' (nep-i-ta fah-sen-ee-ee)
('Six Hills Giant' Nepeta)..........................................Zone 3

2 1/2'-3'; full sun to light shade. Alan Armitage states in his book Herbaceous Perennial Plants that "This is one of the finest plants I have seen". Indeed, 'Six Hills Giant' is a very imposing selection, particularly when planted in broad sweeping masses on either sloping or level terrain. It is also fantastic lining sidewalks and pathways and is as magnificent from a distance as it is up close. 'Six Hills Giant' blooms throughout summer with deep dark vio-

let flowers borne profusely in 9-12 inch tall racemes. When in full bloom, its attractive gray green foliage is virtually smothered. Great companions are other nepetas, daylilies, coneflowers, goldenrod, and of course ornamental grasses—especially mid to large sized cultivars of Panicum and Miscanthus.
Rec. Size: 2 gal    Space:

## Nepeta x faassenii 'Walker's Low' (nep-i-ta fah-sen-ee-ee)
('Walker's Low' Nepeta)..........................................Zone 3

1 1/2'-2'; full sun to light shade. This fragrant leaved sprawling/mounding selection is perfect for moderate to large scale ground covering applications as well as accent and companion planting. 'Walker's Low' is quickly becoming popular for its long bloom season in which it is decorated with lavender-blue trumpet shaped flowers from April through fall. Try it alone or in combination with Achillea, coreopsis, Rudbeckia, ornamental grasses, and sedum. Either way, you are in for a rewarding gardening experience.
Rec. Size: #1 pot (8/flat)    Space: (2'-3')

## Nepeta racemosa 'Blue Ice' (nep-i-ta ray-si-moe-sa)
('Blue Ice' Nepeta) ..........................................Zone 4

8"-12"; full sun to light shade. With dense compact habit, this is a super low maintenance, easy to grow selection. Flowering early and lasting for a very long time, the flowers of 'Blue Ice' aren't blue but snow white and contrast nicely with the gray blue-green fragrant foliage. Nice in combination with all of the blue flowering nepetas such as 'Walker's Low' and 'Blue Wonder', 'Blue Ice' is also great with such favorites as daylilies, iris, sedums, Salvias, and many others.
Rec. Size: 1 gal.    Space: (1 1/2'-2')

GROUND COVERS

**Nepeta subsessilus 'Sweet Dreams'** (<u>nep</u>-i-ta   sub-ses-i-lis)
('Sweet Dreams' Showy Nepeta)..............................................Zone 4

12"-16"; full sun to light shade. The deep green pleasantly fragrant foliage of this fine selection all but goes unnoticed during summer under masses of cheerful pink flowers. A superb and very welcome addition to a genus dominated by blue flowered cultivars, 'Sweet Dreams' is great for mass planting alone or in combination with such companions as ornamental grasses, coneflowers, sedums, and other varieties of nepeta.
Rec. Size: 1 gal    Space: (1 1/2'-2')

**Nepeta yunanensis** (<u>nep</u>-i-ta   yew-na-<u>nen</u>-en-sis)
(Yunan Nepeta).................................................................Zone 4

18"-24"; full sun to light shade. One of the very best nepetas, this one has extremely long lasting flowers. Borne all summer and fall, the flowers are huge, brilliant bright blue, and act as magnets to hummingbirds. The plant itself, clothed in crisp green fragrant foliage, is excellent for dwarf hedging and medium to large scale ground cover use. It is also a great companion to other ground covers including Calamintha, coreopsis, Echinacea, Eupatorium, geraniums, Hemerocallis, Lamium, Leucanthemum, Origanum, Perovskia selections and such ornamental grasses as Calamagrostis, Miscanthus, Panicum, and Pennisetum selections.
Rec. Size: 1 gal    Space: (1 1/2'-2')

**Oenothera berlandieri 'Siskiyou'** (ee-noe-<u>thee</u>-ra   ber-lan-dee-a-ree)
('Siskiyou' Mexican Primrose) ............................................Zone 5

6"-8"; full sun to light shade. Quick to establish, this is an attractive deciduous ground cover that should be contained or given substantial room, and in either case is a plant that is easy to grow and certain to please. It is drought tolerant, dependable, and very colorful for its magnificent, profusely borne, 2 inch wide, sweet scented, rose pink flowers that arise throughout summer.
Rec. Size: #1 pot (8/flat)    Space: (12"-16")

**Ophiopogon planiscapus 'Nigrescens'** (oh-fee-oh-<u>poe</u>-gon plahn-i-<u>skah</u>-pus   nye-<u>gres</u>-ens)
(Black Mondo Grass) ........................................................Zone 5/6

8"-12"; full sun to moderate shade. Black mondo grass is so intensely purple-pigmented that it looks black. In addition, it bears numerous dainty pink and whitish bell shaped flowers upon upright stems in summer, followed by bunches of shiny black pearl-shaped fruit in fall. A slow spreader, black mondo grass is tough, drought tolerant, and carefree. As would be expected, it yields strong color contrast with variegated ground covers such as variegated pachysandra, 'Ralph Shugert' myrtle, sedges, and 'Silvery Sunproof' lily-turf.
Rec. Size: 3 1/4" (18/flat)    Space: (6"-8")

**Origanum laevigatum 'Herrenhausen'** (o-ree-<u>gay</u>-num   lee-vi-<u>gay</u>-tum)
('Herrenhausen' Oregano)...................................................Zone 4

12"-15"; full sun to light shade. Drought tolerant and easy to care for, 'Herrenhausen' oregano is colorful year round. During winter its neat, fragrant evergreen leaves are an attractive burgundy bronze which during the growing season turn to deep green suffused with burgundy. But, mid summer through fall, the foliage goes unnoticed. This is when the massive display of red-purple, butterfly attracting flowers occurs. So prolific is the flower show, single plants are easily visible from 50 yards away.
Rec. Size: #1 pot (8/flat)    Space: (14"-18")

**Origanum x 'Rosenkuppel'** (o-ree-<u>gay</u>-num)
('Rosenkuppel' Oregano)....................................................Zone 4

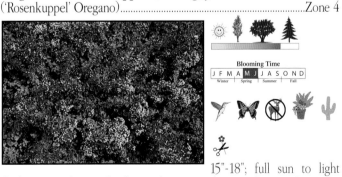

15"-18"; full sun to light shade. Every bit as florific as the extraordinary selection Origanum 'Herrenhausen', 'Rosenkuppel' differs in having flowers of vibrant pink. It too is superior as a butterfly attractant, it tolerates drought, will grow in poor soils, and is a breeze to care for. One of the very finest late summer and fall bloomers, this is a ground cover that should be in every garden.
Rec. Size: #1 pot (8/flat)    Space: (14"-18")

G R O U N D   C O V E R S

## Oxalis crassipes 'Rosea' (ok-<u>say</u>-lis   <u>kras</u>-i-peez)
(Strawberry Shamrock) ...................................................Zone 5

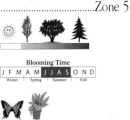

4"-6"; light to dense shade. A member of the wood sorrel family, strawberry shamrock resembles the lovely shamrocks that you see for sale in the supermarket around St. Patrick's Day, except that it is cold hardy. As such, it makes a lovely light green carpet for rich shady settings and is especially nice along woodland paths and around water features. Long blooming, it bears numerous pink, 5 petaled flowers from late spring to fall.
Rec. Size: #1 pot (8/flat)   Space: (12"-14")

## Pachysandra procumbens (pak-i-<u>san</u>-dra   pro-<u>kum</u>-benz)
(Allegheny Pachysandra) NATIVE SPECIES.....................Zone 4

6"-12" tall, spreading about 4 feet across; light to dense shade. Allegheny pachysandra is a sturdy clump forming, dense growing ground cover with sprawling habit. Like the more common Japanese species (P. terminalis), P. procumbens is a reliable foliage plant. It differs, however, in several significant features. Most obviously, its leaves are first light green, mature to bronzy green, and in fall pick up hues of red (P. terminalis stays rich green year round). Moreover its leaves are semievergreen, more coarse textured, and borne upon stems which spread outward to form a defined clump rather than spreading indefinitely by rhizomes. Finally, its purple springborne flower spikes are borne below the foliage.
Rec. Size: 3 1/4" (18/flat)   Space: (8"-12")

## Pachysandra terminalis (pak-i-<u>san</u>-dra   ter-mi-<u>nay</u>-lis)
(Pachysandra) ...........................................................Zone 5

6"-8"; light to dense shade. Pachysandra is considered by many to be the most versatile and reliable evergreen ground cover for the north. Upright white flower spikes appear in May atop rosettes of rich green foliage. Good companions are large bold leaved hostas like 'Elegans' and 'Francis Williams'.
Rec. Size: 100 rc (flat)   Space: (3"-5")
Rec. Size: 50 cell flat   Space: (4"-6")
Rec. Size: 38 cell flat   Space: (6"-8")
Rec. Size: 6-pack (18/flat)   Space: (8"-14")
Rec. Size: #1 pot (8/flat)   Space: (12"-16")

## Pachysandra terminalis 'Green Carpet' (pak-i-<u>san</u>-dra   ter-mi-<u>nay</u>-lis)
('Green Carpet' Pachysandra)..............................................Zone 5

6"-8"; light to dense shade. This relatively slow to moderate growing selection is much like the species but differs in having a slightly more compact, slightly more uniform habit of growth, and seems to retain a darker green color during the winter months. 'Green Carpet' is very low maintenance and bears pleasantly fragrant white floral spikes during early spring.
Rec. Size: 50 cell flat   Space: (4"-6")

## Pachysandra terminalis 'Green Sheen' (pak-i-<u>san</u>-dra   ter-mi-<u>nay</u>-lis)
('Green Sheen' Pachysandra).................................................Zone 5

4"-6"; light to dense shade. 'Green Sheen' pachysandra is substantially different than any other selection of this popular species. In fact, at first glance, you might not recognize it as pachysandra. With smaller, extremely shiny, dark green leaves, the foliage of this slow rhizomatous spreader resembles patent leather. Its flowers of ivory white are short lived but quite fragrant during spring. Use 'Green Sheen' on a small to moderate scale for strong contrast for color and texture.
Rec. Size: 50 cell flat   Space: (3"-5")

## Pachysandra terminalis 'Variegata' (pak-i-<u>san</u>-dra   ter-mi-<u>nay</u>-lis)
(Variegated Pachysandra)................................................Zone 5

4"-6"; light to dense shade. This beautiful cultivar of pachysandra has leaves that are attractively variegated creamy white and green. Like other types of pachysandra, it blooms in spring with fragrant white spikes, but can be used for higher contrast planting where it helps to brighten up shady areas.
Rec. Size: 50 cell flat   Space: (4"-6")

*GROUND COVERS*

## Perovskia atriplicifolia 'Filigran' (pe-rof-skee-a a-tri-plis-i-foe-lee-a)

('Filigran' Russian Sage)......................................................Zone 4

2 1/2'-3'; full sun. Extremely florific with masses of long lasting iridescent lavender blue florets, 'Filigran' is an outstanding late summer and fall blooming ground cover. But it is also a unique foliage plant displaying 'filigree' (of delicate lacy pattern) foliage. Strongly scented when rubbed, the foliage is a soft silvery gray green — easily compatible with a host of other colors and textures.
Rec. Size: #1 pot (8/flat)    Space: (2 1/2'-3')

## Perovskia atriplicifolia 'Little Spire' (pe-rof-skee-a a-tri-plis-i-foe-lee-a)

('Little Spire' Russian Sage).................................................Zone 4

1 1/2'-2' tall; full sun to light shade. Special among the Russian sage cultivars, 'Little Spire' is a true dwarf with compact upright habit that never flops in the wind or rain. A great bloomer, the soft grayish blue stems and leaves of 'Little Spire' are topped with masses of attractive, soft purplish blue florets from mid summer to fall. Great for general ground covering, edging, and companion planting, 'Little Spire' is a good companion to cone flowers, Rudbeckia, mountain garlic, asters, and countless others.
Rec. Size: #1 pot (8/flat)    Space: (2'-2 1/2')

## Perovskia atriplicifolia 'Longin' (pe-rof-skee-a a tri-plis-i-foe-lee-a)

('Longin' Russian Sage) .......................................................Zone 5

3'-4'; full sun. A splendid upright form of Russian sage, 'Longin' has a number of merits, not the least of which is its gray-green pleasantly aromatic foliage. And to anyone who has seen the astounding lavender blue long lasting late summer and fallborne flowers, the plant becomes unforgettable. Needless to say, it is a tremendous companion to the "perennials of fall", pink and white forms of coneflower, Rudbeckia, sedum 'Brilliant', golden rod, and others.
Rec. Size: #1 pot (8/flat)    Space: (2'-2 1/2')

## Persicaria filiformis 'Variegatus' (per-si-kare-ee-a fil-i-form-is)

(Variegated Persicaria) NATIVE CULTIVAR......................Zone 4

2' tall by 2' wide; light to moderate shade. This is a plant that will brighten up the shade garden with its lovely oval shaped, white and green marbled deciduous foliage. Carried upon jointed stems, the foliage is topped with tiny red flowers during summer and fall. Variegated persicaria is rhizomatous but slow spreading. For this reason it is not just a great ground cover for moderate to large scale use, but a good companion to such classics as English ivy, pachysandra, hostas, and ferns.
Rec. Size: #1 pot (8/flat)    Space: (14"-18")

## Persicaria microcephala 'Red Dragon' (per-si-kare-ee-a mi-kro-ceph-i-la)

('Red Dragon' Persicaria) NATIVE CULTIVAR.....................Zone 5

2' tall by 3' wide; full sun to moderate shade. One of the most colorful ground covers ever, 'Red Dragon' is instantly popular and in high demand. In addition to its deep burgundy-purple, maroon, and frosted green arrowhead shaped deciduous leaves, 'Red Dragon' boasts red stems and dainty white summerborne flowers. A robust clump former, it is superb for small to large scale use and is sure to add interest to any landscape.
Rec. Size: #1 pot (8/flat)    Space: (1'-1 1/2')

## Persicaria virginiana 'Lance Corporal' (per-si-kare-ee-a ver-jin-i-aye-na)

('Lance Corporal' Persicaria) NATIVE CULTIVAR..................Zone 5

1 1/2'-2' tall; full sun to moderate shade. A favorite of designers, for its chartreuse green leaves that are overlaid with deep maroon chevrons, 'Lance Corporal' radiates its beauty in sunny and shady settings, is decorated with tiny red flowers during late summer, and is a splendid selection for mass planting and accent use. Good companions include English painted fern, blue leaved hostas, bronze ajuga, 'Chameleon' euphorbia, and the popular sedum selections 'Matrona', 'Vera Jameson', and 'Autumn Fire'.
Rec. Size: #1 pot    Space (14"-18")

GROUND COVERS

## Petasites japonicus 'Giganteus' (pe-ta-<u>sye</u>-teez   ja-<u>pon</u>-i-kus)
(Giant Butterbur)..................................................Zone 4

**Blooming Time**
J F M A M J J A S O N D
Winter  Spring  Summer  Fall

5'-6'; light to dense shade, withstanding full sun. This is an enormous, eye-catching, exotic ground cover. Flowering during late winter and early spring, it displays white to purplish, heavy stalked flowers. Its leaves look like gigantic kidneys, may reach 4 feet across, and lend a lush tropical character to the landscape.
Rec. Size: 5 gal.    Space: (3'-4')

## Petasites japonicus 'Purpureus' (pe-ta-<u>sye</u>-teez   ja-<u>pon</u>-i-kus)
(Purple Leaved Butterbur)..................................Zone 5

**Blooming Time**
J F M A M J J A S O
Winter  Spring  Summer

1 1/2'-3' tall; light-moderate shade. Smaller than giant butterbur, purple leaved butterbur is a rare find that differs in the obvious way, its leaves are purple. Like giant butterbur it also blooms during late winter and spring, but with rich purple flower stalks. Purple leaved butterbur grows well in moist soils as well as normal garden settings, is nice near ponds, and lends a good deal of color contrast when grown near variegated irises and other moisture tolerant ground covers, ferns, and perennials.
Rec. Size: 2 gal.    Space: (2'-3')

## Petasites japonicus 'Variegatus' (pe-ta-<u>sye</u>-teez   ja-<u>pon</u>-i-kus)
(Variegated Butterbur)......................................Zone 4

**Blooming Time**
J F M A M J J A S O N D
Winter  Spring  Summer  Fall

1 1/2'-3' tall; light-moderate shade. Much smaller than giant butterbur, this special selection is a curious foliage plant sure to brighten up the landscape—in sun or shade. Good in regular soils (if kept well watered) and along pondside (or other moist settings), variegated butterbur can be held in check and used as a specimen by surrounding it with a deep edging. Or, let it run (it spreads at a moderate pace by rhizomes) and have one of the most colorful ground covers available to the Midwest. Curious yellow flowers arise before the foliage during late winter and early spring.
Rec. Size: 2 gal.    Space: (3 1/2'-3')

## Phlox paniculata 'Laura' (floks   pa-nik-you-<u>lay</u>-ta)
('Laura' Garden Phlox) NATIVE CULTIVAR ..................................Zone 5

**Blooming Time**
J F M A M J J A S O N D
Winter  Spring  Summer  Fall

2'-2 1/2'; full sun. Particularly impressive for its upright, dense growing habit and mildew resistant foliage, 'Laura' is excellent for ground cover use. It is also among the very best for its character of blooming from midsummer well into fall. This is when it is blanketed with dense panicles of lovely pink-purple, fragrant, butterfly/hummingbird attracting flowers—each with a distinct white star in its center. Use 'Laura' to exceptional effect in broad sweeping drifts, in small groupings for accent, as a backdrop to shorter ground covers, or even as a tall edging plant. Excellent companions include other phlox varieties, Calamagrostis varieties, Deschampsia 'Bronze Veil', fountain grass varieties, and many others.
Rec. Size: #1 pot    Space (14"-18")

## Physostegia virginiana 'Miss Manners' (fi-<u>so</u>-stee-gee-a   vir-jin-ee-<u>aye</u>-na)
('Miss Manners' Obedient Plant) NATIVE CULTIVAR ..................Zone 3

**Blooming Time**
J F M A M J J A S O N D
Winter  Spring  Summer  Fall

18"-24"; full sun to light shade. 'Miss Manners' is exceptional for its clump-forming growth habit (other cultivars spread by rhizomes). Because of this, it not only works well as a moderate to large scale ground cover, but is also effective in combination with other perennials in mixed perennial gardens. 'Miss Manners' displays deep green foliage and numerous pure white flowers from mid- to late-summer.
Rec. Size: #1 pot (8/flat)    Space: (14"-18")

## Polemonium caeruleum 'Snow and Sapphires' (pol-e-<u>moe</u>-nee-um   se-<u>rew</u>-lee-um)
('Snow and Sapphires' Jacob's Ladder)............................................Zone 4

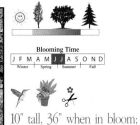

**Blooming Time**
J F M A M J J A S O N D
Winter  Spring  Summer  Fall

10" tall, 36" when in bloom; light-dense shade. Blooming spring to mid-summer, the lovely, fragrant, violet blue, hummingbird attracting flowers of 'Snow and Sapphires' are merely a bonus when compared to the stunning fernlike foliage of this instant classic. Leafy, clean, and always attractive, the fernlike variegated compound leaves are attractive green with a broad crisp edge of ivory white. This is a magnificent companion to ferns, hostas, Heuchera, and others.
Rec. Size: #1 pot (8/flat)    Space: (14"-18")

GROUND COVERS

**GROUND COVERS** (vertical, left margin)

## Polygonatum humile 'Fred Case'
('Fred Case' Dwarf Solomon's Seal)................................Zone 5

6"-9", spreading over 3' across. Light to moderate shade. The typical dwarf Solomon's seal can be slow to establish, but not this one. Via Arrowhead Alpines, who acquired it from wildflower/orchid expert Fred Case, this form displays good vigor, great flower production, and dense habit. A deciduous stoloniferous creeper, dwarf Solomon's seal emerges early spring with its creamy white, bell shaped pendant flowers already formed. By the time it has extended to its 6"-9" height, it is loaded with flowers, in full bloom, and stays this way for a good three weeks. The rest of the year it remains attractive with handsome dark green foliage attractively arranged in alternating fashion upon sturdy upright stems. Dwarf Solomon's seal is a fine small scale ground cover and combines nicely with ferns, hostas, bergenia, and countless wildflowers.
Rec. Size: 3 1/4" (18/flat)   Space: (8"-12")

## Polygonatum odoratum 'Variegatum' (poe-lig-oh-**nay**-tum oh-der-**aye**-tum)

(Variegated Fragrant Solomon's Seal)................Zone 3
24-30" tall; light-dense shade. The classic variegated Solomon's seal, this superb selection displays tall stature, large fragrant white bell-shaped pendant springborne flowers, and large flattend foliage that is handsomely streaked bright white and green.
Rec. Size: #1 pot (8/flat)   Space: (12"-16")

## Pulmonaria longifolia ssp. cevennensis (pul-moe-**nay**-ree-a long-gi-**foe**-lee-a   sev-e-**nen**-sis)
(Cevennensis Pulmonaria) ...........................................Zone 3

15" tall; light-moderate shade. A sturdy disease resistant subspecies, cevennensis is remarkable for its lance shaped, deep green, prominently silver splotched leaves. Above these, during spring, are borne a multitude of steel blue flowers. Excellent when planted on any scale, cevennensis is a superb edging plant, general ground cover, and companion to other ground covers and perennials.
Rec. Size: #1 pot (8/flat)   Space: (12"-16")

## Pulmonaria longifolia 'Diana Clare' (pul-moe-**nay**-ree-a long-gi-**foe**-lee-a)
('Diana Clare' Pulmonaria) .........................................Zone 3

8"-10"; light to moderate shade. From Cotswold Garden in England, 'Diana Clare' is an outstanding selection with brightly silver centered, green-edged elongate leaves and during early spring profusely borne violet-blue flowers. 'Diana Clare' is also one of the more sturdy pulmonaria selections with good mildew resistance and leaves that hold up well through the heat of summer. Its bright silver foliage makes it a great companion to most ferns, bergenia, epimediums, Helleborus, purple leaved Heucheras, blue leaved hostas, Allegheny pachysandra, green and silver striped sedges, Japanese forest grass, and prairie dropseed.
Rec. Size: #1 pot (8/flat)   Space: (14"-18")

## Rhus aromatica 'Grow Low' (roos   air-oh-**mat**-ik-a)
('Grow Low' Fragrant Sumac) NATIVE CULTIVAR.......................Zone 3

1 1/2'-2'; full sun to light shade. This tough ground cover reaches 2 feet tall and up to 8 feet wide. Its deciduous bluish green to coppery green foliage looks like miniature oak leaves and often picks up vibrant hues of yellow or scarlet in autumn ( best coloring occurs in full sun with well drained soil). The flowers are 1 inch long, yellow, and borne in spring before the leaves unfold. Its fruit, consisting of clusters of red hairy drupes (that can be used to make a lemonadelike drink) are effective late summer to early fall.
Rec. Size: 1 gal.   Space: (3'-4')

## Rodgersia aesculifolia (rod-**jer**-si-a   es-kyew-li-fo-**lee**-a)
(Fivefinger Rodgersia)...............................................Zone 5

3'-4'; full sun to dense shade. With great big five-parted compound leaves that resemble those of horse chestnut (for which it takes its scientific name), fivefinger rodgersia is an imposing ground cover for specimen or large scale ground cover use. Its foliage is covered with shaggy brown hair at its base, is very coarse textured and stately, and during late spring is accented with flat topped clusters of tiny white flowers. A well kept secret, this wonderful species is appreciated by everyone who has ever tried it.
Rec. Size: #1 pot (8/flat)   Space: (2 1/2'-3 1/2')

## Rosa x 'Nearly Wild' (row-za)
('Nearly Wild' Rose)..................................................Zone 4

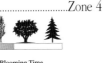

2'-3'; full sun to light shade. An excellent, disease resistant, long blooming, shrubby ground covering rose that has been in the trade since 1941 (reportedly bred from the cross R. 'Dr. W. Van Fleet' x R. 'Leuchstern'), 'Nearly Wild' is, after all these years, becoming very poplar. Rightfully so, for beginning early summer 'Nearly Wild' bears lovely rose-pink, long stemmed fragrant flowers. In West Michigan these typically bloom all summer and well into October — usually still blooming strong a few weeks after fall's first frost.
Rec. Size: 2 gal.    Space: (2 1/2'-3')

## Rubus calycinoides (roo-bus    kal-i-sin-oy-deez)
(Taiwanese Creeper).................................................Zone 5/6

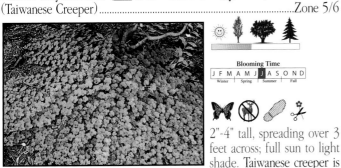

2"-4" tall, spreading over 3 feet across; full sun to light shade. Taiwanese creeper is a neat, attractive, creeping, dense growing woody ground cover clothed in rugged semievergreen, emerald-green, 5-lobed ivy-shaped foliage. During fall and winter the leaves are even more interesting as they become copper colored. But, Taiwanese creeper isn't just a foliage plant. During summer it bears showy white 1/2 inch wide flowers, which later give rise to bright red blackberry-like fruit.
Rec. Size: #1 pot (8/flat)    Space: (1 1/2'-2 1/2')

## Rudbeckia fulgida var. sullivantii 'Goldsturm' (rud-bek-ee-a ful-gi-da)
('Goldsturm' Orange Coneflower) NATIVE CULTIVAR **Perennial Plant of the Year 1999**.................................Zone 4

2'; full sun to light shade. Among the finest companion plants for the perennial border, this superb cultivar of our native black eyed Susan is a tenacious rhizomatous spreader that is also excellent mass planted as a moderate to large scale ground cover. Its roughened deep green leaves are sturdy and pest resistant and from mid summer through fall disappear under masses of deep yellow petaled, black coned, cheerful and very striking daisylike flowers.
Rec. Size: #1 pot (8/flat)    Space: (12"-18")
Rec. Size: 2 gal.    Space: (12"-18")

## Rudbeckia laciniata 'Goldquelle' (rud-bek-ee-a    la-sin-ee-aya-ta)
(Golden Fountain Cutleaf Coneflower) NATIVE CULTIVAR.......Zone 4

2 1/2'-3'; full sun to light shade. Offering cheerful mid to late season flowers, 'Goldquelle' is a nice alternative to the more common black-eyed Susan. Its foliage, a vibrant green, remains clean all season and above it during summer and fall are borne impressive double petaled lemon-yellow flowers. Combining nicely with coneflowers, asters, sedum, and 'Limerock Ruby' coreopsis, 'Goldquelle' is an easy fit in most landscapes and does well on a large scale, when mass planted, or on a smaller scale as a companion plant.
Rec. Size: #1 pot (8/flat)    Space: (14"-18")

## Rudbeckia speciosa 'Viette's Little Suzy' (rud-bek-ee-a spee-see-oh-sa)
('Little Suzy' Dwarf Orange Coneflower) NATIVE CULTIVAR).Zone 4

1 1/2'-2'; full sun to light shade. 'Viette's Little Suzy' is unique for its dwarf compact habit and cheerful golden-yellow petaled, deep brown centered flowers which open over a period of time rather than all at once—giving it a more open and varied floral appearance versus other cultivars that go into flower all at once. This is a plant that has great usefulness and can be planted effectively enmasse as a general cover, as a border edging, for accent, and as a comfortable companion to dozens of other ground covers—some of the best being Salvia 'Marcus', purple coneflower varieties, and various ornamental grasses.
Rec. Size: #1 pot (8/flat)    Space: (12"-16")

## Sagina subulata (sa-jie-na    sub-you-lay-ta)
(Irish Moss) ..........................................................Zone 5

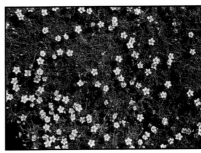

1"-2"; light to moderate shade. A low, mat-forming, evergreen mosslike ground cover, Irish moss reaches under 2 inches tall, spreads indefinitely, and makes a wonderful choice for filling in between stepping stones or the pavers of a patio or walkway, where it holds the soil in place and endures periodic foot traffic. Above the mosslike foliage, during summer, are borne many tiny white star-shaped flowers.
Rec. Size: 6-pack (18/flat)    Space: (6"-10")

## Sagina subulata 'Aurea' (sa-jie-na   sub-you-lay-ta)
(Scotch Moss) .............................................................Zone 5

1"-2"; light to moderate shade. Just like the all-green leaved species, 'Aurea' may be used as a small scale ground cover or filler between the cracks of pavers, patio stones, and walkway cracks and crevices. It also bears white star-shaped flowers during summer, but it differs from the species in that its foliage is golden yellow.
Rec. Size: 3 1/4" (18/flat)    Space: (6"-10")

## Salvia nemorosa 'Blue Hill' (sal-vee-a   ne-mo-roe-sa)
('Blue Hill' Sage) ........................................................Zone 4

1 1/2'-2'; full sun to light shade. An important color breakthrough, 'Blue Hill' flowers true blue above deep green aromatic foliage during early summer. Compact and well behaved, 'Blue Hill' is nice on a small or moderate scale as an edging or general cover. It prefers well drained soil, resists insects and diseases, drought, heat, and wind, and combines well with small ornamental grasses, daylilies, coneflowers, sedums, and other perennials and ground covers.
Rec. Size: #1 pot (8/flat)    Space: (12"-16")

## Salvia nemorosa 'Caradonna' (sal-vee-a   ne-mo-roe-sa)
('Caradonna' Sage) ......................................................Zone 4

1 1/2'-2'; full sun to light shade. Originating in Germany, this is a fabulous Salvia selection unique for its stiff upright stems of bright glowing purple. Its handsome foliage is dark green and leathery and during early summer is contrasted with a multitude of bright violet-purple flower spikes. Attractive to hummingbirds and butterflies, the flowers are long lived and highly effective. Favorite companions are numerous and include such plants as fountain grass, Acorus, sedums, Lamium, Heuchera 'Snow Angel', Dianthus, and many others.
Rec. Size: #1 pot (8/flat)    Space: (12"-16")

## Salvia nemorosa 'East Friesland' (sal-vee-a   ne-mo-roe-sa)
('East Friesland' Sage) ................................................Zone 4

1 1/2'-2'; full sun to light shade. With bright purple summerborne flowers, 'East Friesland' is a popular selection that makes quite a splash when in bloom. Its leaves, a handsome mid-green, are neat, durable, and resistant to drought and disease.
Rec. Size: #1 pot (8/flat)    Space: (12"-16")

## Salvia nemorosa 'Lubeca' (sal-vee-a   ne-mo-roe-sa)
('Lubeca' Sage) ...........................................................Zone 4

1 1/2'-2'; full sun to light shade. Regarded as a longer blooming 'East Freisland', 'Lubeca' is a superior florific sage selection that flowers late spring through mid summer—at which time its fragrant dark green leaves disappear under numerous dense spikes of deep purple blooms.
Rec. Size: #1 pot (8/flat)    Space: (12"-16")

## Salvia nemorosa 'Marcus' (sal-vee-a   ne-mo-roe-sa)
('Marcus' Sage) ...........................................................Zone 4

8"-10"; full sun to light shade. From Haussermann Nursery in Germany, 'Marcus' represents a major breakthrough. It is the first really strong growing, compact, dwarf selection that bears flowers as good as or better then the most popular varieties (like 'East Friesland', from whose seed it originated). Deep dark violet-purple flowering, during early and midsummer, 'Marcus' stays compact and clothes the ground in a rich blanket of purple. It is great in containers and is a superior small scale ground cover, edging, and accent plant. Like its parent, 'East Friesland', 'Marcus' is durable, rich green leaved, and resistant to most common garden pests and diseases. Companions are many and include dwarf ornamental grasses, Salvia 'Rose Wine', sedums, coneflowers, geraniums, and daylilies.
Rec. Size: #1 pot (8/flat)    Space: (12"-16")

G R O U N D   C O V E R S

## Salvia nemorosa 'May Night' (<u>sal</u>-vee-a   ne-mo-<u>roe</u>-sa)
**Perennial Plant of the Year 1997**
('May Night' Sage)..................................................................Zone 4

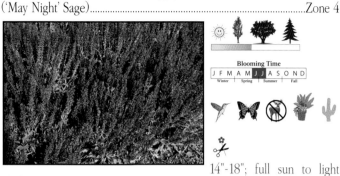

14"-18"; full sun to light shade. Not only does 'May Night' boast handsome disease and insect resistant, fragrant, deep green foliage, during June and July it blooms with a profusion of rich deep purple, hummingbird attracting tubular flowers. It resists drought, is long lived, requires little maintenance, and combines nicely with other Salvia cultivars, sedums, dwarf forms of Pennisetum, cultivars of thyme, and daylilies.
Rec. Size: #1 pot (8/flat)    Space: (12"-16")

## Salvia nemorosa 'Rose Wine' (a.k.a. 'Rosenwein') (<u>sal</u>-vee-a ne-mo-<u>roe</u>-sa)
('Rose Wine' Sage)............................................................Zone 4

14"-20"; full sun to light shade. In a species composed of mostly blue and purple flowered selections, a good pink cultivar is a welcome addition. 'Rose Wine' is a plant that is perfectly named, as it blooms throughout summer with loads of upright spikes of rich deep pink flowers. The substance of its flowers is such that they can be seen from a long distance and their tone is such that they blend nicely with blues, purples, greens, and the silver tones of the landscape. Like other salvias, 'Rose Wine' bears deep green, fragrant, disease resistant foliage. It, like the others, responds well to deadheading (trimming off the flower spikes as they fade) which often results in late season rebloom.
Rec. Size: #1 pot (8/flat)    Space: (12"-16")

## Salvia nemorosa 'Viola Klose' (<u>sal</u>-vee-a   ne-mo-<u>roe</u>-sa)
('Viola Klose' Sage)............................................................Zone 4

12"-16"; full sun to light shade. Maybe the most outstanding of the Salvias in respect to "flower power", while blooming (during summer) 'Viola Klose' absolutely jumps right out of the landscape. Visible from the longest distance, its upright flower spikes are dense and completely loaded with brilliant violet-blue hummingbird attracting flowers. 'Viola Klose' is outstanding on its own, but also combines nicely with other cultivars of sage as well as Dianthus, geranium, Heuchera, iris, Lamium, Leucanthemum, Persicaria filiformis 'Variegata', sedums, Thymus, and many ornamental grasses.
Rec. Size: #1 pot (8/flat)    Space: (12"-16")

## Saponaria lempergii 'Max Frei' (sap-oh-<u>nay</u>-ree-a   lem-<u>per</u>-gee-eye)
('Max Frei' Soapwort).........................................................Zone 3

12"; full sun to light shade. Covered in healthy dark green, teardrop shaped foliage, carried upon stout stems, 'Max Frei' does a nice job of covering the ground. Of course, when it blooms, from midsummer into fall, it is exceptional. During this time it bears a succession of one inch wide cheerful pink flowers. Difficult to propagate, 'Max Frei' would otherwise be extremely common.
Rec. Size: #1 pot (8/flat)    Space: (12"-16")

## Scabiosa columbaria 'Butterfly Blue' (skay-<u>bee</u>-oh-sa   kol-um-<u>bare</u>-e-a)  Perennial Plant of the Year 2000
('Butterfly Blue' Pincushion Flower).......................................Zone 3

6", to 16" — in flower; full sun to light shade. One of the finest small scale ground covers for use in the Midwest, not only is 'Butterfly Blue' easy to culture and maintain, it is exceptionally hardy and attractive. Its deciduous foliage is colored deep green and above it, all summer long, is borne a profusion of balloonlike clusters of lavender-blue flowers.
Rec. Size: #1 pot (8/flat)    Space: (8"-12")

*GROUND COVERS*

**Scabiosa columbaria 'Pink Mist'** (skay-<u>bee</u>-oh-sa   kol-um-<u>bare</u>-e-a)
('Pink Mist' Pincushion Flower)........................................Zone 3

**Blooming Time**

| J | F | M | A | M | J | J | A | S | O | N | D |
| Winter | | | Spring | | | Summer | | | Fall | | |

6" tall, 12"-16" when in flower, full sun to light shade. With true soft pink flowers held well above the rich green foliage upon wiry stems, the flowers of 'Pink Mist' wave about in the wind and create a lovely, long lasting summertime show. The perfect companion to Scabiosa 'Butterfly Blue', 'Pink Mist' also combines nicely with dwarf ornamental grasses, cone flowers, Heuchera, and various types of sedums. It is excellent as a small scale ground cover, edging plant, or accent.
Rec. Size: #1 pot (8/flat)     Space: (8"-12")

An amazing foliage plant, **Sedum repestre 'Angelina'** also has some serious floral impact.

**Sedum spurium 'Fuldaglut'** contrasts sharply with turf, making an effective low maintenance edging.

GROUND COVERS

# SEDUMS

With around 300 species, the genus Sedum provides some of the most interesting, useful, and trouble free ground covers for the Midwestern landscape. Typically they range from one to eighteen inches tall with upright or trailing habit, and they store water in their fleshy stems and succulent evergreen or deciduous leaves. Needlelike to bead-shaped or broad and flattened, the diverse leaves often glisten in the sun as they display their colors that span a spectrum from sky blue (like blue fescue) to light green, dark green, yellow, red, burgundy, purple, silvery, golden, or variegated.

*Sedum 'Matrona'*

Big bloomers too, sedum flowers arise as early as May for S. ellacombianum, to as late as late August for the cultivars of S. spectabile. Sometimes their seed capsules are interesting as with S. middendorfianum var. diffusum (russet-red), and other times they preserve well with appealing winter interest with such cultivars as S. 'Autumn Joy', 'Brilliant', 'Neon', 'Matrona' and 'Pink Chablis'. The sedums described below grow best in full sun to light shade—flowering best with 4 or more hours of direct sunlight each day. They prefer well drained soil and grow well in infertile, sandy, and rocky soils. Seldom do they require irrigation, once established, and their high resistance to disease makes them very low maintenance. Usually a mowing during early April, to tidy them up, is all that is needed. As landscape plants, sedums make excellent general purpose small- to large-scale ground covers. Low growers can be used as fillers between stepping stones or terrace walls, and other larger forms make nice specimen and accent plants. Use your imagination with sedums, combine various colors, forms, and textures, and create a unique signature with your designs. There are a multitude of selections to choose from and surely many will compliment your landscaping needs.

**Sedum 'Autumn Fire'** (<u>see</u>-dum  pur-<u>pur</u>-<u>ee</u>-um)
('Autumn Fire' Sedum)..................................................Zone 3

**Blooming Time**

| J | F | M | A | M | J | J | A | S | O | N | D |
| Winter | | | Spring | | | Summer | | | Fall | | |

14"-20"; full sun to light shade. Developed in Quebec Canada, this selection is billed as an 'Autumn Joy' look-alike with thicker, richer-colored flower panicles during late summer and fall along with a tighter growth habit. It is a very nice drought tolerant plant that is likely to become very popular.
Rec. Size: #1 pot (8/flat)    Space: (12"-16")

**Sedum 'Autumn Joy'** (<u>see</u>-dum  per-<u>per</u>-<u>ee</u>-um)
('Autumn Joy' Sedum)..................................................Zone 3

**Blooming Time**

| J | F | M | A | M | J | J | A | S | O | N | D |
| Winter | | | Spring | | | Summer | | | Fall | | |

1 1/4'-2'; full sun to light shade. Appreciated greatly for its showy late summer- and fall-borne clusters of mauve red flowers, this taller "classic" sedum is a favorite for use in perennial borders, as a moderate to large scale general cover, edging, or rock garden specimen. Needless to say, companions are many and include Russian sage, ornamental grasses, golden rod, coneflowers, and other sedums.
Rec. Size: #1 pot (8/flat)    Space: (12"-16")

*GROUND COVERS*

## Sedum cautacola 'Bertram Anderson' (see-dum)
('Bertram Anderson' Sedum).....................................Zone 4

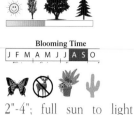

**Blooming Time**
J F M A M J J A S O

2"-4"; full sun to light shade. Neat tidy and very colorful, 'Bertram Anderson' is a pleasing selection for use on a small to moderate scale. It is a slow grower, gradually building attractive round mounds of powder blue to purplish bronze succulent rounded foliage. During summer, it is decorated with dusty rose flowers. Use 'Bertram Anderson' alone as a colorful small scale cover, or combine it with other sedums and succulents, mountain garlic, Dianthus selections, lavender, or Sisyrinchium.
Rec. Size: 3 1/4" (18/flat)    Space: (6"-10")

## Sedum dasyphyllum 'Major' (see-dum das-i-fil-um)
(Thick Leaved Sedum)................................................Zone 5

**Blooming Time**
J F M A M J J A S O N D
Winter    Spring    Summer    Fall

1"; full sun to light shade. Forming a low compact slow creeping cushion of chubby, rounded, succulent, powder blue foliage, thick leaved sedum is decorated during June and July with pale pink florets borne in compact clusters. A fine selection for dry containers, trough gardening, filling cracks between stepping stones, rock gardening, and as a small scale general cover, thick leaved sedum is drought resistent, attractive, and very easy to grow.
Rec. Size: 3 1/4" (18/flat)    Space: (6"-10")

## Sedum hispanicum 'Minus'(see-dum   his-pan-i-kum)
(Ellacombe's Sedum)..................................................Zone 3

**Blooming Time**
J F M A M J J A S O N D
Winter    Spring    Summer    Fall

5"-8"; full sun to light shade. Deciduous and fleshy, the attractive foliage of this popular species is a cheerful light green. Its lemon yellow flowers appear in June, last for a few weeks, then yeild to interesting stalks of coffee brown.
Rec. Size: 50 cell flat    Space: (6"-8")

## Sedum hispanicum 'Minus' (see-dum   his-pan-i-kum)
(Blue Carpet Sedum)..................................................Zone 5

**Blooming Time**
J F M A M J J A S O N D
Winter    Spring    Summer    Fall

1"-2"; full sun to light shade. Clothed in miniature rich-blue fleshy foliage, this low, compact, creeping evergreen ground cover is a good selection for use between stepping stones, in the rock garden, and as a small scale general ground cover. Sometimes becoming more green than blue in the heat of summer, 'Minus' can almost disappear during June and July when it goes into flower and bears its pinkish white florets above the leaves in clusters atop compact branches.
Rec. Size: 3 1/4" (18/flat)    Space: (6"-10")

## Sedum kamtschaticum 'Tekaridake' (see-dum   kam-chat-i-kum   te-kare-i-da-kee)
('Tekaridake' Kamtschatka Sedum)...........................Zone 3

**Blooming Time**
J F M A M J J A S O N D
Winter    Spring    Summer    Fall

8"-10', to 14" in flower; full sun to light shade. Robust and clump forming, 'Tekaridake' sends out stout ascending stems which carry densely set, vibrant green, scallop edged succulent leaves. A recent introduction from Japan, this superb selection is still rare but catching on. Neat, compact, and requiring no maintenance, 'Tekaridake' is a strong bloomer, covered with bright yellow flowers, and makes a nice show during early summer.
Rec. Size: #1 pot (8/flat)    Space: (10"-14")

## Sedum kamtschaticum 'Variegatum' (see-dum   kam-chat-i-kum)
(Variegated Kamtschatka Sedum)..............................Zone 3

**Blooming Time**
J F M A M J J A S O N D
Winter    Spring    Summer    Fall

3"-5"; full sun to light shade. With attractive creamy white and light green variegated evergreen foliage, this is an attractive ground cover for use on a small, medium, or large scale. And its merits aren't limited to foliage. Blooming late spring/early summer, it produces masses of orange-yellow flowers followed by nice russet orange seed capsules. Great in combination with small grasses, tall sedums, and many rock garden plants, this sedum is drought tolerant, dependable, and long lived.
Rec. Size: #1 pot (8/flat)    Space: (10"-14"')

# Sedum 'Matrona' (<u>see</u>-dum)
('Matrona' Sedum)................................................Zone 3

15"; full sun to light shade. 'Matrona' is a sturdy purple-stemmed upright grower with purple blushed, rose pink edged, gray green foliage. Flowering mid to late summer, its large, long lived flower clusters are pleasing pinkish maroon and persist as attractive rich-brown throughout the winter months. Its drought resistance, as with the other sedums, is excellent and it performs well in sandy as well as loamy well drained soils. 'Matrona' is a superb companion to various ornamental grasses, other sedums, golden-rod, asters, Shasta daisy, white coneflower, and yellow flag iris.
Rec. Size: #1 pot (8/flat)    Space: (1'-1 1/2')

# Sedum middendorfianum var. diffusum (<u>see</u>-dum    mid-den-dore-fee-<u>aye</u>-num)
(Diffuse Middendorf's Sedum)................................Zone 3

4"-6"; full sun to light shade. Aggressive but not overly so, this evergreen stonecrop, one of my favorites, is attractive in all seasons. With spring comes new deep green foliage, then in early summer, bright yellow flowers followed by russet seed capsules. In fall the foliage picks up deep hues of purple.
Rec. Size: 38 cell flat    Space: (6"-8")

# Sedum 'Purple Emperor' (<u>see</u>-dum)
('Purple Emperor' Sedum)...................................Zone 3

15", full sun to light shade (best with late afternoon shade). With its extremely deep dark purple leaves, 'Purple Emperor' may be the most intensely purple of the sedum cultivars, and therefore naturally makes for a very high contrast plant—especially when combined with light-green leaved plants. Suitable companions to 'Purple Emperor' include ornamental grasses, other sedums, lily-turf, goldenrod, variegated persicaria and many others. In addition to being a high contrast companion plant, 'Purple Emperor' can stand on its own when planted enmasse as a moderate scale ground cover, for edging, or as a facing plant. Certainly its foliage alone can carry it, but it's also an effective bloomer and during August and September is smoth-

ered in dusty-pink flowers that dry to a pleasing soft tan. Best performance seems to come with full sun with midafternoon shade (as would be the case when sited on the east side of something taller). This allows the deep purple leaves to stay relatively cool and fresh appearing.
Rec. Size: #1 pot (8/flat)    Space: (12"-16")

# Sedum rupestre 'Angelina' (<u>see</u>-dum    rew-pes-tree)
('Angelina' Sedum)................................................Zone 3

2"-3"; full sun to light shade. Discovered in a private garden in Croatia, 'Angelina' is a trailing selection clothed in brilliant golden-yellow spruce-needle shaped foliage. It is superb not only as a general purpose ground cover, but looks great flowing over the side of terraces and retaining walls, as a rock garden specimen, and as an exceptional container plant. Its flowers, borne during June and July, are lemon-yellow upon upright stems 6-8 inches above the foliage. Suitable companions are many but plants with shades of purple, like sedum 'Purple Emperor' and 'Matrona' and Eupatorium 'Chocolate' and Heuchera 'Stormy Seas' and 'Palace Purple' are absolutely excellent. For cool contrast combine 'Angelina' with shades of blue as found in Salvia 'Viola Klose' and Nepeta selections. And, for sharp contrast try it with red or black foliage as found in Imperata 'Red Baron' or Ophiopogon 'Nigrescens'.
Rec. Size: #1 pot (8/flat)    Space: (12"-16")

# Sedum spectabile 'Brilliant' (<u>see</u>-dum    spek-<u>tab</u>-i-lee)
('Brilliant' Sedum)................................................Zone 3

1 1/2'-2'; full sun to light shade. Like 'Autumn Joy' sedum which is described above, this durable, drought tolerant, succulent ground cover is most greatly appreciated for its late season of bloom. At Hortech it begins to flower in late summer and continues well into fall. It differs from 'Autumn Joy' primarily in being slightly shorter, and having pink rather than mauve red flowers.
Rec. Size: #1 pot (8/flat)    Space: (12"-18")

G R O U N D   C O V E R S

### Sedum spectabile 'Neon' (<u>see</u>-dum   spek-<u>tab</u>-i-lee)
('Neon' Sedum).............................................................Zone 3

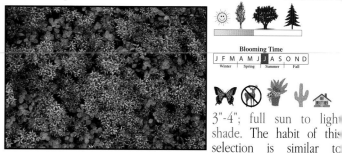

14"-18"; full sun to light shade. Selected as a sport of Sedum 'Brilliant' (at the The Ivy Farm in Locustville, VA) for intense deep purplish pink summer and fallborne flowers, 'Neon' displays flowers that are deeper rose pink arranged in thick rounded clusters. A great item for fall color, 'Neon' can be used on a moderate to large scale for dramatic landscape effect.
Rec. Size: #1 pot (8/flat)    Space: (1'-1 1/2')

### Sedum spectabile 'Pink Chablis' (<u>see</u>-dum   spek-<u>tab</u>-i-lee)
('Pink Chablis' Sedum).................................................Zone 3

14"-18"; full sun to light shade. Selected by Chris Howe, cultural manager of Hortech, 'Pink Chablis' is an exceptional variegated sport of 'Brilliant' and is the natural choice to replace Sedum 'Frosty Morn'. Like 'Frosty Morn', 'Pink Chablis' adorns the late summer and fall landscape with clusters of vibrant pink flowers—preceded by snow white buds. The clusters are larger, however, and like the taller 'Frosty Morn', its white edged blue green foliage is attractive, but broader and carried in more horizontal fashion. The most important difference however, is in the cultural/maintenance aspect of this plant. And, to appreciate this, you first need a little background on the morphology of variegated sedums.

'Pink Chablis', 'Frosty Morn', and other variegated sedums get their multi-colored effect by having two types of cell lines within the same plant—some cells having white tissue (lacking in chlorophyll) and others with green or blue/green tissue (chlorophyll-containing). In the case of 'Frosty Morn' and 'Pink Chablis' the combination of these two tissues (within the same plant) gives the pleasing variegation pattern that makes them so attractive. But, like many variegated plants, the combination of tissues periodically segregates/reverts and gives rise to either all-green- or all-white-leaved new growth. With 'Frosty Morn' and 'Pink Chablis' revertant shoots often appear during the spring. 'Frosty Morn' typically sends up all-green-leaved shoots from the base of the plant and, because these shoots contain more chlorophyll than the other variegated tissue, they are more vigorous and can quickly overrun the parent plant (unless you constantly cut these shoots off season after season). 'Pink Chablis', on the other hand, typically sends up a few all-white (ghost) shoots. These lack chlorophyll and therefore soon wither and die. In a sense, 'Pink Chablis' is self cleaning, and free of the constant maintenance needed to keep 'Frosty Morn' looking good. So, if you are growing 'Frosty Morn', consider 'Pink Chablis' as a replacement. Your job will be easier and your long term satisfaction will be greater.

### Sedum spurium 'Bronze Carpet' (<u>see</u>-dum   <u>spew</u>-ree-um)
('Bronze Carpet' Sedum)..............................................Zone 3

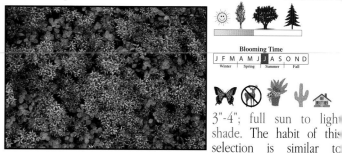

3"-4"; full sun to light shade. The habit of this selection is similar to 'Dragons Blood' but the leaves are broader, more crowded, and more intensely red colored in fall and winter. During the growing season they are purplish bronze, and topped in mid-summer with flowers of pink.
Rec. Size: 38 cell flat    Space: (6"-8")

### Sedum spurium 'Dragon's Blood' (Clone) (<u>see</u>-dum   <u>spew</u>-ree-um)
('Dragon's Blood' Sedum)..............................................Zone 3

3"-4"; full sun to light shade. 'Dragon's Blood' sedum is a classic selection that has been cultivated for several decades. Naturally, to be popular after so many years, 'Dragon's Blood' is a very good plant. It is long lived, drought tolerant, and easy to care for, and it is also very attractive and colorful. 'Dragon's Blood' starts the year with green leaves that are often edged with maroon. By late June it goes into bloom so heavily that its brilliant red flowers nearly obscure the foliage. They remain effective through July and often produce a few residual blooms during August. Finally, during fall, the foliage turns a striking bronzy maroon as a stunning finish to the season.
Rec. Size: 50 cell flat    Space: (4"-6")

*Chris Howe, the discoverer of Sedum 'Pink Chablis'*

Rec. Size: #1 pot (8/flat)    Space: (1'-1 1/2')

**G R O U N D   C O V E R S**

## Sedum spurium 'Fuldaglut' (<u>see</u>-dum <u>spew</u>-ree-um)
('Fuldaglut' Sedum)..................................................Zone 3

3"-4"; full sun to light shade. Remarkable for its deep maroon leaves and deep pinkish rose summerborne flowers, 'Fuldaglut' stonecrop is an exciting new introduction that gives high contrast against light colored backdrops such as stone or cement work. It is relatively fast spreading so fills in quickly and makes a dense ground cover. Excellent interplanted with tall sedums such as 'Autumn Joy', 'Brilliant', 'Meteor', and 'Pink Chablis'.
Rec. Size: 3 1/4" (18/flat)   Space: (8"-10")

## Sedum spurium 'Royal Pink' (<u>see</u>-dum <u>spew</u>-ree-um)
('Royal Pink' Sedum) ..................................................Zone 3

2"-3"; full sun to light shade. This cultivar of two-row stonecrop is one of the best for foliage. Its leaves are vibrant green, densely set, and make a lovely weed-impenetrable mat in light shade as well as full sun. Showy deep pink flowers arise slightly above the foliage during midsummer.
Rec. Size: 38 cell flat   Space: (6"-8")

## Sedum spurium 'Tricolor' (<u>see</u>-dum <u>spew</u>-ree-um)
('Tricolor' Sedum)..................................................Zone 3

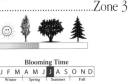

3"-4"; full sun to light shade. This cultivar is much like sedum 'Dragon's Blood' in habit but it is distinct for its variegated foliage of pink, white, and green. Blooming during summer, its flowers are a soft pale pink. No doubt, it is one of the most colorfully foliaged of all ground covers.
Rec. Size: 3 1/4" (18/flat)   Space: (8"-10")

## Sedum x 'Vera Jameson' (<u>see</u>-dum)
('Vera Jameson' Sedum)..................................................Zone 3

9"-12"; full sun to light shade. 'Vera Jameson' is one of the finest clump forming stonecrops for color and ease of care. During midsummer it displays a multitude of 4 inch wide pink flower heads — each nicely set off by the marvelous bluish green succulent foliage.
Rec. Size: #1 pot (8/flat)   Space: (8"-10")

## Sempervivum arachnoideum (sem-per-<u>vie</u>-vum a-rak-noy-dee-um)
(Cobwebbed Hen and Chicks)..................................................Zone 3

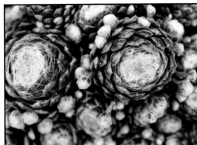

1"-3"; full sun to light shade. Cobwebbed hen and chicks is an amazing and curious plant for its leaftips that are crisscrossed with a dense network of whitish gray spiderweb-like hairs. Each evergreen, succulent blue-green rosette reaches 3/4 to 1 inch wide, and during midsummer the large ones (the hens) send up thin leafy stalks that bear clusters of rose-red flowers at their tops. This is a good little rock garden plant and can be massed on a small scale as a ground cover.
Rec. Size: 3 1/4" (18/flat)   Space: (6"-10")

## Sempervivum 'Purple Beauty' (sem-per-<u>vye</u>-vum)
('Purple Beauty' Hen and Chicks)..................................................Zone 5

3"-4"; full to light shade. This durable selection of hen and chicks is most noteworthy for its vigorous spreading nature and grayish purple foliage. During autumn, winter, and spring, the hues intensify and above the foliage during midsummer it bears its curious flowers upon leafy upright stalks.
Rec. Size: 3 1/4" (18/flat)   Space: (8"-10")

**GROUND COVERS**

**GROUND COVERS**

## Sempervivum 'Silverine' (sem-per-<u>vye</u>-vum)
('Silverine' Hen and Chicks)..........................................................Zone 5

3"-4"; full sun to light shade. This selection of hen and chicks was named for the metallic appearance of the light green, red-tipped foliage. Of the hen and chicks that we offer, this is the fastest spreading and therefore the best choice for use as a turf substitute in small to moderate scale plantings. Its rosettes are tight, about 2 to 3 inches across, and turn darker during the cool months, and like other hen and chicks, it flowers during summer with curious flowers held atop leafy stalks.
Rec. Size: 3 1/4" (18/flat)    Space: (8"-10")

## Sisyrinchium angustifolium 'Lucerne' (sis-i-<u>ring</u>-ki-um an-gus-ti-<u>foe</u>-lee-um)
('Lucerne' Blue Eyed Grass) NATIVE CULTIVAR .........................Zone 5

8"-10" x 4"-6" wide; full sun to light shade. 'Lucerne' not only flowers big, it flowers a lot, and for a long time—bearing its marvelous bright blue, gold-centered,, star shaped flowers above fine, irislike, blue-green foliage for a full ten weeks (May until July). Best in moist to average soil, and superb for edging, this wonderful introduction is long lived, and exceptional in combination with low growing sedums, sedges, thymus, mazus, ajuga, and rupturewort.
Rec. Size: 3 1/4" (18/flat)    Space: (4"-6")

## Smilacina racemosa (smy-la-<u>see</u>-na ray-sa-<u>moe</u>-sa)
(False Solomon's Seal) NATIVE.......................................................Zone 3

2'-2 1/2'; light to moderate shade. Native throughout much of North America, this colonizing (by slow creeping rhizomes) ground cover displays lovely arching habit with pairs of attractive 5"-7" long, elliptical, rich green leaves. A big bloomer, false Solomon's seal flowers during spring with billowy panicles loaded with thousands of tiny, creamy-white, fragrant flowers. Later bearing numerous purple-speckled reddish berries, false Solomon's seal is attractive throughout the growing season and combines nicely with sedges, ferns, and a host of shade loving ground covers, grasses, perennials and wildflowers.
Rec. Size: #1 pot (8/flat)    Space: (12"-16")

## Solidago rugosa 'Fireworks' (so-li-<u>day</u>-go rew-<u>go</u>-sa)
('Fireworks' Goldenrod) NATIVE CULTIVAR..............................Zone 4

3'-4'; full sun to light shade. This is maybe the most impressive Solidago in cultivation—and there are many good ones. It is tall, robust, hardy, and always gives a huge display of late season color. 'Fireworks' is a natural for combining with asters, tall sedums, and ornamental grasses. It tolerates drought and is nice for its neat upright habit and attractive green foliage. In fall, however, it bursts forth with a brilliant crown of magnificently bright yellow flowers. These, by the way, do not cause hay fever (ragweed does), they simply punctuate the fall season with their beauty.
Rec. Size: #1 pot (8/flat)    Space: (18"-24")

## Stachys byzantina 'Silver Carpet' (<u>stay</u>-kis bye-zan-<u>teen</u>-a)
('Silver Carpet' Lamb's Ears)..........................................................Zone 4

6"-10"; full sun to light shade. Given that lamb's ears are grown for their foliage, and their flowers are usually regarded as nonornamental (and create maintenance as they are usually cut off), this usually nonblooming form presents the advantages of a nice clean look with less maintenance. That aside, 'Silver Carpet' displays superior bright silvery blue foliage. It resists the heat of summer and provides a magnificently cool, soft-textural quality to the landscape. Use 'Silver Carpet' as a general cover or as a pathway or patio edging where it softens the hard lines of pavers and timbers. 'Silver Carpet' is a wonderful companion to other blues such as Festuca and Helictotrichon and combines nicely with Amsonia, asters, Caryopteris, Eupatorium, euphorbias, salvias, sedums, and veronica. The occasional flower will be pinkish purple.
Rec. Size: #1 pot (8/flat)    Space: (14"-18")

## Stylophorum diphyllum (sty-<u>lof</u>-oh-rum dye-<u>fil</u>-um)
(Celandine Poppy) NATIVE SPECIES.............................................Zone 4

1'-1 1/2'; light to dense shade. Filling the uncommon niche of being long and showy-blooming, in the shade, Celandine poppy is an attractive foliaged, impressive flowering native ground cover for the shade garden. Celendine poppy blooms throughout mid to late spring with a succession of large cheerful yellow flowers and is great for moderate to large sized areas.
Rec. Size: #1 pot (8/flat)    Space: (12"-16")

G R O U N D   C O V E R S

## Thymus x citriodorus 'Doone Valley' (thy-mus   sit-ree-oh-door-us)
('Doone Valley' Lemon Thyme)..........................Zone 4

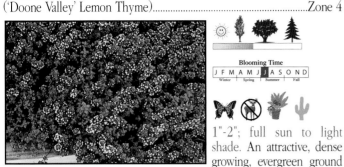

1"-2"; full sun to light shade. An attractive, dense growing, evergreen ground cover, 'Doone Valley' lemon thyme is unique for its dark green lemon flecked, lemon scented leaves. Flowers of pale lilac appear in summer.
Rec. Size: #1 pot (8/flat)   Space: (8"-12")

## Thymus nitens (thy-mus   nye-tens)
(Dwarf Thyme)..........................Zone 5

1/2"-1"; full sun to light shade. Although a rare species, this is an exceptionally fine one. In our trial garden (at Hortech) we have found that Thymus nitens has stayed disease free and has shown no evidence of thinning in the center (a common characteristic of many thymes). Its broadly oval, deep shiny green foliage is densely set upon compact stems which makes a tidy mat that can take a good deal of foot traffic. In summer, Thymus nitens blooms with loads of deep pink, long lasting flowers. During winter its foliage takes on tones of purple. Thymus nitens is a good companion to other varieties of thyme as well as mountain garlic, bell flowers, Gaillardia 'Fanfare', sedums, blue fescue, maritime thrift, and dwarf forms of fountain grass.
Rec. Size: 3 1/4" (18/flat)   Space: (8"-12")

## Thymus pseudolanuginosus (thy-mus   soo-doe-lan-you-ji-noe-sis)
(Woolly Thyme)..........................Zone 5

1/2"-1"; full sun to light shade. Woolly thyme is a wonderful small scale ground cover that makes a superb filler for between stepping- and patio-stones. So soft and velvety is woolly thyme, you will want to walk on it barefoot—because its tiny bluish gray green leaves are covered in soft gray hairs. And, during summer it gets even better, as it becomes decorated with tiny pale pink flowers. Woolly thyme can be combined with other types of thyme for an interesting effect, and it matches up nicely with many sedums which tend to share its cultural needs for well drained soil and sunshine.
Rec. Size: #1 pot (8/flat)   Space: (12"-16")

## Thymus serpyllum (thy-mus   ser-pil-um)
(Creeping Red Thyme)..........................Zone 4

1"-2"; full sun to light shade. Low growing, creeping thyme makes a sturdy and reliable ground cover or lawn substitute for small or moderate sized areas. Planting between stepping stones allows its fragrant foliage to be further appreciated when occasionally crushed. Flowers are purple and borne late spring to late summer.
Rec. Size: 3 1/4" (18/flat)   Space: (8"-12")

## Thymus serpyllum 'Album' (thy-mus   ser-pil-um)
(White Flowered Creeping Thyme)..........................Zone 4

1"-3"; full sun to light shade. With low carpeting habit and the ability to withstand moderate foot traffic, this mosslike ground cover is ideal for planting between stepping- and patio-stones. It is durable, relatively resistant to summer's heat and humidity, and particularly attractive in summer when in bloom and adorned with masses of tiny white flowers. Try planting it in combination with other thymes for a low maintenance lawn substitute.
Rec. Size: 3 1/4" (18/flat)   Space: (8"-12")

## Thymus serpyllum 'Elfin' (thy-mus   ser-pil-um)
('Elfin' Creeping Thyme)..........................Zone 4

1", full sun to light shade. Like the parent species, this cultivar is low growing, creeping, sturdy, and reliable. It may be walked upon and used as a lawn substitute and is great for planting between stepping stones. The difference is that it is slower growing, miniature in every respect, and displays pretty pink flowers during summer.
Rec. Size: 3 1/4" (18/flat)   Space: (6"-8")

## Thymus serpyllum 'Russettings' (<u>thy</u>-mus  ser-<u>pil</u>-um)
('Russettings' Creeping Thyme)..................................................Zone 5

**Blooming Time**

| J | F | M | A | M | J | J | A | S | O | N | D |
|---|---|---|---|---|---|---|---|---|---|---|---|
| Winter | | | Spring | | | Summer | | | Fall | | |

1"-2"; full sun to light shade. Valuable for its late season display of clear pink flowers, 'Russettings' is a slow creeper with crisp shiny green foliage and dense habit which resists opening up in the center (as happens with many thymes). Later, during fall and winter, its foliage turns so deep purple that it appears black. 'Russettings' is an excellent choice as a filler between stepping stones as it tolerates a good deal of foot traffic. It is also great for planting in the cracks of retaining walls and cascading over the tops of planter boxes and containers.
Rec. Size: 3 1/4" (18/flat)    Space: (8"-12")

## Tiarella cordifolia 'Eco Running Tapestry' (tie-a-<u>rel</u>-a  kore-di-<u>foe</u>-lee-a)
('Eco Running Tapestry' Foamflower)..................................Zone 4

**Blooming Time**

| J | F | M | A | M | J | J | A | S | O | N | D |
|---|---|---|---|---|---|---|---|---|---|---|---|
| Winter | | | Spring | | | Summer | | | Fall | | |

2"-4"; light to dense shade. This running (by stolons like strawberries) selection of foamflower is quite different than the others, all of which are clump forming. And because of its running habit, 'Eco Running Tapestry' fills in fast and is useful on a moderate to large scale. But, it is not simply a boring green ground cover. Rather, it is a beautiful foliage plant with broad-maple-shaped evergreen leaves—which during fall and winter are stained deep burgundy black in their centers. Above the foliage, during spring, are borne numerous floral spikes each supporting a multitude of tiny white star shaped flowers.
Rec. Size: #1 pot (8/flat)    Space: (12"-16")

## Tiarella 'Ink Blot' (tie-a-<u>rel</u>-a)
('Ink Blot' Foamflower)..................................................Zone 4

**Blooming Time**

| J | F | M | A | M | J | J | A | S | O | N | D |
|---|---|---|---|---|---|---|---|---|---|---|---|
| Winter | | | Spring | | | Summer | | | Fall | | |

2"-4" tall, 10" in flower; full sun to dense shade. An excellent evergreen ground cover, 'Inkblot' displays 2 1/2 inch wide, maple-shaped foliage, stained deep purplish black around its veins, and by fall this pigmentation intensifies and runs together, covering the entire center of the leaf. At the same time, the leaf edges are vibrant green, the combination making for an attractive variegation pattern. And one more thing, above the foliage during spring are borne beautiful sprays of delicate pink florets.
Rec. Size: #1 pot (8/flat)    Space: (8"-12")

## Tiarella 'Pink Bouquet' (tie-a-<u>rel</u>-a)
('Pink Bouquet' Foamflower)..................................................Zone 4

**Blooming Time**

| J | F | M | A | M | J | J | A | S | O | N | D |
|---|---|---|---|---|---|---|---|---|---|---|---|
| Winter | | | Spring | | | Summer | | | Fall | | |

7"-10", light to dense shade. Spring blooming with numerous compact spikes of fragrant pink florets, 'Pink Bouquet' is a unique selection among the normally white flowered foamflowers. And not only is 'Pink Bouquet' a terrific flowering ground cover, it is a superb evergreen foliage plant. As such, it is clothed in shiny green, deep burgundy-purple centered (and veined), evergreen, maple shaped foliage. Resistant to disease and easy to culture.
Rec. Size: #1 pot (8/flat)    Space: (10"-14")

## Tiarella wherryi (tie-a-<u>rel</u>-a  ware-<u>ee</u>-eye)
(Wherry's Foamflower) NATIVE SPECIES........................................Zone 3

**Blooming Time**

| J | F | M | A | M | J | J | A | S | O | N | D |
|---|---|---|---|---|---|---|---|---|---|---|---|
| Winter | | | Spring | | | Summer | | | Fall | | |

6"-12"; light to dense shade. Wherry's foamflower is lovely in any season. Evergreen and durable, its 3 to 4 inch wide, medium green maple shaped leaves are accented with veins of purple. In spring a new crop of foliage comes up about the edges of the parent plant, and shortly therafter it sends up spikes of white and pink star-shaped florets. With the first few frosts of fall the purple of the midvein spreads outward, creating a deep wine-red central splotch.
Rec. Size: #1 pot (8/flat)    Space: (12"-16")

*GROUND COVERS*

## Tradescantia 'Sweet Kate' (trad-es-<u>kan</u>-shee-a) (syn. 'Blue and Gold')
('Sweet Kate' Spiderwort)............................................Zone 4

**Blooming Time**
J F M A M **J J** A S O N D
Winter Spring Summer Fall

15"-18"; full sun to light shade. The iridescent chartreuse yellow stems and foliage of 'Sweet Kate' are like a beacon in the landscape. And, the contrast they provide for its deep purple-blue summerborne flowers is beyond compare. Use your imagination with this plant, it can be used for high contrast planting to brighten up lightly shaded areas, and for companionship with other spiderworts, sedums such as 'Vera Jameson', 'Bertram Anderson', and 'Lidakense', Salvia cultivars, black lily-turf, bronze ajuga, and 'Kobold' Liatris.
Rec. Size: #1 pot (8/flat)    Space: (10"-14")

## Tradescantia x 'Zwanenburg Blue' (trad-es-<u>kan</u>-shee-a)
('Zwanenburg Blue' Spiderwort)...........................Zone 4

**Blooming Time**
J F M A M **J J** A S O N D
Winter Spring Summer Fall

1 1/2'-2'; full sun to light shade. Another superior selection of spiderwort, 'Zwanenburg Blue' is sturdy, drought resistant, and florific. Flowering mid summer with blossoms of iridescent purple blue, its flowers seem to glow against its soft blue green, gracefully arcing foliage.
Rec. Size: #1 pot (8/flat)    Space: (12"-18")

## Tricyrtis formosana 'Gilt Edge' (tri-<u>ser</u>-tis    for-moe-<u>say</u>-na)
('Gilt Edge' Orchid Flower)......................................Zone 5

**Blooming Time**
J F M A M **J J** A S O N D
Winter Spring Summer Fall

12"; light to moderate shade. I'm exercising my right to create a new common name for this lovely plant. The old name toad-lily is grossly inept at describing a plant that has no toadlike spots on its leaves, as do some members of this genus. Instead, 'Gilt Edge' is clothed in gracefully ornate, rich green lilylike leaves that are trimmed in the neatest, cleanest golden yellow you will ever see. 'Gilt Edge' is robust yet well behaved, and during late summer and fall is graced with a generous compliment of exquisite, rosy purplish pink, orchidlike flowers. 'Gilt Edge' should be used in areas near walkways and patios so that its intriguing foliage and flowers may be viewed close up. In containers, as edging, and as a small to moderate scale ground cover, 'Gilt Edge' orchid flower is a fine choice.
Rec. Size: #1 pot (8/flat)    Space: (10"-14")

## Tricyrtis hirta 'Variegata' (tri-<u>ser</u>-tis    <u>hir</u>-ta)
(Variegated Orchid Flower)......................................Zone 4

**Blooming Time**
J F M A M J J A **S O N** D
Winter Spring Summer Fall

2'-2 1/2'; light to moderate shade. Showy in foliage and curious in flower, variegated toad-lily is a real conversation piece. Its gracefully arching stems carry many closely-set, softly haired, 3-6 inch long, narrow, pointed leaves. Each colored rich green and edged in creamy white, the leaves combine to create a lush, colorful, tropical effect. Then, late summer and fall, for at least 6 weeks, many maroon and pale purple speckled, white, orchid-like flowers are borne in the leaf axils. Planting near walks and pathways is a good practice so that its merits can be viewed close up.
Rec. Size: #1 pot (8/flat)    Space: (10"-16")

## Tricyrtis 'Tojen' (tri-<u>ser</u>-tis)
('Tojen' Orchid Flower)...........................................Zone 4

**Blooming Time**
J F M A M J J A **S O** N D
Winter Spring Summer Fall

24"-30"; light to moderate shade. Producing exquisite fallborne orchidlike flowers of pale lavender with white throat, this superb cultivar shows good vigor and quickly makes rich colonies of arching stems covered with attractive deep green foliage. 'Tojen' is great for accent, edging, and mass planting. It gives a modern feel to the landscape and it is a superb companion to ajuga, astilbe, Asarum, bergenia, Carex, corydalis, Dicentra, geranium, Heuchera, hostas, Lysimachia, Ophiopogon, Pachysandra procumbens, Oxalis, pulmonaria, Tiarella, and Waldsteinia.
Rec. Size: #1 pot (8/flat)    Space: (10"-16")

## Trifolium repens 'Atropurpureum' (tri-<u>foe</u>-lee-um    <u>ree</u>-penz)
(Black Leaved Shamrock)........................................Zone 5

**Blooming Time**
J F M A M **J J** A S O N D
Winter Spring Summer Fall

1"-2"; full sun to moderate shade. This unusual creeping ground cover is a fine selection for high contrast (with such plants as Carex 'Bowles Golden', Carex 'Frosted Curls', and Hosta 'Golden Scepter'), and because it tolerates a bit of foot traffic, it works nicely as a filler between stepping stones. Each 3, often 4-parted leaf of black leaved clover reaches 1 inch wide and is stained deep burgundy blackish purple with a thin iridescent green edge. During spring to fall it sends up sweet scented, white, balloonlike flower heads.
Rec. Size: #1 pot (8/flat)    Space: (8"-12")

**G R O U N D   C O V E R S**

G R O U N D   C O V E R S

## Veronica oltensis (ve-ron-i-ka   ol-ten-sis)
(Turkish Veronica).................................................................Zone 4

1"; full sun to light shade. A true "foot friendly" ground cover, this remarkable species creeps about the ground at a moderate rate and literally blankets the soil with its tiny evergreen foliage. In spring and well into summer, it bears loads of china blue flowers. Turkish veronica is an excellent choice for planting along pathways and between stepping stones. It combines nicely with Allium, coreopsis, Heuchera, Ophiopogon 'Nigrescens', nonrunning sedum selections, and colorful clump forming sedges.
Rec. Size: 3 1/4" (18/flat)   Space: (8"-12")

## Veronica spicata 'Red Fox' (ve-ron-i-ka   spy-kay-ta)
('Red Fox' Veronica) ............................................................Zone 4

12"-15" when in flower; full sun to light shade. With attractive, dark green evergreen foliage this is a nice foliage plant, but it's the flowers that make this plant so exciting. Long lasting (June to early fall), 'Red Fox' bears masses of upright spikes—laden with loads of brilliant red flowers. Visible from a great distance, it is a plant for high contrast lending an exciting color element to the landscape. Relatively tough and drought tolerant, 'Red Fox' can be counted upon for years of troublefree service.
Rec. Size: #1 pot (8/flat)   Space: (10"-14")

## Veronica spicata 'Royal Candles' (ve-ron-i-ka   spy-kay-ta)
('Royal Candles' Veronica)..................................................Zone 3

12"-15"; full sun to light shade. A compact yet robust selection (from Mike and Heather Philpott of England), 'Royal Candles' is special for its abundant spikes of deep violet blue flowers during mid to late summer. Great in the front of the border, enmasse as a general ground cover, in containers, and as a companion, 'Royal Candles' represents an advancement in this species in that it retains its lower foliage, while others varieties often lose theirs and invite weeds to encroach. Preferring moderately fertile, loamy, well-drained soil, this plant deserves a place in all gardens.
Rec. Size: #1 pot (8/flat)   Space: (10"-14")

## Veronica 'Waterperry Blue' (ve-ron-i-ka)
('Waterperry Blue' Veronica)................................................Zone 5

1"-3"; full sun to light shade. With dense trailing habit, 'Waterperry Blue' is a remarkable "foot friendly" ground cover for use around pathways, in a mixed perennial garden, as a lawn substitute, and trailing over planters and retaining walls. It is tough and versatile and resistant to disease, insects, and drought. Not only that, it is a beautiful plant clothed in lovely rich green, sometimes copper-tinged, round-lobed evergreen foliage. During spring and early summer, and again a little in fall, it bears a multitude of lovely lilac blue flowers. Good companions include Agastache 'Blue Fortune', Coreopsis 'Moonbeam', Crocosmia, Eupatorium 'Chocolate', Fallopia 'Variegata', Iris ensata 'Variegata', Liatris, Perovskia, Persicaria 'Variegatus', and such grasses as Calamagrostis, Pennisetum, Panicum, and Miscanthus.
Rec. Size: #1 pot (8/flat)   Space: (12"-18")

## Vinca minor (ving-ka   mye-nor)
(Myrtle, Periwinkle)............................................................Zone 4

4"-6"; full sun to dense shade. A popular trailing evergreen with vibrant spreading nature, myrtle displays dark green, shiny evergreen leaves. Lilac blue flowers appear during April, and provide a lovely beginning to the growing season. In the fall they repeat blooming but to a lesser extent. Myrtle combines nicely with robust hostas, is great for edging and general ground cover use, and is indespensible for erosion control in shady landscapes.
Rec. Size: 38 cell flat   Space: (10"-12")
Rec. Size: 6-pack   Space: (12"-14")
Rec. Size: #1 pot (8/flat)   Space: (14"-18")

## Vinca minor 'Atropurpurea' (ving-ka   mye-nor)
(Purple Flowered Myrtle)......................................................Zone 4

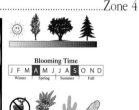

2"-6"; full sun to dense shade. A magnificent variation of myrtle with deep green leaves and rich royal purple spring and fall-borne flowers ('Atropurpurea' literally means very purple in Latin), this lovely selection impresses everyone who sees it.
Rec. Size: #1 pot (8/flat)   Space: (14"-16")

## Vinca minor 'Blue & Gold' (ving-ka mye-nor)
('Blue and Gold' Myrtle)..............................Zone 4

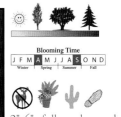

2"-6"; full sun to dense shade. A very showy variegated selection. 'Blue and Gold' displays superb floral and foliar characteristics. Among the finest variegation patterns of any myrtle, this one is medium green surrounded by wide edges of bright golden yellow. Then, during spring and again in fall, it bears numerous large petaled, vibrant bluish purple flowers.
Rec. Size: #1 pot (8/flat)   Space: (14"-16")

## Vinca minor 'Bowlesii' (ving-ka mye-nor)
(Bowles' Myrtle) .............................................Zone 4

4"-6"; full sun to dense shade. In comparison to the species, Bowles' myrtle is a little bit lower and slower growing, somewhat more apt to stay in a clump, possibly a bit deeper green, and perhaps slightly smaller and a bit more glossy in leaf. The primary difference, however, is in its flowering traits. Bowles' myrtle, also spring and fall blooming, blooms more heavily with larger and darker violet blossoms.
Rec. Size: 38 cell   Space: (8"-10")
Rec. Size: #1 pot (8/flat)   Space: (14"-16")

## Vinca minor 'Emily Joy' (ving-ka mye-nor)
(White Flowered Myrtle)..............................Zone 4

2"-6"; full sun to dense shade. With deep green leaves and large white, sometimes pink blushed, springborne flowers, 'Emily Joy' is considered to be the finest white-flowered selection of myrtle and is exceptional when planted alone enmasse or combined with other myrtles including 'Atropurpurea' and 'Bowlesii'.
Rec. Size: #1 pot (8/flat)   Space: (14"-16")

## Vinca minor 'Ralph Shugert' (ving-ka mye-nor)
(Shugert's Variegated Myrtle) ...................Zone 4/5

Ralph Shugert

2"-6"; full to dense shade. Arising as a sport of Vinca minor 'Bowles', this selection is characterized by dark, glossy green, white margined foliage. Its spring and fall-borne deep lilac flowers are numerous and larger than the species. I registered this cultivar during the autumn of 1987 and named it in honor of Ralph Shugert, a dear friend and accomplished American horticulturist.
Rec. Size: 3 1/4" (18/flat)   Space: (8"-12")
Rec. Size: #1 pot (8/flat)   Space: (12"-16")

## Viola coreana (vie-o-la kor-ee-an-a)
(Decorative Violet) .........................................Zone 5

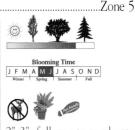

2"-3"; full sun to moderate shade. Blooming a nice violet-blue during spring, the flower is, remarkably, the least ornamental feature of this charming foliage plant. Shaped like little 1 inch wide hearts, the nearly evergreen leaves of this decorative violet are soft jade green overlaid with wide silvery-white veination. It is clearly one of the finest foliage ground covers and makes a nice companion to dwarf grasses, clump forming sedums, black lily-turf, lady's mantle, and mountain garlic.
Rec. Size: 3 1/4 in. (18/flat)   Space: (8"-12")

## Viola 'Purple Showers' (vie-o-la)
('Purple Showers' Hardy Pansy) ...................Zone 5

6"-8"; full sun to light shade. The hardiness of this pansy is impressive and so is its nice clean green foliage and compact habit. Its flowers, however, are in another stratosphere. How about a plant that completely disappears under bright purple flowers during May and June, then keeps flowering (not just sporadically) well into October. It really is remarkable, and deserves every one of the compliments that it receives from those who see it—which essentially is everyone. 'Purple Showers' is, predictably, a plant for high contrast, usually on a small to medium scale as an accent plant, edging, or small scale cover. It has long lived perennial qualities (now 3 years in our trial garden) but gives annuallike floral impact.
Rec. Size: #1 pot (8/flat)   Space: (10"-14")

**GROUND COVERS**

**Waldsteinia ternata (wald-<u>sty</u>-nee-a   ter-<u>nay</u>-ta)**
(Barren Strawberry) ...................................................................Zone 4

**Blooming Time**

| J | F | M | A | M | J | J | A | S | O | N | D |

Winter   Spring   Summer   Fall

4"-6"; full sun to moderate shade. Low, tufted, herbaceous, rhizomatous, and mat forming, this lovely, relatively slow spreading ground cover is attractive in or out of flower. During midspring, its vibrant yellow strawberrylike flowers are borne upon short stalks slightly above the foliage. Once they fade the stage belongs to the shiny evergreen foliage. Broad, wedge shaped, and lobed, the leaves are durable, hold up well throughout the season, and in fall take on lovely shades of bronzy purple. A good general ground cover for small, medium, or large sized areas — particularly among open shrubs and small trees.
Rec. Size: 3 1/4" (18/flat)   Space: (8"-12")

Why not consider **Barren Strawberry** as a substitute for turf?

**Vinca minor**, **Periwinkle**, is tried and proven and remains one of the very best ground covers for erosion control. Here it is nicely accented with specimens of **Hosta 'Patriot'**.

*G R O U N D   C O V E R S*

# Selecting, Using, and Maintaining Ornamental Grasses

*Lagurus ovatus*

Long adored in Europe and the Orient, ornamental grasses have finally become accepted into American gardens. Different from lawn grasses, which are tolerant to foot traffic but are boring and require high maintenance and loads of fertilizer, ornamental grasses are used more for aesthetic purposes and are easy to care for.

They are remarkable plants that come from all corners of the globe. Even some of our native prairie grasses make splendid ornamental specimens. Ornamental grasses range from an inch or so tall to over 20 feet and include the bamboos (woody grasses), many of which are hardy in the midwest.

The color display of ornamental grasses is something to behold. It begins with the leaves which during late winter display attractive shades of straw and tan. Some evergreen species even remain green all winter long. During April these leaves should be removed to make room for the new year's growth, which begins in early May. By mid May the new leaves begin to grow very fast and by early summer they begin to mature.

Most grass leaves are narrow and pointed at their tips, but the similarities end there. Grass leaves are available in about every shade of green and blue, golden and yellow, bronze, red, silver and green striped, gold and green striped, and gold and green banded. They often change color or intensify their colors in fall. This alone is remarkable, but in combination with the flowers, which normally transcend the foliage during summer or fall, the color effect is spectacular. Flowers of grasses include shades of tan, pink, purple, russet, yellow, white, and silver. They are often large, showy, and persistent. And, like the leaves, they often remain effective throughout the winter months.

## Landscaping with Grasses:

Ornamental grasses perform a variety of functions. Like the turf grasses, some of the shorter types can be walked on. The shorter sedges (a genus of grasslike plants) even grow in the shade and only need mowing once a year. Others serve the purpose of conventional ground cover and may be either colonizing spreaders or short growing clump formers that tolerate close spacing. Large, clump forming selections make nice specimen or accent plants and can easily take the place of small to large sized shrubs. These may be massed in thickets for a tropical effect and can even be planted as a hedge.

## Naturalized Plantings:

Certain grasses can be used at home or on a commercial scale in prairie type gardens. Here they combine nicely with other perennial species including a number of native plants.

## Grasses Enmasse as Ground Covers:

Most ornamental grasses lend themselves to planting in large colonies as ground covers. Sometimes, one has to be a bit open minded to visualize a 6 foot tall grass as a ground cover, but when thinking large or commercial-scale, this becomes easy to do. On a residential basis, the smaller types such as Carex, Panicum, and Pennisetum, may be more appropriate choices as ground cover.

## Grasses as Specimens:

Grasses can take the place of shrubs in the landscape and perform the function of a specimen. As such, they can be planted alone and enhance the landscape with their own unique features and architectural merits.

## Grasses for Erosion Control:

Grasses have extensive fibrous root systems and when planted on steep slopes, enmasse, do an excellent job of stabilizing the soil.

## Grasses as Companion Plants:

Grasses are superb companion plants, interacting well with a host of ground covers and perennials. Some of the most popular companions to the grasses are Rudbeckia, cone flower, sedums, Russian sage, oregano cultivars, Lavender, daylilies, geranium cultivars, crownvetch, Caryopteris, Campanula, aster, and golden rod.

## Controlling Weeds in Grass Plantings:

Follow the directions in the ground cover section of this brochure. Additionally, remember that there is no selective control for weed grasses within your grasses. Weed grasses will have to be removed by hand.

## Fertilizing Ornamental Grasses:

Unlike most turf grasses that require fertilizing 3 or 4 times each season, most ornamental grasses are happy with one or two fertilizations per season. Usually they have very deep and fibrous root systems and do a good job of extracting nutrients from the ground. Mid spring and early fall are good times to fertilize. You may do so in the manner described for ground covers previously in this book.

## ORNAMENTAL GRASS SELECTION CHART

Abbreviations: X = Applicable to this plant
P = Partially applicable to this plant

| NAME | GROWTH HABITS | Full Sun | Light Shade | Moderate Shade | Dense Shade | Large area | Moderate area | Small area | Controls erosion | Tolerates foot traffic | Drought tolerant | Moisture tolerant | Tolerates sandy soil | Salt tolerant | Spring Bloom | Summer Bloom | Fall Bloom | Evergreen |
|---|---|---|---|---|---|---|---|---|---|---|---|---|---|---|---|---|---|---|
| Acorus calamus 'Variegatus' | slow spreader | X | X | X | | X | X | X | X | | | X | P | | X | | | |
| A. gramineus 'Pusillus Minimus Aureus' | slow spreader | | X | X | | | X | X | | | | X | | | X | | | |
| Andropogon gerardii | clumper | X | X | | | X | X | | X | | X | | X | | | X | X | |
| Arundo donax 'Variegata' | clumper | X | X | | | X | X | | X | | P | | P | | | | X | |
| Calamagrositis x acutif. varieties | clumper | X | X | | | X | X | | X | | P | | X | | | X | | |
| Calamagrostis arund. var. brachytricha | clumper | X | X | | | X | X | | X | | P | | X | | | | X | |
| Carex buchananii | clumper | X | X | X | | X | X | X | x | | X | | P | | X | | | X |
| Carex caryopylla 'Beatlemania' | clumper | | X | X | | X | X | X | X | P | | P | | X | | | | |
| Carex dolichostachya 'Kaga Nishiki' | clumper | | X | X | | X | X | X | X | P | P | P | | | X | | | X |
| Carex elata 'Bowles Golden' | clumper | | X | X | | X | X | | | | | | | | X | | | |
| Carex hachioensis 'Evergold' | clumper | | X | X | | X | X | X | X | P | X | | X | | X | | | X |
| Carex morowii cultivars | clumper | | X | X | | X | X | X | X | | X | | P | | X | | | X |
| Carex muskingumensis cultivars | clumper | | X | X | | X | X | | | | | | P | | | X | | |
| Carex pennsylvanica | clumper | | X | X | | X | X | X | X | X | X | | P | | X | | | |
| Carex siderosticha 'Variegata' | slow spreader | | X | X | X | X | X | | | | | | P | | X | | | |
| Chasmanthium latifolium | clumper | X | X | X | | X | X | | X | | X | | X | P | | X | X | |
| Deschampsia 'Bronze Veil' | clumper | X | X | | | X | X | X | P | P | X | | X | P | X | | | |
| Erianthus ravennae | clumper | X | X | | | X | X | | X | | X | | X | X | | | X | |
| Festuca glauca 'Elijah Blue' | clumper | X | | | | X | X | X | X | | X | | X | | | X | X | X |
| Festuca idahoensis | clumper | X | X | | | X | X | X | X | | X | | X | | X | | | |
| Hakonechloa macra and 'Aureola' | slow spreader | | X | X | | X | X | | P | | | | | | | X | | |
| Helictotrichon sempervirens 'Sapphire' | clumper | X | X | | | X | X | | X | | X | | X | X | | X | | X |
| Imperata cylindrica 'Red Baron' | slow spreader | X | X | | | X | X | | | | | P | P | | | | | |
| Indocalamus tesselatus | runner | X | X | X | | X | X | | X | | X | | P | | | | | X |
| Isolepis cernua | clumper | X | X | | | | X | X | X | | | X | | | X | X | | |
| Juncus effusus cultivars | clumper | X | X | X | | | | | X | X | | | | | | X | | |
| Lagarus ovatus | clumper | X | X | | | | | X | | | | | | | X | X | | |
| Leymus arenarius 'Blue Dune' | spreader | X | X | | | X | X | | X | | X | | X | P | | X | | P |
| Luzula 'Ruby Stiletto' | slow spreader | | X | X | | X | X | | P | | | | X | | | X | | |
| Miscanthus giganteus | clumper | | X | X | | X | | | X | X | X | P | P | X | | | X | |
| Miscanthus sinensis 'Adagio' | clumper | X | X | | | X | X | | X | | X | P | X | P | | | X | |
| Miscanthus sinensis 'Andante' | clumper | X | X | | | X | | | X | | X | P | P | | X | X | | |
| Miscanthus sinensis 'Bluetenwunder' | clumper | X | X | | | X | | | X | | X | P | P | | X | X | | |
| Miscanthus sinensis 'Cabaret' | clumper | X | X | | | X | X | | X | | X | P | X | P | | | X | |
| Miscanthus sinensis 'Cosmopolitan' | clumper | X | X | | | X | X | | X | | X | P | X | P | | | X | |
| Miscanthus sinensis 'Dixieland' | clumper | X | X | | | X | X | | X | | X | P | X | P | | X | X | |
| Miscanthus sinensis 'Emerald Shadow' | clumper | X | X | | | X | | | X | | X | X | X | P | | | X | |
| Miscanthus sinensis 'Ferner Osten' | clumper | X | X | | | X | X | X | X | | X | P | X | P | | | X | |
| Miscanthus sinensis 'Flamingo' | clumper | X | X | | | X | X | | X | | X | P | X | P | | X | X | |
| Miscanthus sinensis 'Gracillimus' | clumper | X | X | | | X | X | | X | | X | P | X | P | | | X | |
| Miscanthus sinensis 'Graziella' | clumper | X | X | | | X | X | | X | | X | P | X | P | | | X | |
| Miscanthus sinensis 'Grosse Fontäne' | clumper | X | X | | | X | X | | X | | X | P | X | P | | | X | |
| Miscanthus sinensis 'Helga Reich' | clumper | X | X | | | X | X | | X | | X | P | X | P | | | X | |
| Miscanthus sinensis 'Kaskade' | clumper | X | X | | | X | X | | X | | X | P | X | P | | | X | |
| Miscanthus sinensis 'Little Kitten' | clumper | X | X | | | X | X | X | X | | X | P | X | P | | | X | |
| Miscanthus sinensis 'Little Zebra' | clumper | X | X | | | X | X | X | X | | X | P | X | P | | | X | |
| Miscanthus sinensis 'Malepartus' | clumper | X | X | | | X | X | | X | | X | P | X | P | | | X | |
| Miscanthus sinensis 'Morning Light' | clumper | X | X | | | X | X | | X | | X | P | X | P | | | X | |
| Miscanthus sinensis 'Purpurascens' | slow spreader | X | X | | | X | X | | X | | X | P | X | P | | | X | |
| Miscanthus sinensis 'Silver Arrow' | clumper | X | X | | | X | X | | X | | X | P | X | P | | | X | |

# ORNAMENTAL GRASS SELECTION CHART

Abbreviations:  X = Applicable to this plant
P = Partially applicable to this plant

| NAME | GROWTH HABITS | Full Sun | Light Shade | Moderate Shade | Dense Shade | Large area | Moderate area | Small area | Controls erosion | Tolerates foot traffic | Drought tolerant | Moisture tolerant | Tolerates sandy soil | Salt tolerant | Spring Bloom | Summer Bloom | Fall Bloom | Evergreen |
|---|---|---|---|---|---|---|---|---|---|---|---|---|---|---|---|---|---|---|
| *Miscanthus sinensis* 'Silver Feather' | *clumper* | X | X | | | X | X | | X | | X | P | X | P | | X | X | |
| *Miscanthus sinensis* 'Sirene' | *clumper* | X | X | | | X | X | | X | | X | P | X | P | | X | X | |
| *Miscanthus sinensis* 'Strictus' | *clumper* | X | X | | | X | X | | X | | X | P | X | P | | | X | |
| *Miscanthus sinensis* 'Undine' | *clumper* | X | X | | | X | X | | X | | X | P | X | P | | | X | |
| *Miscanthus sinensis* 'Variegatus' | *clumper* | X | X | | | X | X | | X | | X | P | X | P | | | X | |
| *Miscanthus sinensis* 'Weather Vane' | clumper | X | X | | | X | X | | X | | X | P | X | P | | X | X | |
| *Miscanthus sinensis* 'Zebrinus' | *clumper* | X | X | | | X | X | | X | | X | P | X | P | | | X | |
| *Panicum amarum* 'Dewey Blue' | *clumper* | X | X | | | X | X | | X | | X | | X | X | | X | X | |
| *Panicum virgatum* 'Cloud Nine' | *clumper* | X | X | | | X | X | | X | | X | | X | X | | X | X | |
| *Panicum virgatum* 'Dallas Blues' | *clumper* | X | X | | | X | X | | X | | X | | X | X | | X | X | |
| *Panicum virgatum* 'Heavy Metal' | *clumper* | X | X | | | X | X | | X | | X | | X | X | | | X | |
| *Panicum virgatum* 'Northwind' | *clumper* | X | X | | | X | X | | X | | X | | X | X | | | X | |
| *Panicum virgatum* 'Rotstrahlbusch' | *clumper* | X | X | | | X | X | | X | | X | | X | X | | | X | |
| *Panicum virgatum* 'Squaw' | *clumper* | X | X | | | X | X | | X | | X | | X | X | | | X | |
| *Panicum virgatum* 'Shenandoah' | *clumper* | X | X | | | X | X | X | X | | X | | X | X | | | X | |
| *Panicum virgatum* 'Warrior' | *clumper* | X | X | | | X | X | | X | | X | | X | X | | | X | |
| *Pennisetum alopecuroides* | *clumper* | X | X | | | X | X | X | X | | X | | X | P | | | X | |
| *Pennisetum alopecuroides* 'Cassian' | *clumper* | X | X | | | X | X | X | X | | X | | X | | | X | X | |
| *Pennisetum alopecuroides* 'Hameln' | *clumper* | X | | | | X | X | X | X | | X | | X | P | | | X | |
| *Pennisetum alopecuroides* 'Japonicum' | *clumper* | X | | X | | X | X | X | X | | X | | X | P | | | X | |
| *Pennisetum alopec.* 'Little Bunny' | *clumper* | X | | | | X | X | X | X | | X | | X | X | | X | X | |
| *Pennisetum alopecuroides* 'Little Honey' | *clumper* | X | X | | | X | X | | X | | X | | X | X | | X | X | |
| *Pennisetum alopecuroides* 'Moudry' | *clumper* | X | X | | | X | X | X | X | | P | | X | P | | | X | |
| *Pennisetum alopec.* 'Red Head' | *clumper* | X | X | | | X | X | | X | | X | | X | | | X | X | |
| *Pennisetum alopec.* 'Viridescens' | *clumper* | X | X | | | X | X | X | X | | X | | X | P | | | X | |
| *Pennisetum glaucum* 'Purple Majesty' | *clumper* | X | X | | | | X | X | | | P | | P | | | X | X | |
| *Pennisetum orientale* 'Karley Rose' | *clumper* | X | X | | | X | X | X | X | | P | | X | P | | X | X | |
| *Pennisetum setaceum* | *clumper* | X | X | | | X | X | | X | | X | | X | | | | X | |
| *Pennisetum setaceum* 'Rubrum' | *clumper* | X | X | | | X | X | | X | | X | | X | | | | X | |
| *Phalaris arundinacea* 'Feesey's Form' | *spreader* | X | X | | | X | X | | X | | | X | P | | | | X | |
| *Phalaris arundinacea* 'Tricolor' | *slow spreader* | X | X | | | X | X | | X | | | X | P | | | | X | |
| *Pleioblastus auricoma* | *spreader* | X | X | X | | X | X | | X | | X | | X | | | | | P |
| *Pleioblastus fortunei* 'Variegata' | *spreader* | X | X | X | | X | X | | X | | X | | X | | | | | P |
| *Sasa veitchii* | *slow spreader* | X | X | X | | X | X | X | X | | X | | | | | | | X |
| *Schizachyrium scoparium* 'The Blues' | *clumper* | X | X | | | X | X | X | X | P | X | | X | X | | | | X | |
| *Sorghastrum nutans* 'Bluebird' | *clumper* | X | X | | | X | X | | X | | X | | X | P | | | X | |
| *Sorghastrum nutans* 'Sioux Blue' | *clumper* | X | X | | | X | X | | X | | X | | X | P | | | X | |
| *Sporobolus heterolepis* | *clumper* | X | X | | | X | X | X | X | | X | | X | P | | | X | |

**Miscanthus sinensis 'Malepartus'** is one of the very most colorful Japanese Silver Grasses.

# ORNAMENTAL GRASSES AND SEDGES

ORNAMENTAL GRASSES

## Acorus calamus 'Variegatus' (a-<u>kore</u>-is  <u>kal</u>-i-mus)
(Variegated Sweet Flag) NATIVE CULTIVAR.............................Zone 5

18"-24"; full sun to moderate shade. Keeled, leathery, upright, and straplike, the rugged leaves of variegated sweet flag are colorfully striped white and green and do not fade as the season progresses. Variegated sweet flag tolerates moist soils but is very comfortable in regular garden settings. It is a wonderful companion plant, compatible with dozens of ground covers, grasses, and perennials, and may be mass planted as a ground cover. Its summerborne flowers, greenish yellow and tiny, are carried in 1/2 inch wide, upright 3 1/2 inch long spathes.
Rec. Size: #1 pot (8/flat)    Space: (12"-18")

## Acorus gramineus 'Pusillus Minimus Aureus' (a-<u>kore</u>-is grah-<u>min</u>-ee-us)
(Miniature Golden Sweet Flag).............................................Zone 4

3"-5"; light to moderate shade. Strikingly golden, the foliage of this fabulous little grasslike plant screams for attention—making it a good choice for high contrast, accent, landscape brightening ground covering effect. Miniature golden acorus is interesting in that it creeps slowly from a central rhizome to form very dense grasslike carpets. It can take a little bit of foot traffic and tolerates saturated soils. For that matter, it is not drought tolerant and its soil should be kept moist at all times. The flowers of miniature golden acorus are interesting little spaths and can be found, upon close observation, during late spring. Companions include ferns, ginger, Amsonia, epimediums, Heucheras, dwarf hostas, creeping Charley, black mondo grass, foamflower, Japanese forest grass, and sedges.
Rec. Size: #1 pot (8/flat)    Space: (8"-10")

## Andropogon gerardii (an-dro-<u>poe</u>-gon  jer-<u>ard</u>-ee-eye)
(Big Bluestem) NATIVE SPECIES.........................................Zone 3

5'-8'; full sun to light shade. Deemed "Monarch of the Prairie Grasses" by prairie expert, Neil Diboll, this fabulous species is native to moist and dry soils of prairies and open woodlands from central Mexico throughout much of the U.S. and Canada, including the Great Lakes Region. Called big bluestem for its bluish green foliage and stems, and its position as the largest (tallest) member of the genus, big bluestem sends up vertical flowering stems during late summer and fall. Each of these bears an inflorescence which is shaped like the three-parted foot of a turkey, hence its other common name turkey tracks. While interesting, the flowers are not especially showy. Rather, it is the strong vertical effect and sturdy long lived nature that makes this plant so popular. It is often planted in naturalized gardens and prairie restorations and should not be overlooked in more conventional landscapes where it makes a wonderful screen as well as a fine companion to sedums, Liatris, goldenrod, coneflowers, asters, and other ornamental grasses.
Rec. Size: #1 pot (8/flat)    Space: (2 1/2'-3')

## Arundo donax 'Variegata' (a-<u>run</u>-doe  <u>doe</u>-naks)
(Variegated Giant Reed)......................................................Zone 6

5'-7'; full sun to light shade. Variegated giant reed is a stunning foliage plant that combines well with a host of tall, colorfully flowered (blues, pinks, reds and purple) summer and fall-blooming perennials. Stout stalked and brightly white and green striped, this is an unusual selection excellent for specimen and accent use. Its fallborne plumes are seldom produced in midwestern landscapes.
Rec. Size: 2 gal.    Space: (3'-5')

## Calamagrostis acutiflora 'Avalanche' (kal-a-moe-gros-tis a-kue-ti-flow-ra)
('Avalanche' Variegated Feather Reed Grass)................Zone 5

1 1/2' (the foliage), 3'-3 1/2' (in bloom); full sun to light shade. 'Avalanche' represents the exact opposite color pattern as 'Overdam'. Instead of having leaves green centered with white edges, it has white centered leaves with deep green edges. This may sound trivial, but 'Avalanche' is more subdued in the intensity of its whiteness, and grows a bit taller, especially when in flower. This is particularly evident in mass plantings and groupings for accent. 'Avalanche' blooms early summer when topped with lovely creamy white spikes that mature to an attractive straw shade–carried into the last weeks of autumn. Companions include summer and fall blooming perennials, ground covers, and ornamental grasses.
Rec. Size: #1 pot (8/flat). Space: (2'-3')

## Calamagrostis acutiflora 'Karl Foerster' (kal-a-moe-gros-tis a-kue-ti-flow-ra) Perennial Plant Of The Year 2001
(Karl Foerster's Feather Reed Grass)................Zone 5

4'-5' in flower; full sun to light shade. For the impatient this is the right plant, since unlike many grasses, it flowers early. Indeed, as early as May the erect stemmed, narrow panicled flowers become noticeable. By mid June, they have achieved a height of 4 to 5 feet and have colored a soft shade of green. By the first of July, they are rosy purple, and by the first of August, they have turned a lovely shade of straw brown which they will remain all winter.
Rec. Size: #1 pot (8/flat) Space: (2 1/2'-3 1/2')
Rec. Size: 2 gal. Space: (2 1/2'-3 1/2')

## Calamogrostis acutiflora 'Overdam' (kal-a-moe-gros-tis a-kue-ti-flow-ra)
(Variegated Feather Reed Grass)................Zone 5

18" (the foliage), 36" (in bloom); full sun to light shade. Unique and attractive, variegated feather reed grass displays a tufted habit of lovely, narrow green and white striped foliage. Above the leaves, mid to late summer, are borne spike-shaped inflorescences colored first rosy purple then light tan.
Rec. Size: #1 pot (8/flat) Space: (2'-3')

## Calamagrostis arundinacea variety brachytricha (kal-a-moe-gros-tis ah-run-din-aye-see-a bray-kee-trik-a)
(Fall Blooming Feather Reed Grass)................Zone 5

2 1/2'-3 1/2' in flower; full sun to light shade. Feather reed grass leafs out early and spends the spring and summer as a pleasing clump of upright to arching rich green foliage. But the real action occurs in fall when the light green, pink blushed flower spikes unfurl in a glorious display of season punctuating color. And yet, the display does not stop here. The flowers and foliage, which matures to bright yellow, persist well into the winter months adding interest and vertical dimension to the wintertime landscape.
Rec. Size: #1 pot (8/flat) Space: (2 1/2'-3 1/2')

## Carex buchananii (kay-reks bue-kan-a-nee-eye)
(Leatherleaf Sedge)................Zone 5/6?

1 1/2'-2'; full sun to moderate shade. The hardiness of this plant is traditionally listed as Zone 7. I've grown it for years, in Zone 6, without a hint of winter damage. And lately, its been showing up in lots of Zone 5 gardens. So Zone 6 I'm comfortable with, Zone 5 maybe. That said, leatherleaf sedge is reddish bronze with curly leaf tips, lending superior contrast and interest when combined with other sedges, grasses, and perennials. Its inconspicuous florets are borne during spring.
Rec. Size: #1 pot (8/flat) Space: (12"-18")

## Carex caryophyllea 'Beatlemania' (kay-reks kar-yoe-fil-ee-a)
('Beatlemania' Spring Sedge)................Zone 4

6"; light to moderate shade. 'Beatlemania' is attractive and unique for its gracefully arching bright gold edged, deep green centered foliage. Carried in a mop like mound, like the hair of The Beatles (back in the 60's), its evergreen leaves create a wonderful mounded effect when used as a ground cover, edging to a sidewalk or garden path, or in small groupings for accent. During spring 'Beatlemania' bears upright spikelets of tiny yellow flowers. Comfortable companions include ferns, bergenia, Brunnera 'Jack Frost', other sedges, and countless woodland wildflowers.
Rec. Size: #1 pot (8/flat) Space: (12"-18")

## Carex dolichostachya 'Kaga Nishiki' (a.k.a. 'Gold Fountains')
(kay-reks  dol-i-ko-stay-kee-a)
('Gold Fountains' Sedge) .................................................Zone 5

**Blooming Time**
J F M A M J J A S O N D
Winter   Spring   Summer   Fall

8"-10"; light to moderate shade. Gold fountains sedge is a neat, classy colorful sedge. It is sort of like an understated 'Evergold', not quite as bright yellow striped, but still very effectively variegated (gold and green). This lower contrast makes it an easier plant to work with from a design standpoint. Blooming during spring, subtly in yellow, it is superb for edging and ground cover use and makes a pleasing companion to other sedges, grasses, and ground covers.
Rec. Size: #1 pot (8/flat)   Space: (12"-18")

## Carex elata 'Bowles Golden' (kay-reks  or  kair-ex  ee-lay-ta)
('Bowles Golden' Sedge) .................................................Zone 5

**Blooming Time**
J F M A M J J A S O N D
Winter   Spring   Summer   Fall

1 1/2'-2'; light to moderate shade. You might want to put on your sun glasses before viewing this brilliant yellow selection. It is very bright. Discovered in the UK, 'Bowles Golden' is named for its famous discoverer E.A. Bowles and is characterized by longitudinally thin green striped, brilliant yellow leaves. Most colorful in constantly moist soil in the coolest part of the garden, it may become lime green in too much shade or burn if too dry and hot. Its subtle lime green floral spikes are borne early spring and soon become buried under its lovely foliage.
Rec. Size: #1 pot (8/flat)   Space: (8"-12")

## Carex hachioensis 'Evergold' (kay-reks  or  kair-ex  hah-chee-oh-en-sis)
('Evergold' Japanese Sedge) .............................................Zone 5

**Blooming Time**
J F M A M J J A S O N D
Winter   Spring   Summer   Fall

8"-10"; light to moderate shade. Certainly one of the brightest yellow plants available for ground cover use, 'Evergold' Japanese sedge is also one of the toughest — even tolerating limited foot traffic. Its springborne flowers are small and brownish (if formed at all) but no matter, it is the lush arching, bright creamy yellow, center-striped, green margined foliage that makes this such a prize. It tolerates gravelly, sandy, and rich soils, prefers modest moisture and yet is reasonably drought tolerant for short periods of time. Maintenance is seldom necessary.
Rec. Size: #1 pot (8/flat)   Space: (10"-14")

## Carex morrowii 'Goldband' (kay-reks  moe-row-ee-eye)
('Goldband' Sedge) .................................................Zone 5

**Blooming Time**
J F M A M J J A S O N D
Winter   Spring   Summer   Fall

8"-10"; light to moderate shade. Believe it or not, this sedge is brighter than 'Evergold'! That's because instead of having golden yellow/deep green striped leaves (as is the case with 'Evergold'), its leaves are striped golden-lemon yellow/medium green. When viewing individual plants the difference is subtle. But, planted enmass, 'Goldband' is significantly brighter and really jumps out of shady areas. It also provides sharp contrast with dark green and brown elements of the landscape. It combines nicely with other sedges, Japanese forest grass, and Sporobolus, and naturally, it is good with bronze leaved ajugas, astilbes, bergenia, epimediums, geranium, Helleborus, Heuchera, hostas, Lysimachia, Mazus, Mitchella, Ophiopogon 'Nigrescens', and Allegheny pachysandra.
Rec. Size: #1 pot (8/flat)   Space: (10"-14")

## Carex morrowii 'Ice Dance' (kay-reks  moe-row-ee-eye)
('Ice Dance' Sedge) .................................................Zone 5

**Blooming Time**
J F M A M J J A S O
Winter   Spring   Summer   Fall

12"; light to moderate shade. This is a very impressive sedge with sturdy 1/2 inch wide, evergreen white and green striped leaves. 'Ice Dance' is eye catching, spreads by rhizomes (at a relatively slow pace) and makes a nice ground cover for small to medium sized areas. It combines nicely with taller ferns, such as Dryopteris filix-mas 'Undulata Robusta', Osmunda regalis, O. cinnamomea, and O. claytoniana. And, with robust shade loving perennials, such as Cimicifuga racemosa 'Atropurpurea' and Ligularia 'The Rocket' it is exceptional. Floral spikes are borne during spring.
Rec. Size: #1 pot (8/flat)   Space: (8"-12")

ORNAMENTAL GRASSES

## Carex morowii 'Silver Scepter' (kay-reks or kair-eks moe-row-ee-eye)
('Silver Scepter' Sedge) ...........................Zone 5

**Blooming Time**
J F M A M **M** J J A S O N D
Winter  Spring  Summer  Fall

12"; full sun to dense shade. This beautiful sedge is characterized by narrow, soft-green leaves with crisp white edges. It is fine textured, slow spreading, effective at brightening up shady areas and is an excellent small to moderate scale foot friendly ground cover. It is also a nice accent plant and companion to green-leaved sedges, Japanese forest grass, and such shade lovers as ferns, gingers, bergenia, Crocosmia, epimedium, geranium, Heuchera, hostas, lily-turf, Rodgersia, Tiarella, and Stylophorum. Yellow floral spikes are borne during spring.
Rec. Size: #1 pot (8/flat)    Space: (12"-16")

## Carex muskingumensis 'Ice Fountains' (kay-reks or kair-ex mus-kin-gum-en-sis)
('Ice Fountains' Palm Sedge) NATIVE CULTIVAR .......................Zone 4

**Blooming Time**
J F M A M J **J A** S O N D
Winter  Spring  Summer  Fall

1 1/2'-2'; light to moderate shade. 'Ice Fountains' is an uncommon selection that begins the year with bright white variegation around the edges of its rich green, tropical, palm tree like foliage. Eventually, during the summer months, the variegation picks up chlorophyll and changes to green. 'Ice Fountains', like others within this species, tolerates relatively wet soil as well as typical garden conditions (slightly moist but well drained). It combines effectively with hostas, Heucheras, Tiarella, Allegheny pachysandra, bergenia, brunnera, and various ferns.
Rec. Size: #1 pot (8/flat)    Space: (10"-14")

## Carex muskingumensis 'Little Midge' (kay-reks mus-kin-gum-en-sis)
('Little Midge' Palm Sedge) NATIVE CULTIVAR ...........................Zone 4

**Blooming Time**
J F M A M J **J A** S O N D
Winter  Spring  Summer  Fall

10"; light to moderate shade. A charming yet sturdy sedge with fascinating bright green bamboolike foliage, 'Little Midge' is a favorite for edging ponds and pathways, planting in containers, and mass planting as a ground cover where it lends an extremely fine textural quality. Its yellow flowers, which it bears

during summer, are ornamentally insignificant. But, that doesn't matter, this is an exceptional foliage plant. Companions include other sedges, Japanese forest grass, hostas, pulmonaria, epimedium, wood spurge, Heuchera, Tiarella, and variegated Solomon's seal.
Rec. Size: #1 pot (8/flat)    Space: (10"-14")

## Carex muskingumensis 'Oehme' (kay-reks mus-kin-gum-en-sis)
('Oehme' Variegated Palm Sedge) NATIVE CULTIVAR................Zone 4

**Blooming Time**
J F M A M J **J A** S O N D
Winter  Spring  Summer  Fall

1 1/2'-2'; light to moderate shade. This pleasing selection of our native palm sedge was found in the garden of Wolfgang Oehme (the talented East Coast designer and author of Bold Romantic Gardens). Named by Tony Avent of Plant Delights Nursery, 'Oehme' variegated palm sedge carries its foliage in horizontal fashion radiating around its triangular stems like the leaves of a palm tree. Each leaf arches gracefully at its tip and is cleanly edged in a broad margin of clear yellow (the yellow margin lasting throughout the entire season). Tiny flowers arise during summer adding further interest. 'Oehme' will grow at the base of a pond or in a regular garden setting, greatly benefiting from incorporated organic material and constant moisture. It is good as an accent or specimen plant, edging, or ground cover and is great near high traffic areas for up-close viewing.
Rec. Size: #1 pot (8/flat)    Space: (14"-18")

## Carex pennsylvanica (kay-reks or kair-ex pen-sil-van-i-ka)
(Pennsylvania Sedge) NATIVE SPECIES .........................................Zone 4

**Blooming Time**
J F M A **M** J J A S O N D
Winter  Spring  Summer  Fall

6"-8"; light to moderate shade. Pennsylvania sedge hails from thickets and woods of eastern North America and is tolerant of a good deal of drought. It isn't a big plant, but it is tough. For this reason Pennsylvania sedge is a good choice as an alternative to conventional turf grass and as such requires minimal watering and little care. You may walk on it and mow it, however, for times when you want to throw a summertime barbecue and set up some picnic tables on it. Of course, it is also useful as a ground cover, edging, or accent to wildflowers, ferns, astilbes, and hostas.
Rec. Size: 3 1/4" (18/flat)    Space: (10"-14")

## Carex siderosticha 'Variegata' (kay-reks sih-der-oh-sti-ka)
(Variegated Broad-leaved Sedge) ................................................Zone 5

6"-8"; light to dense shade. This striking deciduous sedge is clothed in hand-some green and white striped leaves that reach 3/4 inch wide by up to 16 inches long! In the moist shady woodland garden it may be used as a colorful edging or ground cover where it slowly spreads into broad colonies. In late fall the foliage turns a lovely tawny shade. The following spring it emerges showy pink before taking on its characteristic green and white striping. The springborne flowers of this fine selection are brownish black spikes, carried upon 6 to 12 inch, thin wiry stems.
Rec. Size: #1 pot (8/flat)    Space: (10"-14")

## Chasmanthium latifolium (chaz-man-thee-um lat-i-foe-lee-um)
(Northern Sea Oats) NATIVE SPECIES ...............................Zone 3

2'-4'; full sun to moderate shade. Northern sea oats is one of our most endearing harbingers of autumn—and is one of the few grasses that performs well in shade. Especially valuable for its flattened fishscale-shaped, dangling floral spikelets, these first appear pale green in midsummer before changing to reddish brown then maturing to soft tan during fall. They are carried upon thin nodding stems, well above its fresh vibrant green foliage, and dry nicely—therefore contributing to winter effect.
Rec. Size: #1 pot (8/flat)    Space: (14"-18")

## Deschampsia caespitosa 'Bronze Veil' (a.k.a. 'Bronzeschleier')
(deh-shamp-see-ah or des-kamp-see-a, seez-pi-toe-sa)
('Bronze Veil' Tufted Hairgrass) NATIVE CULTIVAR ..................Zone 4

2 1/2'-3' in flower. Full sun to light shade. Preferring constantly moist organically enriched soil, 'Bronze Veil' is a popular selection that is extremely cold hardy, quick to regrow in the spring, and during summer, loaded with bronzy inflorescences which it carries high above its foliage. These maintain their bronze color for several weeks before drying to a wonderful tawny tint whereby they continue to decorate the garden through the remainder of summer and well into fall.
Rec. Size: #1 pot (8/flat)    Space: (12"-16")

## Erianthus ravennae (a.k.a. Saccharum ravennae) (air-ee-an-thus ra-ven-ee)
(Plume Grass) ................................................................Zone 5

8'-12' in flower; full sun to light shade. Tall and robust, ravennae grass is exceptional for its height and late season floral display. Large plumes are borne during late summer on upright stalks and ascend to 12 feet. It is excellent as a specimen or hedge, and needs well-drained sandy soil for best growth.
Rec. Size: #1 pot (8/flat)    Space: (3'-4')

## Festuca glauca 'Elijah Blue' (fes-tew-ka glaw-ka)
('Elijah Blue' Fescue) ....................................................Zone 4

8"-12" tall by 1 to 1-1/2' wide; full sun. This outstanding, clump forming, self-sterile cultivar has soft powdery blue evergreen foliage, neat compact habit, and is likely the most showy of the fescue cultivars. During early summer it bears bluish spikelike flowers which soon mature and turn to a soft tan. 'Elijah Blue' performs best in moderately moist, well drained soil, in full sun, and is ideal for mass planting or accent.
Rec. Size: #1 pot (8/flat)    Space: (12"-16")

## Festuca idahoensis (fes-tew-ka eye-da-hoe-en-sis)
(Idaho Fescue) NATIVE SPECIES ......................................Zone 5

14", 2' in flower; full sun to light shade. Although named for Idaho, this cool season species is native to open woods and rocky slopes form British Columbia southward to California and Colorado. Like the more common blue Fescues, the vibrant green foliage of F. idahoensis grows quickly during early April, when most other plants are still asleep. Then, to keep things rolling, during early May it sends up spiky floral stems that bear loads of soft greenish gray flower heads. In time these turn a nice shade of soft tan and about then the flower stalks begin to take on tones of rich red and burnt orange. The entire effect is rather dramatic. Other nice attributes of the plant are that it resists summer heat and humidity, and in comparison to other fescues, it is more tolerant of short periods of excess soil moisture.
Rec. Size: #1 pot (8/flat)    Space: (12"-16")

ORNAMENTAL GRASSES

## Hakonechloa macra (ha-kone-ee-<u>kloe</u>-a   <u>mak</u>-ra)
(Japanese Forest Grass).........................................................Zone 5

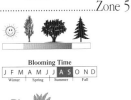

12"-18"; light to moderate shade. Japanese forest grass is one of the most graceful of all slow spreading grasses. With lovely drooping foliage arranged in neat parallel rows, it looks like a bamboo and is an essential element of the Japanese theme garden. Hakone grass bears small greenish yellow flowers during late summer and fall and although interesting, these are not of real ornamental significance. This is truly a foliage plant and exceptional for edging shady walks, lending accent to hostas and pulmonarias, and and as a delicate facing to trees and shrubs.
Rec. Size: #1 pot (8/flat)   Space: (10"-16")

## Hakonechloa macra 'Aureola' (ha-kone-ee-<u>kloe</u>-a   <u>mak</u>-ra)
(Golden-leaved Japanese Forest Grass)...........................Zone 5

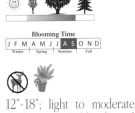

12"-18"; light to moderate shade.   Golden-leaved hakonechloa displays pendant, bamboolike leaves colored bright yellow with thin green lines running longitudinally through them. Viewed from a few feet away it creates an effect that is spectacular — perfect for accent and specimen planting in shady settings, especially Japanese theme gardens. Golden leaved hakonechloa prefers a moist, organically rich, moderately acidic to slightly alkaline soil and spreads at a slow pace. Whispy spikelike flowers are borne in summer and fall.
Rec. Size: #1 pot (8/flat)   Space: (10"-16")

## Helictotrichon sempervirens 'Sapphire' (a.k.a. 'Saphirsprudel') (he-lik-toe-<u>try</u>-con   sem-per-<u>vye</u>-renz)
('Sapphire' Blue Oat Grass) .........................................Zone 4

1 1/2'-2'; full sun to light shade. Tufted and slowly expanding from its base, this durable, vibrant sky blue, coarse textured, spiky evergreen leaved grass is one of the finest. Its arching spring- and summertime flower heads rise high above the foliage and dramatically contribute their own unique qualities.
Rec. Size: #1 pot (8/flat)   Space: (2'-3')
Rec. Size: 2 gal.   Space: (2'-3')

## Imperata cylindrica 'Red Baron' (im-per-<u>aye</u>-ta   si-lin-<u>dri</u>-ka)
(Japanese Blood Grass)...................................................Zone 5

12"-18"; full sun to light shade, preferably with afternoon shade. No other plant displays such bright red leaves as Japanese blood grass. Emerging green in spring, as the season progresses the leaf tips, then the rest of the blades, become wine red before changing to deep blood red by fall. A natural for lending strong color contrast, Japanese blood grass can be used in small clumps or large sweeping masses. It seldom if ever flowers, spreads at a slow pace, needs little maintenance, and does best in well drained moisture retentive soils..
Rec. Size: #1 pot (8/flat)   Space: (1'-1 1/2')

## Indocalamus tesselatus (in-doe-<u>kal</u>-i-mis   tes-e-<u>lay</u>-tis)
(Broadleaf Bamboo)........................................................Zone 6

3'-4'; full sun to moderate shade. This is one of the most extraordinary of the hardy bamboos—maybe one of the most extraordinary of any running grass for that matter. What's so fascinating about this plant is that it looks like it should be in the jungle. That's because its leaves are huge, tropical looking, vibrant green, and downward hanging, like so many of the conservatory tropicals. Yet, broadleaf bamboo is not limited to conservatory use. On the contrary, broadleaf bamboo is suited to drought, heat, and cold—withstanding Zone 6 conditions (with winter mulching being a good idea).
Rec. Size: 2 gal.   Space: 3'-4'

## Isolepis cernua (ice-oh-<u>lep</u>-is   sir-<u>new</u>-a)
(Fiber Optic Grass) Tender Perennial.............................Zone 8

6"-10"; full sun to light shade. From open peaty or sandy coastal soils of the British Isles, this magnificent frost-tender rush is a runaway success for seasonal interest. Wire thin, like fiber optic wire, its fresh green stems are leafless and tipped with curious golden brown spiklets — just heavy enough to cause a gentle cascading mop-head effect. It is this characteristic that makes fiber optic grass ideal for spilling over the edges of containers and planters and especially nice for growing between rocks and at waters edge. Interesting companions include Bergenia purpurascens, Heucheras, small blue-leaved cultivars of Hosta, iris, Acorus, Juncus 'Unicorn' and miniature cattail.
Rec. Size: #1 pot (8/flat)   Space: (12"-16")

ORNAMENTAL GRASSES

## Juncus effusus 'Curly Wurly' (jung-kus e-few-sus)
('Curly Wurly' Corkscrew Rush) NATIVE CULTIVAR.................Zone 5

8"-12"; full sun to moderate shade. An off-the-wall plant that makes people smile and laugh, 'Curly Wurly' is fun, interesting and unusual, and aptly named. 'Curly Wurly' is a leafless rush (all the chlorophyll is contained in its green stems) with tightly rolled, spiraling wirelike stems. When picked and dried, the stems shorten and the spirals become even tighter. Use this plant in containers and as a curious accent or small scale ground cover in areas that are up close and easily viewed—so that as many people as possible can appreciate its unique character. Tiny brown flowers are borne during late summertime. Grows well in normal garden settings and tolerates moist soils.
Rec. Size: #1 pot (8/flat)    Space: (8"-12")

## Juncus effusus 'Unicorn' (jung-kus e-few-sus)
(Unicorn Rush) NATIVE CULTIVAR.......................................Zone 5

1'-2'; full sun to moderate shade. 'Unicorn' is perfectly named and just plain fun. Its green, elongated, leafless stems spiral in the shape of a unicorn's horn. Anyone with a flair for the unusual, and especially children, will appreciate the curious whimsical nature of this "one of a kind" plant. Treasured among flower arrangers, the stems of unicorn are fantastic in a vase or bouquet. In the landscape 'Unicorn' is an effective specimen, accent, or ground cover when mass planted. Be sure to plant it in a location where its stems are silhouetted against a light colored backdrop or with plants of different texture and color—so as to show off its features all the more. Grows well in normal garden settings and tolerates moist soils. Good companions include ajuga, bergenia, Cornus, Delosperma, Gaultheria, Ophiopogon 'Nigrescens', Lysimachia, Isotoma, and Leptinella.
Rec. Size: #1 pot (8/flat)    Space: (1'-1 1/2')

## Lagurus ovatus (la-gur-is oh-vay-tus)
(Annual Bunny-tail Grass) ......................................Annual/NOT HARDY

6"-8"; full sun to light shade. From the Mediterranean region, this lovely annual grass is a delight for seasonal color. Velvety soft, its pale green leaves are the perfect backdrop to its countless, ever present (spring through fall), fuzzy cotton-ball tufts of pure white florets carried 4-10 inches above the foliage. Bunny-tail grass is as charming as they come, guaranteed to make you smile. What's more, it is complimentary to such great companions as Bergenia purpurascens, Iris cristata, lavenders, Ophiopogon 'Nigrescens', purple leaved Heucheras, Salvias, clump forming sedums, sedges, and Imperata 'Red Baron'.
Rec. Size: #3 1/4 (8/flat)    Space: (10"-14")

## Leymus arenarius 'Blue Dune' (ley-mus ar-i-nare-ee-us)
('Blue Dune' Wild Rye)..........................................................Zone 4

2'-3'; full sun to light shade. Of the brightest blue grasses, 'Blue Dune' is slow spreading, and shows a greater propensity to send up its interesting blue green late-summerborne flower stalks. 'Blue Dune' is excellent in parking areas where it tolerates heat, drought, and some foot traffic. It is easy to care for, reliable for many years, and is nice in combination with tall daylilies, Helianthus cultivars, coneflowers, feather reed grass, Miscanthus cultivars, and tall asters.
Rec. Size: #1 pot (8/flat)    Space: (12"-16")

## Luzula 'Ruby Stiletto' (lewz-ew-la)
('Ruby Stiletto' Wood Rush)...................................................Zone 5

8"; full sun to moderate shade. A neat, new, compact, colorful, ever-changing selection of wood rush that was discovered in the mountains of British Columbia by Graham Ware, 'Ruby Stiletto' is one of those pleasing cool-season plants that every garden needs to get it jump started in early spring. It is a plant that comes on strong during April with a burst of fresh new silvery green, rich ruby tipped foliage. Then, by mid May, it is in full bloom with its foliage nearly disappearing under compact spikes of bronzy gold. Next, attractive reddish seed pods have made their appearance. And, finally, during fall it will often give a final burst of red tones to the foliage.
Rec. Size: #1 pot (8/flat)    Space: (12"-16")

ORNAMENTAL GRASSES

# Miscanthus – the queen of ornamental grasses.

*Miscanthus sinensis 'Silver Feather'*

*Miscanthus is, arguably, the most popular and most beautiful of the ornamental grasses. Collectively the genus is sometimes called the queen of ornamental grasses and goes by such common names as Japanese silver grass, maiden grass, and eulalia. Miscanthus is composed of only a few species, and of these nearly all ornamental selections come from the species M. sinensis.*

*The selections that you will find listed here represent the very best of this extraordinary genus. They are durable hardy plants that range from a few feet to over 12 feet tall. They are the most disease resistant of dozens that have been extensively tested. Aside from 'Giganteus' and 'Gracillimus', they bloom early enough so that even during unusually cool summers, they will flower beautifully. What's more, these selections have good separation between their foliage and flowers, a trait necessary to adequately show off their flowers. They are clump forming and well behaved (except for 'Purpurascens' which travels a bit, but isn't weedy by any means), and exhibit superior color during summer. They also have striking fall foliar color. And, last but not least, they are selections that resist flopping and hold up well throughout the winter months.*

*Cultivars of Miscanthus are very versatile, fun, and exciting. They are probably the most wind responsive plants available, swaying gracefully to the most gentle breeze, and providing a soothing sound as the wind passes through their foliage. Miscanthus selections may be employed as specimens, accent plants, hedges, massed as ground covers, and used to provide a tropical-like screening effect.*

*Miscanthus is a plant for full sun or light shade—flowering best with four or more hours of direct sunlight each day. Dramatic effects can be created with back- and side-lighting, at night and during the day, especially when plants are sited near water or dark colored elements in the landscape. Cultivars are prized for their strong architectural merits and graceful habit. Japanese silver grass is excellent on golf courses, around water features and patios, and is tolerant of moderate periods of both drought and wetness (capable of tolerating wet soil for several weeks).*

*Suitable companions to the maiden grasses are many. Such tall perennials as Eupatorium 'Gateway' and tall cultivars of sunflower combine nicely with the taller and mid-height selections of Miscanthus. Shorter companions, often used in the foreground of Miscanthus include sedum, coneflower, asters, coreopsis, Chelone, crown vetch, compact Japanese fleeceflower, Origanum, Russian sage, Rudbeckia, and of course, other types of grasses.*

**ENVIRONMENTAL AWARENESS** Miscanthus expert Mary Hockenberry Meyer of Minnesota Landscape Arboretum has extensively studied the seed producing ability of Miscanthus. From her research she states that "Miscanthus cultivars are fine for use in managed areas where plants can be watched for self-seeding (i.e. managed areas such as home and commercial landscapes, parks, public gardens, etc.)." Individual cultivars tend to be self sterile and seed production is none or minimal. If a seedling were to occur, it could easily be removed or transplanted for enjoyment elsewhere in the garden.

It is the wild type M. sinensis that has shown a propensity to self-seed, particularly in mild climates of the mid-Atlantic states. Although I know of no nursery that grows this plant in the Great Lakes area it may be offered in seed packets via mail order. The best thing to do is to use container grown plants from garden centers or landscapers. These are cultivars that have been vegetatively (not seed) propagated by division.

ORNAMENTAL GRASSES

**ORNAMENTAL GRASSES**

| | GREEN | WHITE/GREEN | YELLOW/GREEN |
|---|---|---|---|
| **Dwarf (1'-3')** | (3') 'Little Kitten' — upright vase, silver plumes<br>(3 ½') 'Adagio' — broad form, silver plumes | | (3 ½') 'Little Zebra' — upright vase purple plumes |
| **Mid-Size (4'-6')** | (4) 'Sarabande' — upright vase, long lived bronzy plumes<br>(5') 'Ferner Osten' — upright vase, thin leaves, silver and purple plumes<br>(5') 'Helga Reich' — upright vase, thin leaves, coppery silver plumes<br>(5½') 'Gracillimus' — broad vase, thin leaves, late bloom<br>(6') 'Bluetenwunder' — upright vase, silky silvery plumes<br>(6') 'Flamingo' — upright, wide leaves, early bloom<br>(6') 'Graziella' — upright vase, thin leaves, silver plumes good fall color<br>(6') 'Malepartus' — upright vase, tropical leaves, early bloom, great fall color<br>(6') 'Purpurescens' — spreader, bright red fall color, silver plumes,<br>(6') 'Silver Feather' — stately, with large silvery plumes<br>(6') 'Sirene' — upright vase, purple and silver plumes | (4 ½') 'Dixieland' — upright vase, burgandy plumes<br>(5') 'Morning Light' — purple plumes, thin leaves, late bloomer<br>(6') 'Cabaret' — wide leaves, broad habit | (6') 'Strictus' — upright vase, coppery silver plumes |
| **Tall (7'-9')** | (7') 'Grosse Fontane' — upright vase, silver plumes, good fall color<br>(7') 'Undine' — upright vase, silver plumes high above leaves<br>(7'-8') 'Andante' — upright vase pinkish plumes age to silver | (7xx) 'Silver Arrow' — upright habit, purplish plumes<br>(8') 'Cosmopolitan' — broad form, wide leaves, purplish plumes<br>(8') 'Variegatus' — broad form, med-width leaves purplish plumes | (7') 'Zebrinus' — broad form, pinkish coppery plumes |
| **Very Tall 10'+** | (12') M. giganteus — late bloomer, broad leaves, tropical | | |

ORNAMENTAL GRASSES

## Miscanthus giganteus (mis-<u>kan</u>-thus ji-gan-<u>tee</u>-is)
(Giant Chinese Silver Grass)..................................................Zone 4

8'-12' in leaf; full sun to light shade. The grandaddy of the silver grasses, giant Chinese silver grass is enormous! Slowly spreading to make broad 8 foot wide thicketlike clumps, it goes from nothing to 12 feet in a single season. Then in fall, provided the weather has been hot, it sends up large fluffy plumes 1 to 2 feet above the foliage. Flowers or no flowers, it imparts a magnificent tropical-like presence and is exceptional near water — especially in large landscapes.
Rec. Size: 5 gal.    Space: (5'-7')

## Miscanthus sinensis 'Adagio' (mis-<u>kan</u>-thus sye-<u>nen</u>-sis)
('Adagio' Japanese Silver Grass)..........................................Zone 5

2 1/2'-3' in flower; full sun to light shade. Tough drought tolerant and hardy, this superb cultivar is exceptional. Not only is it dwarf and compact, making it excellent in the smaller landscape, it gives a lovely display of narrow silvery gray foliage topped during early fall by pink florets that turn white in maturity.
Rec. Size: #1 pot (8/flat)    Space: (2'-2 1/2')

## Miscanthus sinensis 'Andante' (mis-<u>kan</u>-thus sye-<u>nen</u>-sis)
('Andante' Japanese Silver Grass)........................................Zone 5

7'-8'; full sun to light shade. Proclaimed by grass expert Kurt Bluemel as the "best specimen Miscanthus on the market", 'Andante' has a lot to live up to. I have found this plant to be an excellent selection that begins flowering during early fall with lovely pink plumes that age to silver. Borne well above the foliage, the flowers are graceful and showy. The foliage, a pleasing mid-green, is attractive spring through fall and lovely, as soft tan, throughout the winter months. It is, as Kurt says, a superior specimen, but it should not be overlooked for hedging and mass planting. Nor should it be overlooked as a brilliant companion to other grasses, Amsonia, asters, Campanula, Calamintha, coreopsis, daylilies, iris, Shasta daisy, Perovskia, and tall sedums.
Rec. Size: #1 pot (8/flat)    Space: (3'-4')

## Miscanthus sinensis 'Bluetenwunder' (mis-<u>kan</u>-thus sye-nen-sis)
('Bluetenwunder' Japanese Silver Grass)...........................Zone 5

6'; full sun to light shade. Known to be a massive bloomer, 'Bluetenwunder' is exceptional for bearing spectacular silky silvery plumes, late summer and fall, above lovely blue-gray foliage. Its habit is upright and strong—giving it a neat clean appearance and making it a good selection for hedge, specimen, or accent use. Interesting companions include asters, coreopsis, Crocosmia, Liatris, Eupatorium, Fallopia, Hemerocallis, sedums, and other grasses.
Rec. Size: #1 pot (8/flat)    Space: (3'-4')

## Miscanthus sinensis 'Cabaret' (mis-<u>kan</u>-thus sye-<u>nen</u>-sis)
('Cabaret' Japanese Silver Grass).........................................Zone 5

5'-6' in flower; full sun to light shade. 'Cabaret' displays big, bold, broad leaves with wide creamy white center stripes and bright green margins—prompting claims that this is the most spectacular of all variegated Miscanthus cultivars. 'Cabaret' blooms during September and October and like Miscanthus 'Gracillimus' may not flower during cool summers—a great merit to designers when looking primarily for a colorful backdrop.
Rec. Size: #1 pot (8/flat)    Space: (3'-4')
Rec. Size: 2 gal.    Space: (3'-4')

## Miscanthus sinensis 'Cosmopolitan' (mis-<u>kan</u>-thus sye-nen-sis)
('Cosmopolitan' Variegated Japanese Silver Grass)...........................Zone 5

6'-8' in flower; full sun to light shade. 'Cosmopolitan' is among the most impressive of all variegated grasses. Its substantial foliage is exceptionally wide and marked with vibrant creamy white and dark green longitudinal striping. Flowering during early fall, it produces broad silvery plumes.
Rec. Size: 2-5 gal.    Space: (4'-5')

*ORNAMENTAL GRASSES*

## Miscanthus sinensis 'Dixieland' (mis-kan-thus sye-nen-sis)
('Dixieland' Japanese Silver Grass)..................................Zone 5

3'-4', 4 1/2' in flower; full sun to light shade. 'Dixieland' is a dwarf form of 'Silver Arrow' with broad leaved, bright white and green streaked foliage. A compact upright grower that never flops over, 'Dixieland' is an excellent choice for the smaller garden and for use as a low hedge or screen. It flowers early fall with burgundy plumes and combines well with other grasses and many perennials and ground covers.
Rec. Size: #1 pot (8/flat)    Space: (2 1/2'-3')

## 'Miscanthus sinensis 'Emerald Shadow' (mis-kan-thus sye-nen-sis)
('Emerald Shadow' Japanese Silver Grass).......................Zone 5

7'-9'; full sun to light shade. Originating as an all-green-leaved sport of 'Cosmopolitan', 'Emerald Shadow' is even more robust in its growth rate and habit, and truly is an exceptional specimen, companion, or screening plant. Displaying extra wide, pendant, rich green leaves which look like a lush cascading waterfall, 'Emerald Shadow' has a tropical quality to it and exudes a bold commanding effect. Great companions include 'Gateway' and 'Chocolate' Joe-Pye, tall sunflowers, Russian sage, Rudbeckia, and other ornamental grasses.
Rec. Size: 5 gal.    Space: (5"-7")

## Miscanthus sinensis 'Ferner Osten' (mis-kan-thus sye-nen-sis)
(Far East Japanese Silver Grass)......................................Zone 5

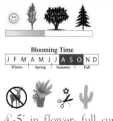

4'-5' in flower; full sun to light shade. 'Ferner Osten', meaning far east, is among the most remarkable ornamental grasses ever. It blooms early for a Miscanthus, beginning during late summer, and does so in a very pleasing manner. First silvery purple, its lovely compact inflorescences change to shiny silver as they age. Often both colors are present at the same time which creates a striking multicolored effect that contrasts nicely with the graceful, dark green, silver-midribbed foliage.
Rec. Size: #1 pot (8/flat)    Space: (3'-4')

## Miscanthus sinensis 'Flamingo' (mis-kan-thus sye-nen-sis)
('Flamingo' Japanese Silver Grass).................................Zone 5

5'-6' in flower; full sun to light shade. Maybe the earliest blooming of the silver grasses, this extraordinary specimen begins flowering mid summer with heavy substanced, pink-tinged flowers that mature first to silver then soft tan. Carried above medium green silver-midribbed foliage, the flowers are durable and lend interest throughout the fall and winter months.
Rec. Size: #1 pot (8/flat)    Space: (3'-4'

## Miscanthus sinensis 'Gracillimus' (mis-kan-thus sye-nen-sis)
(Narrow Leaved Japanese Silver Grass)............................Zone 5

4 1/2'-5 1/2' in flower; full sun to light shade. Here is a lovely grass that not only entertains with its fine textured leaves, but with the gentle motion they display in response to breezes. Interestingly, its autumnal floral display is effective only after a long hot summer. This is appreciated by designers primarily interested in a foliage back drop. 'Gracillimus' forms lovely vase shaped clumps, is tolerant of dry sandy soils, and withstands having its roots in water for short periods of time.
Rec. Size: #1 pot (8/flat)    Space: (2 1/2'-3 1/2')
Rec. Size: 2-5 gal.    Space: (2 1/2'-3 1/2')

## Miscanthus sinensis 'Graziella' (mis-kan-thus sye-nen-sis)
('Graziella' [Grace] Japanese Silver Grass).....................Zone 5

5'-6' in flower; full sun to light shade. With exceptional production of unusually white late-summerborne flower panicles above graceful slender foliage, 'Graziella' is among the most florific and popular selections of Miscanthus. During fall its foliage and stems turn lovely shades of yellow, orange, and reddish purple.
Rec. Size: #1 pot (8/flat)    Space: (2 1/2'-3 1/2')
Rec. Size: 2-5 gal.    Space: (2 1/2'-3 1/2')

ORNAMENTAL GRASSES

## Miscanthus sinensis 'Grosse Fontäne' (mis-kan-thus sye-nen-sis)
(Giant Fountain Japanese Silver Grass)......................Zone 5

**Blooming Time**
J F M A M J J A S O N D
Winter | Spring | Summer | Fall

6'-7' in flower; full sun to light shade. A superb selection with magnificent early fallborne silvery plumes that extend well above its cascading foliage, 'Grosse Fontäne' is one of the finest choices for planting in groups, massing as a screen or hedge, or using alone as a specimen. It lends itself well to the large scale landscapes and looks marvelous throughout the winter months.
Rec. Size: 2-5 gal.    Space: (4'-5')

## Miscanthus sinensis 'Helga Reich' (mis-kan-thus sye-nen-sis)
('Helga Reich' Japanese Silver Ggrass)......................Zone 5

**Blooming Time**
J F M A M J J A S O N D
Winter | Spring | Summer | Fall

4'-5' in flower; full sun to light shade. 'Helga Reich' epitomizes gracefulness in every respect. First, during spring and early summer, it decorates the landscape with very thin, fine-textured silvery green foliage which responds to the most gentle breeze. Then, late summer, it puts on a lovely unpretentious show of slender coppery-silver plumes which change to silver then soft tan as they age. Preserving well, they are carried in this fashion throughout the winter months.
Rec. Size: #1 pot (8/flat)    Space: (2 1/2'-3 1/2')

## Miscanthus sinensis 'Kaskade' (mis-kan-thus sye-nen-sis)
('Kaskade' Japanese Silver Grass)......................Zone 5

**Blooming Time**
J F M A M J J A S O N D
Winter | Spring | Summer | Fall

5'-6' in flower; full sun to light shade. Among Miscanthus selections, this one stands out for its unusual pink tinged summerborne flowers which cascade over in graceful pendant fashion. An early bloomer, it can be counted upon to flower year after year, and prior to blooming, it is a pleasing foliage plant with tight vase shaped habit of narrow silvery green leaves.
Rec. Size: #1 pot (8/flat)    Space: (3'-4')

## Miscanthus sinensis 'Little Kitten' (mis-kan-thus sye-nen-sis)
('Little Kitten' Japanese Silver Grass)......................Zone 5

**Blooming Time**
J F M A M J J A S O N D
Winter | Spring | Summer | Fall

1 1/2'-3'; full sun to light shade. The tiniest of the silver grasses, 'Little Kitten' is exceptionally small, and therefore an excellent choice as a dwarf hedge, accent plant, or perennial garden sepcimen. Its narrow leaves are attractive for their silver midribs, and its early fallborne flowers are carried at a height of 24" — setting them well above the foliage where they can sway gracefully in the wind.
Rec. Size: #1 pot (8/flat)    Space: (1 1/2'-2")

## Miscanthus sinensis 'Little Zebra' (mis-kan-thus sye-nen-sis)
('Little Zebra' Dwarf Zebra Grass)......................Zone 5

**Blooming Time**
J F M A M J J A S O N D
Winter | Spring | Summer | Fall

3'-4' in flower; full sun to light shade. This miniature zebra grass holds its green and yellow banding all season. That makes it a superior selection as other dwarf varieties often fade to all green during the summer months. What's more, 'Little Zebra' has the desirable trait of flowering during late summer—so its lovely reddish purple plumes are borne reliably every year, even during seasons of cool weather. 'Little Zebra' is perfect for accent or specimen use in ornamental grass and perennial border plantings, rock gardens, and even as a dwarf hedging or large scale ground cover. It is neat, tidy, reliable, and easy to maintain.
Rec. Size: #1 pot (8/flat)    Space: (2'-3')

## Miscanthus sinensis 'Malepartus' (mis-kan-thus sye-nen-sis)
('Malepartus' Japanese Silver Grass)......................Zone 5

**Blooming Time**
J F M A M J J A S O N D
Winter | Spring | Summer | Fall

5'-6' in flower; full sun to light shade. 'Malepartus' is a unique cultivar in that its broadly white centered green leaves are oriented at right angles to the stalks. This creates a rather intriguing bamboolike appearance. Its early fallborne flowers, first pinkish purple, peak during mid-fall, turn an attractive silver, then mature to attractive straw brown as they age.
Rec. Size: #1 pot (8/flat)    Space: (3'-4')
Rec. Size: 2-5 gal.    Space: (3'-4')

## Miscanthus sinensis 'Morning Light' (mis-<u>kan</u>-thus sye-<u>nen</u>-sis)
('Morning Light' Japanese Silver Grass)..........................................Zone 5

4'-5' in flower; full sun to light shade. Compact with fine textured, gently arching, silvery foliage, this selection combines well with other pastels such as the flowers of Russian sage or Sedum 'Brilliant'. It also tolerates a bit of shade and like the other species of Japanese silver grass, it is easy to grow and adds interest to the winter landscape. Although sometimes blooming well in fall, 'Morning Light' is grown mainly for its foliage.
Rec. Size: #1 pot (8/flat)    Space: (2 1/2'-3')
Rec. Size: 2 gal.    Space: (2 1/2'-3')

## Miscanthus sinensis 'Purpurascens' (mis-<u>kan</u>-thus sye-<u>nen</u>-sis)
(Flame Japanese Silver Grass).........................................................Zone 5

4 1/2'-6' in flower; full sun to light shade. Flame grass differs from other Miscanthus cultivars in two important ways. First, it is a bit of a runner and will spread to several feet across to form lush, leafy thickets. Second, in addition to providing a superb autumnal floral display of tight silvery plumes that arise some two feet above the leaves, it boasts magnificent red late season foliage.
Rec. Size: #1 pot (8/flat)    Space: (3'-4')
Rec. Size: 2-5 gal.    Space: (3'-4')

## Miscanthus sinensis 'Silver Arrow' (mis-<u>kan</u>-thus sye-<u>nen</u>-sis)
('Silver Arrow' Japanese Silver Grass)..............................................Zone 5

5'-7' in flower by 5'-6' wide; full sun to light shade. An extraordinary choice for specimen, accent, or mass planting, silver arrow grass is distinguished by its neat vase shaped habit and superb foliage with white central stripes surrounded by borders of vibrant green. During August it begins to bloom and its silvery plumes remain effective through fall and winter.
Rec. Size: #1 pot (8/flat)    Space: (3'-4')
Rec. Size: 2-5 gal.    Space: (3'-4')

## Miscanthus sinensis 'Silver Feather' (mis-<u>kan</u>-thus sye-<u>nen</u>-sis)
('Silver Feather' Japanese Silver Grass)............................................Zone 4

6'-7' in flower; full sun to light shade. 'Silver Feather' Miscanthus is a stately selection with large feathery golden plumes in late summer. Flowering early like this, it is reliable during even the coolest summers, and it is one of the most hardy selections with a rating of Zone 4. In foliage, 'Silver Feather' is effective as well. Broad leaved with prominent white midrib, the rich green leaves of 'Silver Feather' are disease resistant and durable. During fall they turn an attractive harvest yellow and the golden plumes age to a soft tan.
Rec. Size: #1 pot (8/flat)    Space: (3'-3 1/2')

## Miscanthus sinensis 'Sirene' (mis-<u>kan</u>-thus sye-<u>nen</u>-sis)
('Sirene' Japanese Silver Grass)........................................................Zone 5

5'-6' in flower; full sun to light shade. Characterized by attractive compact habit of deep green, wide white midribbed foliage, held horizontally to give it a tropical look, 'Sirene' is a superb summer-time foliage plant. Then, late summer, it begins to flower with showy rich purplish plumes that mature to silky silver. Below the mature silver plumes are borne a second tier of immature purple plumes. This is one of the finest grasses available.
Rec. Size: #1 pot (8/flat)    Space: (2 1/2'-3')

## Miscanthus sinensis 'Strictus' (mis-<u>kan</u>-thus sye-<u>nen</u>-sis)
(Porcupine Japanese Silver Grass)....................................................Zone 4

4'-6' in flower by 3'-5' wide; full sun to light shade. Compact and clump forming, this selection is neat and easily managed. Its foliage is interesting for its display of bright yellow, one inch horizontal bands between bands of bright vibrant green. Flowering is just as impressive. Beginning in September (and remaining through the winter months), the plumes of porcupine grass are coppery silver and silky textured, then during fall they dry to a soft fluffy tan.
Rec. Size: #1 pot (8/flat)    Space: (3'-3 1/2')
Rec. Size: 2-5 gal.    Space: (3'-3 1/2')

## Miscanthus sinensis 'Undine' (mis-<u>kan</u>-thus   sye-<u>nen</u>-sis un-deen)
('Undine' Japanese Silver Grass)..............................Zone 5

6'-7' in flower; full sun to light shade. With its lovely, low growing, compact foliar habit and full plumes of silvery white late summerborne flowers carried several feet above the foliage (upon slender, gracefully arching stems), 'Undine' is as lovely and graceful as any other grass. The great distance between the flowers and leaves makes this an ideal selection to use for creating a soft, sophisticated veiled effect when planted in the foreground of other plants.
Rec. Size: #1 pot (8/flat)   Space: (3 1/2'-4 1/2')
Rec. Size: 2-5 gal.   Space: (3 1/2'-4 1/2')

## Miscanthus sinensis 'Variegatus' (mis-<u>kan</u>-thus   sye-<u>nen</u>-sis)
(White Variegated Japanese Silver Grass)..............................Zone 5

6'-8' in flower; full sun to light shade. A striking selection, white variegated Japanese silver grass is outstanding as a specimen or enmasse. Cultivated since 1900, this popular cultivar is named for its vibrant white and green striped foliage. It is robust in habit (broader in form than 'Silver Arrow'), thrives in most any soil, and puts on a nice display of first reddish, then silver fallborne flowers.
Rec. Size: #1 pot (8/flat)   Space: (3'-4')
Rec. Size: 2-5 gal.   Space: (3'-4')

## Miscanthus sinensis 'Weather Vane' (mis-<u>kan</u>-thus   sye-<u>nen</u>-sis)
('Weather Vane' Japanese Silver Grass)..............................Zone 5

6'-7' in flower; full sun to light shade. Along with 'Flamingo', this is perhaps the earliest blooming silver grass in our product line—actually in peak bloom from mid July to mid August! Not only is it an early bloomer, but a very effective bloomer with full bodied plumes of silver florets that age to soft tan. In addition, the flowers are carried unusually high above the broad, cascading, lime green foliage (brilliant reddish purple in fall)—giving 'Weather Vane' a unique tropical look.
Rec. Size: #1 pot (8/flat)   Space: (2 1/2'-3 1/2')

## Miscanthus sinensis 'Zebrinus' (mis-<u>kan</u>-thus   sye-<u>nen</u>-sis)
(Zebra Grass)..............................Zone 5

5'-7' in flower; full sun to light shade. Large, robust and stately, zebra grass takes its name for the bright yellow horizontal bands that decorate the vibrant green arching leaves. A prodigious bloomer, zebra grass makes quite a show during early fall with flowers that are first pinkish copper then silvery before maturing to a pleasant shade of tan.
Rec. Size: #1 pot (8/flat)   Space: (4'-5')
Rec. Size: 2-5 gal.   Space: (4'-5')

## Panicum amarum 'Dewey Blue' (<u>pan</u>-i-kum   a-<u>mare</u>-um)
('Dewey Blue' Switch Grass) NATIVE CULTIVAR..............................Zone 2

3'-4'; Full sun. Descended from a native beach grass (dunes and shore lines from Louisiana to Connecticut), 'Dewey Blue' was chosen for its gracefully fountainlike habit and broad leaved, soft powder blue foliage. Its blue green flowers are open and airy, emerge during late summer, and persist as a light beige color through the winter season. The name 'Dewey Blue', chosen by Rick Darke (well known authority on ornamental grasses), commemorates the shoreline community Dewey, Delaware. Naturally, 'Dewey Blue' performs well in dry sterile sandy conditions, is great for soil stabilization, and combines nicely with crown vetch, Shasta daisy, various coneflowers, and numerous other ornamental grasses.
Rec. Size: 2 gal   Space: (2 1/2'-3')

ORNAMENTAL GRASSES

## Panicum virgatum 'Cloud Nine' (pan-i-kum   vir-gay-tum)
('Cloud Nine' Switch Grass) NATIVE CULTIVAR.........................Zone 4

**Blooming Time**
J F M A M J J A S O N D
Winter  Spring  Summer  Fall

5'-7'; full sun to light shade. The largest and maybe the most florific switch grass, 'Cloud Nine' is awe inspiring. Its sturdy habit is tight and vase shaped, staying vertical in windy settings, and it looks neat, robust, and strong. Colored light blue, its stems and foliage are easy companions to other perennials and grasses. And, late summer and early fall, it bears masses of golden flower panicles — nice through fall and into winter.
Rec. Size: 2 gal.    Space: (3'-4')

## Panicum virgatum 'Dallas Blues' (pan-i-kum   vir-gay-tum)
('Dallas Blues' Switch Grass) NATIVE CULTIVAR ........................Zone 4

**Blooming Time**
J F M A M J J A S O N D
Winter  Spring  Summer  Fall

4'; full sun. This plant is extraordinary and so different from any other switch grass that it takes a close look to even guess the genus. A switch grass it is, however, and a dramatic one at that. Relatively tall, very full and broad, 'Dallas Blues' boasts wide leaf blades of purplish blue—characteristics that establish it as unusual. But, most importantly, it bears huge 2 feet tall, foot-wide late summer and fallborne panicles of iridescent rose-purple. Wind responsive, in an extreme way, the flowers are out of this world.
Rec. Size: 5 gal.   Space: (2 1/2'-3')

## Panicum virgatum 'Heavy Metal' (pan-i-kum   vir-gay-tum)
('Heavy Metal' Switch Grass) NATIVE CULTIVAR ........................Zone 4

**Blooming Time**
J F M A M J J A S O N D
Winter  Spring  Summer  Fall

3'-3 1/2' in flower; full sun to light shade. A unique variation upon our sprawling native prairie species, this unusual selection is interesting for its neat compact upright habit and unusual metallic blue foliage. Later, during August, it becomes even more interesting as its open panicles of purple florets unfurl above the foliar mass. Finally, during fall, the leaves turn a pleasant shade of yellow.
Rec. Size: #1 pot (8/flat)   Space: (2 1/2'-3')

## Panicum virgatum 'Northwind' (pan-i-kum   vir-gay-tum)
('Northwind' Switch Grass) NATIVE CULTIVAR ............................Zone 4

**Blooming Time**
J F M A M J J A S O N D
Winter  Spring  Summer  Fall

5'-6'; full sun to light shade. This is really a terrific Panicum selection for form, function, and sheer beauty. Standing upright with tight vase shaped habit through the strongest winds, 'Northwind' is drought tolerant, colored rich blue green, and during late summer and fall bears lovely upright floral spikes. It is great for hedging, accent, and specimen use and combines beautifully with other Panicum selections—especially the red ones like 'Shenandoah' and 'Rotstrahlbush', and of course other grasses and the "classic" late season perennials including asters, sedums, Rudbeckia, Solidago, and Echinacea.
Rec. Size: #1 pot (8/flat)   Space: (2'-2 1/2')

## Panicum virgatum 'Rotstrahlbusch' (pan-i-kum   vir-gay-tum   rot-stral-bush)
(Red Switch Grass) NATIVE CULTIVAR..........................................Zone 4

**Blooming Time**
J F M A M J J A S O N D
Winter  Spring  Summer  Fall

3'-4' in flower; full sun to light shade. With upright broad vase shaped habit and spread of 3 feet, this popular drought tolerant selection displays attractive medium grayish green foliage during the growing season and interesting open, airy flower panicles in mid summer — which persist through fall and well into winter. Then in fall the leaves turn bright red, the brightest red fall color of the Panicum selections.
Rec. Size: #1 pot (8/flat)   Space: (2 1/2'-3')
Rec. Size: 2 gal.   Space: (2 1/2'-3')

## Panicum virgatum 'Shenandoah' (pan-i-kum   vir-gay-tum)
('Shenandoah' Switch Grass) NATIVE CULTIVER .........................Zone 4

**Blooming Time**
J F M A M J J A S O N D
Winter  Spring  Summer  Fall

3' in flower; full sun to light shade. 'Shenandoah' might be considered a taller, more durable substitute for Imperata 'Red Baron' as its foliage becomes red by June and becomes even more intensely colored as the season progresses. From Germany and introduced by Dr. Hans Simon, 'Shenandoah' flowers bright red in late summer and is a fine companion to other fall blooming grasses and perennials.
Rec. Size: #1 pot (8/pot)   Space: (2'-2 1/2')

# Panicum virgatum 'Squaw' (pan-i-kum vir-gay-tum)
('Squaw' Switch Grass) NATIVE CULTIVAR .................Zone 4

3'-4'; full sun to light shade. This strong growing selection is characterized by a broad compact habit of rich green leaves, red autumnal tones, and strong pinkish purple tones in its fallborne flowers. The compactness of 'Squaw' makes it a good companion to other taller, more upright grasses and other forms of switch grass, great for contrast in the landscape. Another advantage is that it never flops over as sometimes can be the case with taller selections. This makes it a nice plant in broad sweeping beds as a ground cover, great as a facing to tall grasses like Panicum 'Cloud Nine' and 'Dewey Blue', Miscanthus selections, and very tall perennials like Eupatorium 'Gateway' and Helianthus cultivars.
Rec. Size: #1 pot (8/pot)  Space: (2 1/2'-3')

# Panicum virgatum 'Warrior' (pan-i-kum vir-gay-tum)
('Warrior' Switch Grass) NATIVE CULTIVAR.................Zone 4

4'-5'; full sun to light shade. With robust growth to 5' tall, 'Warrior' displays broad vase shaped habit and rich green foliage that is blue on its underside. This alone is not exceptionally unique among the taller switch grasses, except that the other tall selections stay green or blue right up to frost. 'Warrior', on the other hand, begins to color up with red tones in late summer. These intensify during autumn for a nice punctuation to the growing season. 'Warrior' is also a good bloomer with attractive purplish toned sprays carried above the foliage during late summer and fall.
Rec. Size: #1 pot (8/pot)  Space: (2 1/2'-3')

# Pennisetum alopecuroides (pen-i-see-tum al-oh-pek-you-roy-deez)
(Fountain Grass).................Zone 5

2 1/2'-3 1/2' in flower; full sun to light shade. Loosely tufted, fountain grass derives its name from the late summer flower heads which bend outward gracefully like water flowing from an upright fountain. They are feathery, 6-8 inches long, purplish brown, and very attractive. Fountain grass is great for accent, edging, and mass planting as a ground cover. It is also excellent for erosion control.
Rec. Size: #1 pot (8/flat)  Space: (2 1/2'-3 1/2')
Rec. Size: 2 gal.  Space: (2 1/2'-3 1/2')

# Pennisetum alopecuroides 'Cassian' (pen-i-see-tum al-oh-pek-you-roy-deez)
('Cassian' Fountain Grass).................Zone 5

12"-24"; full sun to moderate shade. With compact upright vase shaped habit, 'Cassian' is a much sought after, very useful, semi-dwarf selection. Most unique about it, however, is its amber infused foliage and dark sand colored summer- and fallborne flower spikes
Rec. Size: #1 pot (8/flat)  Space: (2'-2 1/2')

# Pennisetum alopecuroides 'Hameln' (pen-i-see-tum al-oh-pek-you-roy-deez)
('Hameln' Dwarf Fountain Grass).................Zone 5

2 1/2' in flower by 2 1/2' wide; full sun to light shade. This superb selection differs from the species in being more compact with darker green foliage. The flower spikes are 3" to 4" long, pale green in mid-summer, and mature to a creamy tan. 'Hameln' is best in moist, fertile, well drained soils, but tolerates a wide range of soil conditions. Popular for mass planting or accent, 'Hameln' is a good choice where a neat, compact, low maintenance plant is desired.
Rec. Size: #1 pot (8/flat)  Space: (2'-3')
Rec. Size: 2 gal.  Space: (2'-3')

# Pennisetum alopecuroides 'Japonicum' (pen-i-see-tum al-oh-pek-you-roy-deez)
(Japanese Fountain Grass).................Zone 5

4'-4 1/2' in flower; full sun to light shade. Among the fountain grasses this is the big one, taller, broader, and larger flowered than all others. With broad vase shaped habit of vibrant green leaves it is lovely spring through mid summer. Then, late summer through fall it becomes loaded with enormous fluffy spikes of dark tan feathery flowers. Each morning these are covered with dew which gives it even more appeal as they glisten in the early morning sun.
Rec. Size: 2 gal.  Space: (2 1/2'-3')

## Pennisetum alopecuroides 'Little Bunny' (pen-i-see-tum al-oh-pek-you-roy-deez)

('Little Bunny' Fountain Grass)..............................Zone 5

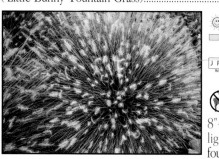

8"-12" in flower; full sun to light shade. The smallest fountain grass, 'Little Bunny' is aptly named for its soft textured foliage and fuzzy late summer and fall-borne floral spikes. It needs virtually no care and is excellent as a ground cover or foreground plant to other grasses and fall blooming perennials.
Rec. Size: #1 pot (8/flat)    Space: (10"-14")

## Pennisetum alopecuroides 'Little Honey' (pen-i-see-tum al-oh-pek-you-roy-deez)

(Dwarf Variegated Fountain Grass)..............................Zone 5

6"-10" in flower; full sun to light shade. The silver variegated equivalent of 'Little Bunny', this lovely little dwarf is neat, compact, and mid summer to fall is covered with fuzzy white flower spikes. A tidy clump former, 'Little Honey' may be mass planted for a soft silvery effect, used as a neat dwarf edging, or combined for accent with other perennials and grasses.
Rec. Size: #1 pot (8/flat)    Space: (10"-14")

## Pennisetum alopecuroides 'Moudry' (pen-i-see-tum al-oh-pek-you-roy-deez)

(Black Flowered Fountain Grass)..............................Zone 5

2 1/2'-3'; full sun. 'Moudry' is drought tolerant, reliable, and attractive even not in flower, which leads to the topic of bloom time. This fountain grass is showy in bloom, but it is later blooming than other fountain grasses in our line. Practically speaking this means that during long hot summers it will give a nice floral display in the fall. During years of cool summers it may not flower much. With this in mind, the cultivar 'Viridescens' may be a better choice in northern areas or areas of cool summer temperatures.
Rec. Size: #1 pot (8/flat)    Space: (2 1/2'-3')

## Pennisetum alopecuroides 'Red Head' (pen-i-see-tum al-oh-pek-you-roy-deez)

('Red Head' Fountain Grass)..............................Zone 5

3' tall, 4' in flower; full sun to light shade. Flowering during August and September, 'Red Heads' flower plumes are amazing deep reddish purple, 8-inch-long, 3-inch-wide bottle brush spikes which remain prominent well into winter. The foliage of 'Red Head' is nice as well. A rich deep green during the growing season, it turns lovely golden tones during fall and maintains a nice tawny shade all winter.
Rec. Size: 2 gal.    Space: (5'-6')

## Pennisetum alopecuroides 'Viridescens' (pen-i-see-tum al-oh-pek-you-roy-deez)

(Early Blooming Black Flowered Fountain Grass) ..............................Zone 5

2'- 2 1/2' in flower; full sun to light shade. With superb densely set, glossy green leaves, this sturdy mound forming cultivar is a splendid foliage plant from spring through late summer. In early fall, however, it becomes a spectacle of floral delight as its extraordinarily showy, fuzzy, near-black bottle brush shaped inflorescences unfurl well above the foliage.
Rec. Size: #1 pot (8/flat)    Space: (2 1/2'-3')
Rec. Size: 2 gal.    Space: (2 1/2'-3')

## Pennisetum glaucum 'Purple Majesty' (pen-i-see-tum glaw-kum)

('Purple Majesty' Flax) ..COLD TENDER/USE FOR ANNUAL COLOR

4'-5'; full sun to light shade. 'Purple Majesty' flax causes people to stop and ask: what is that? It is that unique. Its uniqueness is the result of extreme purple pigmentation in its stems, foliage, and flower spikes--making it absolutely excellent for annual color, both in the ground and in containers. At first, prior to bloom, you might think that 'Purple Majesty' resembles corn, albeit purple corn. But, during mid to late summer when its magnificent 12-16 inch long, upright purple foxtail floral spikes arrive, it looks 100 % like flax. The floral spikes eventually become yellow frosted (due to the developing anthers), and finally change to soft tan as the anthers mature. This effect is ongoing with all three color stages often present at once.
Rec. Size: 6-pack.    Space: (1 1/2'-2')

## Pennisetum orientale 'Karley Rose' (pen-i-<u>see</u>-tum or-ee-en-<u>tale</u>-ee)
('Karley Rose' Oriental Fountain Grass) ........................Zone 5

2 1/2'-3'; full sun to light shade. Considered by many to be the most showy species of fountain grass, 'Karley Rose' Oriental fountain grass is noteworthy for clump forming habit and vibrant green attractive leaves carried upon gently arching stems to a height of 2 1/2 feet. Above them, during mid-summer through fall, are borne soft rose colored, fuzzy foxtail plumes that later mature to creamy light brown.
Rec. Size: #1 pot (8/flat)    Space: (14"-20")

## Pennisetum setaceum 'Rubrum' (pen-i-<u>see</u>-tum se-tay-<u>see</u>-um)
(Purple Leaved Fountain Grass).TENDER: USE FOR ANNUAL COLOR

2 1/2'-3' in flower; full sun to light shade. Although tender, purple leaved fountain grass is so extraordinary, for its deep purple leaves and summerborne flowers, that is has become popular simply for seasonal effect. A staple ingredient in the designs of our country's top landscape architects, and universally included in perennial plantings of leading botanic gardens, I know of no other plant that is so reliably showy.
Rec. Size: #1 pot (8/flat)    Space: (2 1/2'-3')

## Phalaris arundinacea 'Feesey's Form' (<u>fal</u>-a-ris or <u>fa</u>-lare-is a-run-di-<u>nay</u>-see-a, <u>fee</u>-seez)
(Strawberries and Cream Ribbon Grass) ................Zone 4

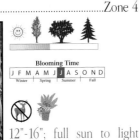

12"-16"; full sun to light shade. Striking for accent and high contrast, 'Feesey's Form' (named after the German nurseryman Herman Feesey) emerges with vibrant green and white striped foliage. It is exceptional planted in the foreground of pink, red, purple, and blue foliage and flowers and by late spring its leaves may pick up hints of pink and rose, for which it takes its common name strawberries and cream. By mid summer it is decorated by pink tinged flowers.
Rec. Size: #1 pot (8/flat)    Space: (12"-16")

## Phalaris arundinacea 'Tricolor' (<u>fal</u>-a-ris or <u>fa</u>-lare-is a-run-di-<u>nay</u>-see-a)
('Tricolor' Ribbon Grass) ................................Zone 4

1 1/4'-2'; full sun to light shade. Like 'Feesey's Form', 'Tricolor' is an attractive green and white striped spreading grass. Similary, 'Tricolor' is hardy, reliable, and excellent for creating contrast and brightening up the landscape. It also bears pink tinged flowers in summer but differs in that it is a little more compact and during spring its new growth is colored rosy pink, white, and green (hence the name 'Tricolor').
Rec. Size: #1 pot (8/flat)    Space: (12"-16")

## Pleioblastus auricoma (a.k.a. P. viridistriata) (<u>ply</u>-oh-blas-tus awe-ri-<u>koe</u>-ma)
(Dwarf Yellow-stripe Bamboo) ........................Zone 5

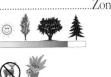

2'-3'; full sun to moderate shade. With vibrant bright green and golden leaves, this running bamboo is an assertive spreader that is easy to grow and superb for contrast. Its colorful variegation is effective at brightening up shade. And, in addition to growing in typical garden settings, it is relatively moisture tolerant. For this reason, dwarf yellow-stripe bamboo is excellent planted next to a pond or pool where its lovely colors can reflect off the surface of the water. This, and other spreading bamboos may be controlled with a deep edging or by planting in a container.
Rec. Size: #1 pot (8/flat)    Space: (1'-1 1/2')

### Sasa veitchii, Kuma Bamboo, displays the curious trait of drying along its leaf edges during fall and winter.

*O R N A M E N T A L   G R A S S E S*

## Pleioblastus fortunei 'Variegata' (ply-oh-blas-tus fore-<u>too</u>-nee-eye)
(White-stripe Bamboo)................................................Zone 5

1 1/4'-1 1/2'; full sun to moderate shade. Nicely painted white and green, the fine textured evergreen foliage of this ground covering bamboo is cheerful and attractive throughout the growing season. It can be used for all the same applications as dwarf yellow stripe bamboo, and tends to brighten up shady areas even more. This, and other spreading bamboos may be controlled with a deep edging or by planting in a container.
Rec. Size: #1 pot (8/flat)   Space: (1'-1 1/2')

## Sasa veitchii (<u>sa</u>-sa vee-<u>chee</u>-eye
(Kuma Bamboo)..............................................Zone 5 or 6

1'-3'; full sun to moderate shade. Like most bamboos, this one was originally thought to be less hardy than what it actually is. As it turns out, kuma bamboo is hardy to Zone 5 or 6, and for this we are lucky. Kuma bamboo is a plant that is reliable, relatively slow spreading, and hugely interesting. It lends itself to shade gardens and Oriental style gardens and is easily contained by surrounding it with an edging. Its leaves, oval and 8 inches long, are tropical looking, colored deep green, and have the marvelous trait of turning straw-colored about their edges in fall and winter.
Rec. Size: #1 pot (8/flat)   Space: (1 1/2'-2')

## Schizachyrium scoparium 'The Blues' (skits-ah-<u>keer</u>-ee-um skoh-<u>pair</u>-ee-um)
('The Blues' Little Bluestem) NATIVE CULTIVAR................Zone 4

**Blooming Time**
J F M A M J J A S O N D
Winter  Spring  Summer  Fall

1 1/2'-2 1/2'; full sun. 'The Blues' is an amazing selection of our own native bluestem. It is terrific for its late season bloom time, sending up masses of silvery blue racemes during early fall. These open to expose attractive silvery flowers which eventually dry to an attractive tawny shade—staying this way to decorate the landscape throughout the winter months. The flowers are remarkable, but couple this with the foliage which is a rich iridescent steel blue that becomes suffused with tones of yellow and burgundy during fall, and you have a plant of exceptional worth.
Rec. Size: #1 pot (8/flat)   Space: (2 1/2'-3')

## Sorghastrum nutans 'Sioux Blue' (sor-gas-trum <u>noo</u>-tanz)
('Sioux Blue' Indian Grass) NATIVE CULTIVAR................Zone 4

**Blooming Time**
J F M A M J J A S O N D
Winter  Spring  Summer  Fall

3'-4 1/2', to 6' in flower; full sun to light shade. Rick Darke of Longwood Gardens made this selection for its upright habit and its leaves, colored bright powder blue-gray, lovely, and wind responsive. Above them during late summer are borne showy tan-yellow, foot-long panicles. Not only are they attractive but extremely silky to the touch. In maturity the flowers turn a soft delicate tan and about this time the fall foliar color comes into play. Yellowish with burnt orange, the autumnal effect is superb.
Rec. Size: #1 pot (8/flat)   Space: (18"-24")

## Spodiopogon sibiricus (spoe-dee-oh-<u>poe</u>-gon sye-<u>beer</u>-i-kus)
(Frost Grass)....................................................Zone 4

**Blooming Time**
J F M A M J J A S O N D
Winter  Spring  Summer  Fall

4'; full sun to light shade. Aptly named frost grass for the way the flower panicles glimmer (as though frosted) when backlit by the sun. Flowering occurs mid summer through fall with silvery spikes carried well above the wonderful foliage. Its bamboolike leaves are slender, flattened, and acutely pointed. At first they grow upright then become almost horizontal. Each is colored a rich green, is decorated by a prominent white midrib, and during fall becomes rich burgundy in color. Suitable companions are asters, goldenrod, cone flowers, daylilies, coreopsis, and other ornamental grasses.
Rec. Size: #1 pot (8/flat)   Space: (1 1/2'-2')

## Sporobolus heterolepis (spor-<u>ah</u>-bol-us het-er-oh-<u>lep</u>-is)
(Prairie Dropseed) NATIVE SPECIES................................Zone 4

**Blooming Time**
J F M A M J J A S O N D
Winter  Spring  Summer  Fall

1 1/2'-2', to 3' in flower; full sun to light shade. This handsome grass slowly forms dense, arching clumps of fine-textured, emerald green leaves. Each clump reaches 1 1/2 to 2 feet tall and infuses a comfortable cool green feel to the landscape. The foliar mass turns deep orange during October or November, then light coppery tan for the winter months. Flowering too, is quite impressive. This occurs during late summer, first with the emergence of thin cylindrical stalks which quickly elongate to 30 inches. At their tops are born whispy, curiously scented, silver, wind responsive inflorescences.
Rec. Size: #1 pot (8/flat)   Space: (18"-24")

# Common Name Index

# Common Name Index (continued)

# Common Name Index (continued)

# Common Name Index (continued)

# Common Name Index (continued)

# Scientific Name Index

# Scientific Name Index (continued)

# Scientific Name Index (continued)

# Scientific Name Index (continued)

# USDA Plant Hardiness Zone Map

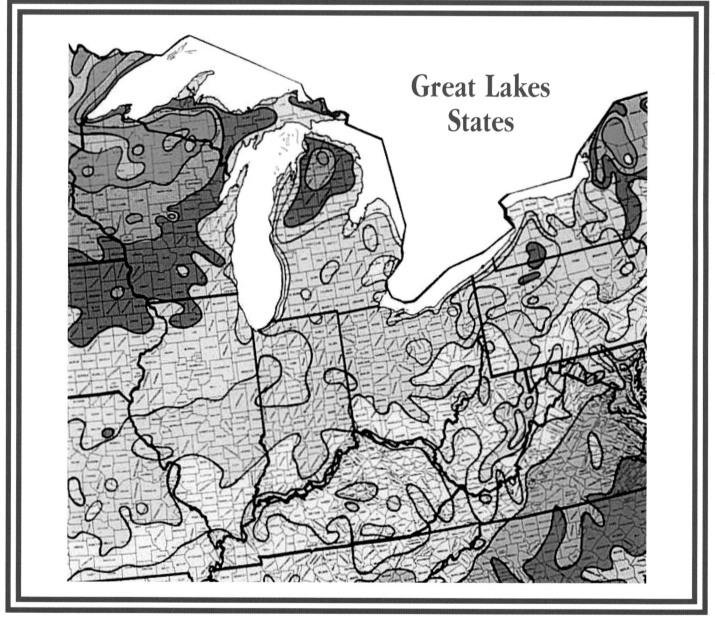

Great Lakes States

**AVERAGE ANNUAL MINIMUM TEMPERATURE ZONE**

| 1 Below -50 | 2A -45 to -50 | 2B -40 to -45 | 3A -35 to -40 |
|---|---|---|---|
| 3B -30 to -35 | 4A -25 to -30 | 4B -20 to -25 | 5A -15 to -20 |
| 5B -10 to -15 | 6A -5 to -10 | 6B 0 to -5 | |